WALKING POINT

WALKING POINT

AMERICAN NARRATIVES

OF VIETNAM

THOMAS MYERS

NEW YORK   OXFORD

OXFORD UNIVERSITY PRESS

1988

Oxford University Press

Oxford   New York   Toronto
Delhi   Bombay   Calcutta   Madras   Karachi
Petaling Jaya   Singapore   Hong Kong   Tokyo
Nairobi   Dar es Salaam   Cape Town
Melbourne   Auckland

and associated companies in
Berlin   Ibadan

Copyright © 1988 by Oxford University Press, Inc.

Published by Oxford University Press, Inc.
200 Madison Avenue, New York, New York 10016

Oxford is a registered trademark of Oxford University Press

Library of Congress Cataloging-in-Publication Data
Myers, Thomas.
Walking point : American narratives of Vietnam/Thomas Myers.
p.   cm.   Bibliography: p.   Includes index.
ISBN 0-19-505351-6 (alk. paper)
1. American prose literature—20th century—History and criticism.
2. Vietnamese Conflict, 1961–1975—Literature and the war.
3. War stories, American—History and criticism.   4. Vietnamese Conflict,
1961–1975—Personal narratives, American.   I. Title.
PS366.V53M94   1988
818'.5408'080358—dc19   87-30285   CIP

Parts of Chapter 1 are based on previously published material by the
author which appeared in *Modern Fiction Studies*, Vol. 30, No. 1,
Spring 1984. Copyright © 1984 by Purdue Research Foundation,
West Lafayette, Indiana 47907. Reprinted with permission.

2 4 6 8 9 7 5 3 1
Printed in the United States of America
on acid-free paper

To My Mother and Father

PREFACE

This study of American writing on the Vietnam War has had an unusually long gestation period. I first became involved with the Vietnam War and its history not in a scholarly way, but in a personal one. Paul Guimond, a classmate at Our Lady Gate of Heaven Elementary School and Mount Carmel High School in Chicago, became a soldier in Vietnam when I became an undergraduate student at De Paul University. On very different operations, I completed my degree in English literature, but Paul did not finish his shorter tour of duty in Indochina.

Killed near the end of his tour of duty, he became—like many Americans, well after the fact—one of the names on the black stone Vietnam Veterans Memorial in Washington, D.C. As I was metamorphosed into someone with a crude dexterity with image patterns and rhyming couplets, Paul was transformed into yet another small national sacrifice, one that seemed to disappear from American consciousness as quickly as it occurred.

I wrote an elegy for Paul that became part of De Paul's annual literary magazine; the poem was a rough, youthful effort, an inadequate but necessary personal response. I had no real knowledge of the roots of American involvement, nor any solid sense of why young men like Paul were becoming daily figures in the rising national body count. The official explanations of strategy and overall purpose changed quite often during those years. As I drove through Grant Park in Chicago during the 1968 Democratic National Convention, seeing the domestic battle lines being drawn, I did sense that this war was not a stable American narrative. Certainly in those days, it seemed to be a story with no possible or acceptable closure.

After the secret Cambodian operations and the new, horrific American iconography at Kent State University, I became more involved in campus politics, more certain—or so I thought—of my own views on the war. But as the new mass demonstrations took place, as the bullhorns boomed across America's campuses, as the official response from the Nixon White House became more recalcitrant—malevolently surreal it seemed at that time—deaths seemed to count less than ever. As deep canyons of political division appeared in America, those continually rising figures of body count— American and Vietnamese—often seemed clouded in opaque verbiage, new shrouds of ideological abstraction. New peace plans were cast, new domestic upheavals occurred, but in the painful point-counterpoint of national pragmatism and idealism—a new American schizophrenia of will and conscience—the human factor, the hard truth of individual life and death, was too often lost in larger arguments on who had the true sight line on humanity and inhumanity.

Well after the often promised "Peace with Honor" was achieved, the news that Saigon had fallen in 1975 produced only small, anticlimactic wrinkles in the fabric of American historical memory. To the country at large, the war already seemed ancient history, a television series that, having run too long, had been granted a merciful cancellation. For the returned American veterans, however, and for the families of those who did not journey back to "the World," the battle for recognition, readjustment, or merely acceptance was just beginning. There were no parades. There was a long list of physical and psychological infirmities. Rage, silence, profound disorientation were the legacies of the most recent American conflict. If the Vietnam veteran had been forever transformed by a crucial national experience, so had been the culture he reentered. Well after the jarring images disappeared from our television screens, well after college campuses became uneasily bucolic again, I found that Paul remained my only true war story, that his passing—that his experience—remained both an unanswered question within my private memory and a missing chapter within the collective national record.

More recently, as I worked on this manuscript for the past three years, I have taught a special course called "Literary Responses to the Vietnam War" (more properly, 232D) for the English Department of Purdue University. The course, begun by Professor William J. Palmer in 1980 when few academic offerings on Vietnam existed anywhere, was a most fortuitous inheritance, one that has become my second true war story. A generation removed from Paul's experience, my present students were four to eight years old when the last American troops returned from Vietnam. None was alive when Presidents Kennedy and Diem were assassinated; few, when the first Marines landed near Da Nang in 1965. For them, the war and the cultural context of the late 1960s and early 1970s are a largely unexplored American archive, no small historical lesson in itself.

Many of the students enter the class with some personal connection to the war or some shards of historical knowledge, but most reveal that their high-school history courses either never "got to Vietnam" or dealt with it quickly or superficially. They sit patiently for the first few weeks as I discuss Vietnamese cultural history: the origin of the country before the birth of Christ; its long history as a divided country with a fear of foreign intruders; the century of voracious French colonialism in Indochina; the post–World War II foreign policy of the United States toward Southeast Asia. What they want, however, are the war stories, those immediate accounts in the novel and personal memoir that offer them what Americans felt, thought, and did in Vietnam, the symbolic history that is the subject of this book.

Some of my students have read Cooper, Melville, and Crane; others, Hemingway or Dos Passos, Mailer or Jones; a very few, Heller, Vonnegut or Pynchon. Even those students with no knowledge of the tradition of American war writing, however, respond immediately to the new corpus of American stories of Vietnam. They are intrigued and puzzled, entralled and horrified, numbed and moved. Hearing their questions—some asked hesitantly, others passionately—reading their essays and exams, I find that Hemingway's assertion that a novel is "truer than anything factual can be" remains a valid one, that one *Rumor of War* or *Going After Cacciato* may be worth more than a hundred considerate, "objective" seminars or documentaries on the Vietnam "experience." The work of art retains—in a way more necessary than ever—its chimerical power to become a unique historical voice.

College campuses are quieter these days, and odd transformations have taken place. Brush haircuts and jungle fatigues are as familiar to this generation of students as long hair and patched jeans were to mine. Still, rumors of future wars, debates on congressional funding for military aid, and media disclosures of new secret histories proliferate. No matter what future American history holds in the way of new narratives of men or women at arms, the students in 232D—and many others like them across the nation—are a reminder that no history can remain untold, that each succeeding generation deserves a full examination of the record.

My students reveal that they are tired of hearing that they are politically apathetic; they often inform me that they know they are lacking in important recent cultural knowledge. They have seen *Apocalypse Now*, *The Deer Hunter*, *Rambo*, *Platoon*, and *Full Metal Jacket* and are conscious of the disparity among those cinematic versions of Vietnam. It comes as little surprise to them—and perhaps as some alleviation of historical anxiety—that I discuss the Vietnam War not as "story" but as "stories," a network of sometimes complementary, often competing narratives. The newest American war stories, like the overall tradition they both extend and refashion, compose a wide spectrum of modal and thematic choices, a full deck of aesthetic differences as historical testimony. If for my generation, the Vietnam War was, as Michael Herr suggests, Wallace Stevens's jar (it did take dominion everywhere), for the new one, the students who garner their experience of the war second hand, it is the impossibility of a single, stable narrative. If that realization deflates a number of contemporary texts—both within popular culture and within official quarters—such reading can only be welcomed.

This book, then, originates from the meeting of two generations: the one of Paul Guimond, which saw the war close up—and too frequently died within its history—and the new "veterans" of 232D, who chose to read the novels and memoirs, that very personal record of Vietnam that is a crucial component within the larger one. Fixed blocks of stone notwithstanding, there can be no finer or necessary memorial by one generation to the memory of another.

West Lafayette, Indiana   T. M.
September 1987

ACKNOWLEDGMENTS

This discussion of some recent American war stories owes its existence to a number of people. I would like to express my gratitude to Leonard Neufeldt for suggestions and support extending far beyond this study, to G. Richard Thompson for being both valued friend and demanding critic, to Lester Cohen for suggesting by example new pathways into the realm of facts and fictions, and to William J. Palmer for his suggestion during our shared semester of teaching that I never get off the boat.

I also thank the Graduate School of Purdue University for the financial support it generously provided, William Stafford and *Modern Fiction Studies* for allowing me to reprint the Del Vecchio discussion, the Committee on American Studies at Purdue for its patience and interest, and Philip Beidler of the University of Alabama for his advice and generosity.

My deepest gratitude as well to Brooke Horvath for his friendship, advice, and ability to scoop them up at first, to Sandberg for keeping me on schedule, and to Catherine Price for a small galaxy of reasons. One always finds the most necessary point men if he asks for volunteers.

CONTENTS

I envisage a war, of justice or strength,
of a logic beyond all imagining.
It is as simple as a musical phrase.

RIMBAUD

WALKING POINT

Introduction

WALKING POINT
IN THE AMERICAN ARCHIVE

It was a war whose symbolic power always seemed to exceed its narrative stability. Announcing itself continually as a new category of American story in which the essential contrasts and contradictions were impossible to miss, the Vietnam War flashed across American television screens as tight concentrations of violent images, an often surreal dreamscape in which language could never hope to keep pace with the cinematic potential of the event. Aerial views offered tons of American bombs swallowed by a primordial jungle that seemed the final check on grand technological assumptions, while on the ground small columns of men disappeared behind an opaque green curtain, flesh-and-blood GI Joe figures cast as actors in someone's heart-of-darkness scenario. The war offered the most unwelcome iconography: the mythic American soldier wielding a Zippo lighter against thatched village huts, a filmed public execution of one Vietnamese by another in the streets of Saigon, tired soldiers sitting among bomb craters like astronauts without protective suits on the dark side of the moon. These were disconnected images, however, no more than powerful, disquieting snapshots in a new national album, quick cuts in an ongoing newsreel.

The familiar face of the American soldier was there—black, white, and Hispanic faces with similar, fear-inducing expressions—but the context always seemed wrong. The helmet cover above that cinematic face might bear a peace symbol; the flak jacket at the bottom of the picture would offer a contradictory inscription: "Born to Kill" or "We are no sons of America—we are head-hunters." The jacket invariably included as well some version of the short-timer's calendar— each man's personal chronometer of 365 days—which was the most visible symbol of how mere survival had supplanted tangible victory as the grunt's special mission. Clusters of small, aberrant narratives within a larger one, the Vietnam War seemed from the outset unlikely historical data for the well-worn contours and conventions of the traditional war novel.

Always a battle of language—a true test of whose lexicon, the grunt's or the manager's, would produce the more powerful key terms—the Vietnam War was a cultural crisis that required an ever-expanding glossary. "Free-fire zone," "winning hearts and minds," "light at the end of the tunnel," "strategic hamlet," "Peace with Honor"—ingenious phrases seemed to justify a new American enterprise, but as euphemism or deflection they only further scrambled an already skewed text. The grunt's vocabulary—"Freedom Bird," "There it is," "Don't mean nothin'," "the World"—was immediately ironic and phenomenological. Vietnam shorthand, the soldier's historical response was linguistic invention and transmission from the war's dark center, the necessary counter-language to that which would cloak the undeniable personal realities, the new data. Official language always had the upper hand during the war, however, for mainstream journalism most often recorded the creator's language, not the agent's. The soldier's own testimony was a story waiting for a storyteller, a tale whose ultimate message would reside in its tone and style as much as its content. If the Vietnam War was a dark monument to the powers of American imagination, so would imagination be the most necessary tool for its faithful recording.

Previous wars had displayed a gap between official encapsulations and the infantryman's slang, but Vietnam produced an ever-widening gulf between antagonistic historical statements. Strategic summary and spontaneous testimony did not correlate well. The opposed metaphors were striking—Americans hovered in retributive technology above the green landscape while the enemy elaborately tunneled within it—but such symbolic energy never was channeled into a comforting American story. More than anything else, the war was perceived through time as a national aberration, an unwanted conflict so strikingly different in content and style from previous American stories of men at arms that its future in traditional history or fiction was more than problematic. If the war defied conventional attempts to record it, however, it simultaneously demanded connection to and placement within the heritage of its creators. Beneath its inherently imagistic surface, at its linguistic core of official euphemism, puzzling acronym, and crisis-laden coinage, the Vietnam War demanded what all previous conflicts have received: permanent historical documents that are both the object and the reservoir of collective memory. In regard to specific narrative inevitabilities, the Vietnam War was, despite its claims to difference, the extension and evolution of a number of deeply rooted American traditions, a crucial national experience requiring both text and context.

Wars are always fought within two kinds of battlefields. The first, of course, is the clearly bound one in which campaigns are waged, lives are sacrificed or saved, and immediate national assertions of purpose and value are written. This is the field of troop movements, tactical decisions, and strategic overviews, and its history is immediately recordable and verifiable. The historical text may be the necessary itemization of pain and loss—the most costly of many national books of lists—but it is finally only a naming of parts. The immediate history of the happenings within that battlefield—whether it be Château-Thierry, Omaha Beach, the Chosin Reservoir, or Khe Sanh—is that of the journalist's pad, the photograph, and, more recently, the television camera. If the field of action is one of events frozen in time, a grid of inherently stable, reliable surfaces, the historical voice that speaks of that field is invariably a consistent, confident one, but also one of limited cultural range and resonance. The first-level history is a sepia-colored photograph of war suggesting but not revealing its buried story. Its taunt lies in its provocative, mute surface. If asked to render a larger, interpretive significance, it responds, like Melville's Bartelby, with the admission that it would prefer not to.

The second battlefield—one of high organicism, instability, and ever-receding closure—has no geopolitical reference points, for its only map coordinates are those of collective memory and imagination. The physical battlefield engenders formal military histories, columnar chronologies in reference works, and tidy summaries in secondary-school texts. The battle for collective memory—an ongoing pitched battle for the correlation of new emotional, psychological, and spiritual data within larger mythic narratives—is the production of texts that are less finished and, from a limited historiographical perspective perhaps, less trustworthy. It is no small irony, however, that the most significant battles a nation will endure—those fought for long-term possession of collective memory—are often waged within the symbolic histories that are traditionally appraised as documents least worthy of deposit into the national archive.

The battle for public memory has little to do with the faithful recording of objective realities, the verification of body counts. Well after geographical battlefields have become symbolic memorials, the postbellum creators of harmonious narratives of national experience in war—two dimensional ones within popular culture or within the official quarters of national policymakers—invariably edit, revise, or ignore the aspects of the new experience that threaten the preexisting national story, the bright master narrative of collective self-image. Popular myth is inherently conservative—even defensive or resistant— when it is truly threatened by new cultural data, when the fresh chapters of national sacrifice are not softened or sentimental stories are not easily appended to preexisting ones.

The power of popular myth is located within the very narrowness and consistency of its narrative renderings. Collective wish fulfill- ment, it inevitably offers updated reflecting surfaces for long-standing images of national virtue and purpose; it rewards a mass readership with what it most deeply desires to feel or to believe. Popular culture in the narrowest bands of its mythic transmissions offers the B movie, the television series, the supermarket pulp romance, the comic book, but thinness of conventional expression does not preclude prodigious mythic power or telling ideological persuasion. Can there be any question, for instance, that American historical memory of World War II is largely mythic, one in which Roosevelt, Hitler, and Chur- chill contend with John Wayne, Audie Murphy, and Dana Andrews as historical actors? Popular myth does not contradict the formal, verifiable history of war that precedes it and fuels it; rather, most often it validates national sacrifice as it leavens and reshapes the original experience into harmonized, sealed narratives within a larger one. Gary Cooper was both a one-man army and a powerful symbol of militant American pastoralism in *Sergeant York*. Henry Fonda died on a destroyer off Okinawa in *Mister Roberts*, a sacrifice to private virtue and team spirit that transformed Jack Lemmon into the new nemesis of James Cagney, a clear symbol of creeping totali- tarianism in the American military. More recently, Sylvester Stallone's *Rambo* saga has mythically rewritten the Vietnam War by rescuing the American MIAs of victimization and virtue within a cinematic dream mill. If such characterizations are one-sided and two-dimensional, they do indicate that popular myth is powerful salve for both old and new wounds, that it is invariably the voluntary ally of the larger story that precedes it.

The often ignored ideological power of popular culture is only enhanced by the myth-making energies within legitimized seats of political power within American society. With easy access to and even implicit control over mainstream media conduits, both print and electronic, national political figures control the past as much as they govern the present and shape the future. Like the thin, harmonious artifacts of popular culture, a campaign speech, a press conference, a State of the Union address, or a televised summary of a party platform is a powerful historical tool, an often irresistible agent of ideological coercion. An event as subversive of national mythic stories as the Vietnam War may be edited, rewritten, or cosmetically treated to make it not only acceptable, but also usable as a creative narrative for future foreign policy, future history. Popular culture and official history share two vital aspects: the tendency to ignore the deeper, disquieting elements within the mythic history they write; and the likelihood of finding an enthusiastic mass audience for the finished texts. Vietnam was a political torch passed through several administrations from Truman to Nixon, but the Reagan administration has written a history of the war as potent as any penned while Americans still fought and died in the jungle, a history that invents a past as it suggests a future. Odd junctures of mythic influence and new history confront us with increasing frequency. An American medical student on Grenada remarks that approaching helicopters remind him of *Apocalypse Now*. Richard Nixon uses the film *Patton* as a cinematic tape loop to galvanize a crumbling administration. Our most powerful, accessible images coax, seduce, and convince. Memory resides within a prison house of thin but impenetrable walls.

If wars are invariably fought on solid ground and within the creative imagination, each battlefield also features a key figure who undertakes the most hazardous but necessary duty. The forward element of this unit, the eyes, ears, and brain for the soldiers who depend on his intuition, his powers of observation, and his creative decisions, the point man shoulders a huge responsibility. Probing new terrain rife with potentially deadly surprises, he must use his finely tuned senses to record and to assess changing situations, unexpected problems, but he must also use his imagination to shape that data into a meaningful design. Walking point, a soldier is both guide and protector, for at any given moment his position defines the outer circumference of his unit's knowledge and experience in foreign territory. Within the physical battlefield, he is the temporary custodian of human lives; within the imaginative one, he is the author and caretaker of a credible collective memory. In the physical realm, the point man seldom knows the strength or location of his adversaries. In the thick undergrowth of mythic space, however, the enemy is clearly positioned and well equipped, a foe of prodigious power with a familiar face.

Flanked by the harmonious mythologies of popular culture and of official reification, America's most capable literary point men have traditionally faced numerically superior forces with the energy of the creative imagination, the necessary saving power of art. The historical novel—the field weapon of the literary point man—is a different kind of mythic narrative, one that replies to the forced harmony of popular culture and official revision with the deep probing and aesthetic rendering of the most significant information within new historical experience. Since 1814, however, when Sir Walter Scott's Waverley claimed independence from the purely social fiction of the eighteenth century of Fielding and Smollett, the historical novel has traditionally been appraised as a bastardized narrative form, a creation with the distinct features of both imaginative and historical writing but without the right to claim either as its legitimate progenitor. If it did garner praise, it was because it had become, simply, a novel, a work of sufficient complexity and craftsmanship that its historical pretensions could be overlooked.

Hayden White, however, in Metahistory: The Historical Imagination in Nineteenth-Century Europe, offers a definition of historical writing that erases the traditional boundary between historical and imaginative writing. For White, the historical text is "a verbal structure in the form of a narrative prose discourse that purports to be a model, or icon, of past structures and processes in the interest of explaining what they were by representing them" (2, White's italics). The key terms in his statement are "purports" and "icon," words that suggest elements of imagination and meaningful social ritual, and "explaining" and "representing," descriptions of the reciprocal bond between historical interpretation and aesthetic creation. White's expansive definition does more than allow safe passage of the self-conscious historical novelist into the kingdom of traditional historical writing; it also suggests an additional definition of his often denigrated narrative project. The complex historical novel announces its true value when it is appraised as a narrative prose discourse offering itself as a meaningful social artifact—a text that is both a genuine historical hermeneutic and a self-conscious aesthetic expression. Seen in this light, the historical novel transmutes suspicion into strength. It announces that its hybrid nature—its unique blend of fact and fiction—is not the cloaking of the ground truth of historical event but a deeper probing of it. It also grants itself a special textual status; as necessary compensatory history, it demands inclusion within any collective archive that would ignore it.

In *The Armies of the Night*, an exploration of the relation of history to the novel within the context of the October 1967 march on the Pentagon, Norman Mailer offers a succinct statement on the novel as compensatory history. Discovering the narrative tools of the traditional historian inadequate for the task at hand, he concludes,

> Forget that the journalistic information available from both sides is so incoherent, inaccurate, contradictory, malicious, even based on error that no accurate history is conceivable. More than one historian has found a way through chains of false fact. No, the difficulty is that history is interior—no documents can give sufficient intimation: the novel must replace history at precisely the point where experience is sufficiently emotional, spiritual, psychical, moral, existential, or supernatural to expose the fact that the historian in pursuing the experience would be obliged to quit the clearly demarcated limits of historic inquiry. (284)

Mailer's suggestion is a challenge to any historical novelist, but it could not speak more directly to the literary point men of the Vietnam War, those imaginative recorders of an event whose "interior" history always threatened to overload traditional recording devices. As the most recent bearers of a particularly resonant form of the historical novel—the fully realized war narrative—they not only dive deeply into new disturbing data, but also provide lineal connections to a great tradition.

The war novel has always had a special value among historical novels. Because the origin of its aesthetic representation is a historical configuration of maximum crisis, the disruption of the apparent harmony or congruity of a culture, the war novel incorporates within its historical and aesthetic project unique problems and advantages. Beyond its obvious dramatic possibilities, war makes readable and testable the deepest structures of national myth and belief. The facts of war, the lived drama of national trauma, bring into high relief complexes and intersections of ideological presupposition, collective purpose, and group identity that might otherwise recede into perceptions of apparent national harmony or constancy. War is not only a story of nations at arms. It is invariably a signifier of violent shifts within culture and within individual sensibility.

War applies a variety of pressures to a culture beyond the expenditure of natural, industrial, and human resources. It demands not only definition but also implementation of religious, racial, economic, social, and philosophical beliefs and practices that in peacetime may remain uncorrelated but in war become the intertwined threads of national policy. The war novel in its most fully realized form as a historical and aesthetic enterprise is the imaginative inscription of both configurations: the clearly demarcated grouping of elements that are the lived history of the war; and the larger, more elusive components of national myth and belief that are tested, reaffirmed, cast off, or revised in the broadest cultural sense. In short, the war novel makes the leviathan of the national cultural paradigm sound and surface, and as a meaningful social ritual, the novel announces its value in two ways: it is a significant record of immediate history as it renders the aspects of experience that evade other varieties of historical writing; and it is a lasting cultural document as it responds to the rending and reconstituting of national mythos.

In *American War Literature: 1914 to Vietnam*, Jeffrey Walsh considers the dual nature of the war novel and suggests,

> Every war has two histories in literature: it has its own internal history in which literature may record a particularity of circumstance; and it has another history, its place in that wider history of events and nations that transcends the immediate and interprets situations more comprehensively in time. The most effective war writers are generally those who manage to live long enough after their military service to unite both kinds of history. (25)

The war novel does not merely enfold the two histories, however. Rather, in its modal, thematic, and stylistic elements, it often mirrors the crisis of the lived history that it seeks to represent. If the buried structures of culture are made visible by war, so are the aesthetic strategies of the text in which they finally reside. The more extensive and violent are the cultural disturbances within individual and collective sensibility, the more desperate or acute will be the search for appropriate textual forms to record those profound seismic effects. The war novel in its full flower is the representation of three simultaneous crises: one immediately historical, one broadly and deeply cultural, and one self-consciously aesthetic. The fully realized American war novel has always been a unique study in the reciprocity of form and substance, of art and history, of new individual experience and collective belief systems.

Despite the number and magnitude of the wars in the nation's short history and the continuing popularity of the theme of men at war, Americans do not think of themselves as a warlike people. As a component of the master national narrative—that collection of mythic story elements that consistently emphasizes American exceptionalism in regard to virtue, goodness, and the proper application of power—war has been defined within the national consciousness in a number of ways: a crusade, a tragic inevitability, a nasty job to be finished as quickly as possible. But overriding all these interpretations is the larger apprehension that war is an aberration within American civilization, not its most typical and readable recurring practice. Americans choose to think of themselves most often as peace-loving examples to more martial nations, as individual emissaries of culture who will fight out of necessity against a clear and present danger and will implement the most pragmatic patterns of an indigenous idealism to settle matters cleanly and with dispatch. Americans seem to subscribe to the notion of war discoverable in Thomas More's *Utopia*, for More argued that diplomacy is always favorable to conflict, but that once war ensues, every means available may be used to write its historical conclusion. Harry Truman's emphasizing that the atomic fireballs over Japan were necessary tools to end a war is a prime example of the strange blend of idealism and pragmatism inherent in American views on war, views that achieved supreme international importance after World War II when the United States— and its mythic self-image—emerged as a world power of seemingly unlimited potential.

Daniel Boorstin has argued that "what a nation means by war or peace is as characteristic of its experience and as intimately involved with all its other ways as are its laws and its religion" (375), and

American wars recede into the collective historical consciousness as crusades to assert independence, to save the Union, to preserve shared Western values and culture, to defeat fascism and totalitarianism, to contain monolithic world Communism, to guarantee the integrity of an emerging Third World. The recent reinterpretation within the Reagan administration of the Vietnam experience as a "noble" one is merely the latest in a long history of collective revisions that attempt to correlate harmoniously new national experience in war with larger American narratives, to expunge with the wave of a wand areas of ambiguity, the persistent gray areas of most historical experience.

Extensive propaganda campaigns were necessary to orient the American population for involvement in both world wars; once involved, Americans found the realities of trench warfare, automatic weapons, indiscriminate artillery barrage, and carpet bombing to be real horrors, but collective memory has always placed national ideals in a mythic, adversary position to such realities rather than aligned with them. The London blitz and the Dresden fire bombing may be similar technological practices, but contentions of a larger relationship between them as twentieth-century tragedy are most often inadmissible historical readings in the closely guarded national archive of means and ends. Americans do not practice war. In their own minds, they are reluctant warriors who may become ferociously professional when the need presents itself. Once committed, however, they do not find traditional concepts of honor and bravery antiquated notions within the realities of modern or contemporary warfare. When they are called on to serve, it is invariably a response to ills fostered by other nations, other cultures. Public guilt and expiation for complicity in the tragedy are not part of the mythos. Pershing II missiles may be deployed in Western Europe and the American heartland may bristle with nuclear silos, but the renouncement of a first-strike policy is as much an extension of national tradition as it is contingent on present historical configurations. If the ante continues to be raised within lived history, the mythic elements that enfold the historical gamble remain operative and readable.

The finest American war fiction traditionally has offered itself as a corrective to the leveling effect of popular myth, to official or institutional tendencies to expunge ambiguity, to deny complicity in the horror of modern war, to write history in black and white while recoiling from the problematic shadings of ethical and moral gray.

Collective memory seeks to universalize, to place specific historical configurations within a simplified grid of national experience. It seeks continuity rather than disruption; it ignores crevices and promontories for the sake of leveled, well-traveled terrain. Within popular culture, it is no accident that the film *The Green Berets* looks remarkably similar to *The Sands of Iwo Jima* or that both seem the progeny of *Fort Apache* or *They Died with Their Boots On*, for collective memory desires not only to find its visage reflected in new experience, but also to transmute new, disturbing data into more familiar and comforting story elements. Popular myth is difficult to modify or to dislodge, and its power—its ability to order and to codify the unresolved tensions within new experience—will always ensure its position over the complex, self-conscious historical narrative as the national story form. As the American film director John Ford said, "When there is a choice of the legend or the truth, print the legend."

The self-conscious American war novel, however, does not merely stand in opposition to the appropriation of lived history within popular mythic texts. Most often, it enfolds the major components of popular myth within its own textual strategies to do battle with it. The best of American war fiction invariably deals specifically and deliberately with the linguistic strategies, both popular and official, that are the fuel for collective memory and offers itself as a fully realized metalanguage of warfare. And it is for this reason that the finest examples of American war writing often seem so startlingly new in terms of form and style, that historical and aesthetic shifts are invariably simultaneous operations. To respond adequately to the leveling process of popular myth and official reification, the novelist must light out for new aesthetic territory and begin anew.

Art as a social and historical response to war in the United States became a serious endeavor after the Civil War. The half-developed modernist tendencies of John William De Forest, the more fully developed ones of Ambrose Bierce and Stephen Crane, and the chiseled images of the war poetry of Whitman and Melville were new ways of speaking artistically of war, but intimations of this incipiently modernist chorus were present in other texts. It is Natty Bumppo, the perpetual frontiersman and mythic paladin, who traces once and for all the tensions between idealism and pragmatism that characterize American ambivalence toward warfare. Natty, among his other textual functions, may be seen as Cooper's aesthetic resolution of the real discrepancies between American collective self-image and historical reality. Part of both Indian and white culture but affiliated fully with neither, Natty is Cooper's historical statement as heroic impulse, a figure who is finally both a denial and a recognition of omnivorous Western settlement and racial dominance. If Natty simplifies by remaining forever outside them the more troublesome aspects of European territorial expansion crystallized by the Indian wars, he is nevertheless pursued inexorably to the plains by the real history he both opposes and illuminates throughout the *Leather-Stocking Tales*. He was the first and most prominent reminder that, despite the power of legend, history is always immanent in the text as a true adversary.

If Cooper's frontier never existed in fact, it might also be argued that lived history lay just beyond the tree line, its demanding visage visible through Cooper's mythic branches. When Mark Twain revised the Arthurian legends by inserting within them the new horrors of mass industrial warfare, he offered a fully wrought historical novel whose history is by no means faithful to traditional apprehensions of verisimilitude. Hank Morgan's history lesson in *A Connecticut Yankee in King Arthur's Court* lies in Twain's response to the nature and practice of modern warfare in his day. His apparent fabulation, like Cooper's romance, declares itself finally as meaningful historical iconography.

Another figure caught up in the drift of mass military operations and cultural upheaval is Israel Potter, a character whose sacrifice and commitment are overlooked by the Hegelian world figures who dominate Melville's rendition of the Revolutionary War. Wayne Charles Miller argues that in *Israel Potter*, "Melville describes war making not as heroic adventure but as an economic function to rid the nation of its poor" (30), a suggestion that becomes a major theme in subsequent American war fiction and a full-blown credo for many characters within the Vietnam War novel. Potter, as one of the war's throwaway people, reveals himself finally as an emblem of the inherent tension in all of American war fiction between the mythic celebration of the sacrifice of the common man and the historical imperative of the military establishment within society. In *White Jacket* and *Billy Budd*, Melville offered real warnings of the dangers inherent in the encroachment of the military establishment within society. Billy's death is an example of the unholy compromises created by institutional modes of thought that function only in terms of strict order and mass men, and the overall significance of Melville's man-of-war as world lies in the deliberate historical response it poses to the incipient strategies of Hank Morgan and his ilk. General Cummings in Mailer's *The Naked and the Dead* suggests to the ineffectually liberal Lieutenant Hearn that the American army might be viewed as a portrait of the future, but his insight was nothing new. Melville's nineteenth-century loomings, his representations of the would-be hero and would-be innocent overtaken by the nature of modern military thinking and institutions, were in direct historical opposition to the chivalric hero and effectual frontiersman of national myth, but the unstable relationship between the shared belief in noble, individual sacrifice and the historical intimation of useless mass death was a configuration demanding further development, aesthetic explorations it would find in the emergent modernist sensibility within Civil War fiction.

In *Patriotic Gore: Studies in the Literature of the American Civil War*, Edmund Wilson argues that John William De Forest was the first American writer to deal with the new aspects of mass warfare (670). Although the preponderance of Civil War fiction attempted to reaffirm collective romantic notions of the individual chivalric aspects of combat, to reify categories of noble action and just cause from both northern and southern perspectives, De Forest endeavored in *Miss Ravenel's Conversion from Secession to Loyalty* not only to treat the physical and psychological realities of mass industrial slaughter in a new way, but also to cast warnings similar to Melville's of the increasing militarism within American society. De Forest's Colonel Carter is an early example in American fiction of the career military man with totalitarian tendencies; the precursor of Mailer's Cummings and Joseph Heller's Lieutenant Scheisskopf, he would restructure De Forest's imaginary New England state of Barataria into a model of Prussian efficiency. De Forest was not entirely consistent in his treatment of war, and residual romantic tendencies reside side by side with realistic ones within his fiction, but his vivid descriptions of the dead and wounded offered without sentiment were preludes to the more extensive aesthetic innovations of the World War I protest novel.

Ambrose Bierce, in *In the Midst of Life: Tales of Soldiers and Civilians*, offered a graphic portrayal of war that in its darkly ironic aspects is rivaled in American war fiction only by the works of Dalton Trumbo, Joseph Heller, Kurt Vonnegut, and a few of the Vietnam writers. If De Forest's fiction contains residual traces of war as modern chivalry, Bierce's was distinctly new and unrelentingly horrific. Uninterested in overt ideological or political analysis, Bierce made his immediate historical and larger cultural statements through a series of tales that paint mass warfare as absurd and completely callous to the needs, fears, and aspirations of the soldiers trapped within it. Bierce viewed the nature of the new warfare firsthand, and his tapestry of death, dismemberment, and psychological breakdown is a true gothic fiction of war, the most viscerally powerful nineteenth-century warning to the soldiers of future American wars. In "The Coup de Grâce," Bierce offered this description of events after a battle:

> The dead were collected in groups of a dozen or a score and laid side by side in rows while the trenches were dug to receive them. . . . There was little attempt at identification, though in most cases, the burial parties being detailed to glean the same ground which they had assisted to reap, the names of the victorious dead were known and listed. The enemy's fallen had to be content with counting. But of that they got enough: many of them were counted several times, and the total, as given afterward in the official report of the victorious commander, denoted rather a hope than a result.
> (72)

If the language of the passage is not completely contemporary, some of the official facts and fictions of the Vietnam War are certainly foreshadowed, for Bierce's Civil War body count was a prototype of the future imagery of kill ratios and free-fire zones.

Bierce's gallery of horrors was an aesthetic breakthrough in Civil War fiction, but Henry Fleming's battlefield initiation in Stephen Crane's *The Red Badge of Courage* cast the mold of the American *Bildungsroman* that would become the primary narrative structure of war writers from World War I through Vietnam. More so than their European counterparts, American war writers have employed one initiate or a small group of sensibilities through which to filter their cultural statements. The epic sweep and social texture of *War and Peace* are rarely discernible. Rather, the solitary soldier becomes the emblem and prism of historical statement. Fleming, absorbed by a military that Crane describes in alternating organic and mechanical metaphors, finds his crisis not only in the realities of mass warfare, but also in the ambiguous relationship of the individual to the group. *The Red Badge of Courage* both reverberates with the warnings of Melville and De Forest and offers for the first time a complete delineation of the tension between the individual and the collective impulses and imperatives that are at odds not only within the debilitating facts of war, but also within the very fabric of American culture and society. Crane's curiously skewed *Bildungsroman* brings into high relief the delusory nature of individual aspirations to vainglory and chivalric action in post–Industrial Revolution America. Crane, along with De Forest, Bierce, and a few others, attempted to deflate indigenous notions of war as a collective crusade or as an opportunity for individual heroism, but in regard to entrenched national myths, their pleas were to remain generally unheard or disregarded. The American soldiers who boarded the troopships for France in 1917 embarked in a national atmosphere characterized by a renewed vision of the crusade and a commitment to rescue shared Western values. Popular and official mythology were again in grand ascendancy.

In *Waiting for the End*, Leslie Fiedler argues of the new protest fiction of World War I that "the anti-war novel did not end war, but it memorialized the end of something almost as deeply rooted in the culture of the West: the concept of honor" (30). The modernist configuration of protest occupied by Hemingway, Cummings, Dos Passos, Faulkner, William March Campbell, Laurence Stallings, and others was the aesthetic restructuring of the representation of war in American fiction and an analysis of the deeper cultural rifts made readable by the war, but it also must be understood as the flip side of the crusade anthems played by both the early ambulance-service volunteers and the enlisted men of the American Expeditionary Force. Fiedler is correct in identifying the paradigm of protest as a collective social outcry and a rigorous cultural dissection, but the protest fiction was preceded by a large number of works that upheld the official explanations and the collective approval of the American war effort. Troy Belknap in Edith Wharton's *The Marne* and George Campton and Claude Wheeler in Willa Cather's *A Son at the Front* and *One of Ours* all feel to varying degrees a sense of commitment to the preservation of values that the defense of France symbolizes. In *The American Soldier in Fiction, 1880–1963: A History of the Attitudes Toward Warfare and the Military Establishment*, Peter Aichinger notes that "for all the late vogue of disillusionment fostered by Cummings, Hemingway, and Dos Passos, the idealism and simplicity of spirit expressed in the works of Miss Cather and Mrs. Wharton represent accurately the mood of the young men who went away to war" (6).

The notion of the selfless military quest in a new age of mechanized warfare, however, was an impossible one to maintain aesthetically once the true horrors of prolonged trench warfare were manifested. In technique and aesthetic innovation, works such as *A Farewell to Arms*, *The Enormous Room* and *Soldier's Pay*, *Three Soldiers* and *Company K*, and *Plumes* and *Johnny Got His Gun* took divergent paths that met in the collective clearing of a fully realized modernist sensibility. Hemingway stripped the American idiom of vainglorious modification and portrayed the new strategy of the separate peace; Cummings and Faulkner fragmented and dispersed traditional narrative to render the unseen, spiritual effects of war that collective memory would fail to mythologize; Dos Passos and Campbell explored the possibilities of multiple-perspective narrative for their historical analysis; and Stallings and Trumbo inverted the very metaphorical complexes of crusade writing as a powerful tool against it. There is no passage or group of passages that may quickly encapsulate the nature and purpose of the modernist project, but Frederic Henry's linguistic analysis in *A Farewell to Arms* captures the prime imperative of all the protest writers, the need to refashion the American war novel as a meaningful counterstatement to the mythic apparatus that helped to create Verdun, the Somme, and Flanders Field:

> I was always embarrassed by the words sacred, glorious, and sacrifice and the expression in vain. We had heard them, sometimes standing in the rain almost out of earshot, so that only the shouted words came through, and had read them, on proclamations that were slapped up by billposters over other proclamations, now for a long time, and I had seen nothing sacred, and the things that were glorious had no glory and the sacrifices were like the stockyards at Chicago if nothing was done with the meat except to bury it. . . . Abstract words such as glory, honor, courage, or hallow were obscene beside the concrete names of villages, the numbers of roads, the names of rivers, the numbers of regiments and the dates. (184–85)

This is the conclusion of Bierce and Crane reenunciated, an appraisal of language that transformed the crusading of Troy Belknap into the debilitation of Hemingway's Nick Adams, Dos Passos's John Andrews, Faulkner's Donald Mahon. The revised initiate of the American war *Bildungsroman* was still a crusader, and his mythic narrative, as described by Joseph Campbell in *The Hero with a Thousand Faces*, remained solving the riddle, defeating the enemy, and dispensing the great boon to mankind. But for Hemingway, Cummings, and the rest, the riddle deciphered was the dangerous illusion of popular myth, the defeated enemy was less the Hun than the carefully assembled ideological and economic arguments that produced the war, and the boon was the modernist voice that attempted to initiate a new, fully historicized cultural crusade, the forging of a collective memory that would learn from rather than deny the realities stacked like cordwood in the fields of Europe.

The war literature of World War II is much more diversified than that of the previous war, a body of work that displays not only a marked split between liberal and conservative tendencies, what Wayne Charles Miller calls "a divided stream," but also a penchant for focusing on specific problems within an increasingly militarized American society: problems of an ethnic or a racial nature; the separate societies and visions of the career officer and the temporary enlisted man; the nature of the military structure and the military mind at its upper levels; a renewed examination of totalitarian tendencies within a newly powerful American state. There was again a pronounced protest impulse, but overall the writers did not display the initial sense of shock and outrage or the later disillusionment of their earlier counterparts. There was a radical shift from the World War I modernist perspective, for as a group, the new novelists treated war as a regrettable but predictable manifestation of American culture. The American war novel of World War II as powerful symbolic history announced clearly that warfare had become a permanent state of mind.

In *Fiction of the Forties*, Chester E. Eisinger suggests that the American soldier of World War II was less disillusioned by the realities of war because he was far less idealistic than his predecessor. Conditioned by a Depression economy and having a greater sense of alienation and cultural disjointedness, the new soldier was both more cynical and more sophisticated (23–24). Despite the dire effects wrought by the new engines of mass warfare—the mass bombing of civilian populations, the Promethean flashpoints of Hiroshima and Nagasaki—the American soldier accepted both popular and official arguments for defeating Germany and Japan. As the most visible agent and emblem of a collective effort, the American fighting man did experience consistent movement toward the validation of the master mythic narrative. Whether fighting from island to island in the Pacific or moving from North Africa through Sicily, Italy, and France into Germany, soldiers wrote a narrative with a beginning, a middle, and, most important, an end. As Peter Aichinger suggests, "World War I was a long and bloody stalemate; in World War II the machine functioned, victories were clear-cut, the team rolled forward" (65).

It should not be suggested, however, that American writers of World War II did not discover a number of problems concerning the nature of the war or fashion a number of aesthetic innovations and structures by which to address them. More and more, war was perceived to be an emblem of larger social ills, and if General Cummings's description in *The Naked and the Dead* of the American military as a vision of the future is the most inclusive charge, many more specific criticisms are discernible. The delineation of racial inequities—of the Jewish soldier in Irwin Shaw's *The Young Lions*, David Davidson's *The Steeper Cliff*, and Saul Bellow's *Dangling Man*, and of the black in John Cobb's *The Gesture* and John Oliver Killens's *And Then We Heard the Thunder*—is prominent. These works and others like them composed the significant collective assertion that the inequalities inherent within American society were exacerbated rather than diminished within military institutions. James Jones's *From Here to Eternity* not only features the freewheeling prejudicial nature of the army barracks, but also offers the sacrifice of Prewitt, the would-be career enlisted man whose refusal to defer to officer machinations results in his death.

The platoon or squad as a unit for sociological discourse and cultural analysis was a significant new convention of the World War II novel, and it was a filtering device for a wide spectrum of insights. If Norman Mailer employed it as a warning of totalitarian drift, Leon Uris in *Battle Cry* conveyed admiration for the well-functioning unit and offered more than tacit approval of the discipline and rigidity of the military as social microcosm. More typical, though, may be the tone of Harry Brown's *A Walk in the Sun*, a work that offers implicit acceptance of the inevitability of war and the necessity of professionalism in the field. Brown refrained from judging the war; rather, he accepted it as the waking dream of the twentieth century, a fact of life to be dealt with as cleanly and as quickly as possible. Buried within Brown's concrete delineation of one day of war experienced by a rifle platoon is the suggestion that survival is the only meaningful ideology, an idea that would become much more overt in second-generation World War II works, such as Kurt Vonnegut's *Slaughterhouse-Five*, Joseph Heller's *Catch-22*, and James Jones's *The Thin Red Line*.

Both the sociological unit of the platoon and the delineation of racial issues are components of World War II writing that would be recycled in new forms in the Vietnam novel, but the group of novels dealing with the American occupation contain foreshadowing of other major Vietnam themes. Malcolm Cowley, in "War Novels: After Two Wars," argues that the American soldiers of World War II "accepted the war as they might have accepted an earthquake and tried to do their best in the circumstances" but that "they proved irresponsible and corrupt as garrison forces in conquered territory" (300). If the majority of World War I protest novels portray the American soldier as victim, works such as John Hersey's *A Bell for Adano*, Alfred Hayes's *The Girl on the Via Flaminia*, and John Horne Burns's *The Gallery* offer the American forces of occupation as a significant corrupting influence in the older, established cultures they subdue but take no pains to understand. The writers argued that America as victor offered itself only as a sterile, rigid model of order for the rest of the world, that the subtlety and sophistication of both Eastern and Western traditions were placed in jeopardy by the new savior. In *The Gallery*, one of Burns's more analytical characters suggests,

> We're destroying all the new ideas and all the little men of the world to make way for our mass production and our mass thinking and our mass entertainment. Then we can go back to our United States, that green little island in the midst of a smoking world. Then we can kill all the Negroes and the Jews. Then we'll start on the Russians. (76)

The argument of Burns and the other garrison writers becomes especially acute in the Vietnam novel, for the nature of the Vietnam War was such that American forces were simultaneously combat troops and an army of occupation. Not only bearer of bullets and bombs, America would attempt to implant in Southeast Asia the seeds of its own cultural imperatives.

The Soviet consolidation of Eastern Europe after World War II, the political transformation of mainland China, and the successful test of the Russian atomic weapon in 1949 were all contributing factors to a drift in the United States toward what Morris Janowitz calls the "garrison state," the existence and collective apprehension of the military as the dominating institution within American society and of war itself as a permanent shadow. The veterans of World War II who as reserve forces were called up for service in the Korean War, if willing to put on uniforms once more, were resentful and confused that America should be involved in another major conflict so soon. In war novels such as James Michener's *The Bridges at Toko-Ri* and William Styron's *The Long March*, the action centers on the adjustment of a veteran to the new military and a different kind of warfare. Michener's Harry Brubaker becomes a reconciled member of the team, but Styron's Al Mannix is a historically trapped dissenter and malcontent, an emblem of the collective knowledge that war has become a way of life, the one constant in an international arena of political and ideological variables.

A conflict whose progress and final features were determined as much by the bargaining table as by tactical decisions in the field, the Korean War was a prelude of larger things to come, but if there was a powerful, portentous image of that war, it was probably not in the literature. In the final reel of the film *Pork Chop Hill*, Gregory Peck and the few surviving members of his rifle company attempt to repel a human wave of Chinese Communist soldiers while negotiators remain immersed in ideological gamesmanship at Panmunjom. Seeing the film in the context of Vietnam is stunning, for the iconography of the Paris talks of Henry Kissinger and Le Duc Tho leaps off the screen, but the distance between the screen image of Peck's final victorious walk down the hill in Korea and the collective memories of the departure of American forces from South Vietnam seems light-years. If the Korean War was unwelcome, it was resolved satisfactorily within national myth and quickly enough so that domestic reaction remained controlled. The Vietnam War—a military, ideological, and cultural enterprise of confusing origins, shifting practices, and ever-receding closure—would be an experience that would illuminate, test, and revise not only the newly forged components of Cold War mythology, but also those buried elements of national belief and self-image that had been operative since the elegaic death of Natty Bumppo on the plains.

Any reader seeking the essential history of the Vietnam War, an Ur-text of overall significance, would be well advised to confront a symbolic riddle residing in Washington, D.C. A permanent reminder of the problems of secure historical closure, a challenge on the level of reader response, the black stone Vietnam Veterans Memorial, carrying the names of the 58,132 American dead in Vietnam, is the most difficult kind of text. Its polished black surface both reflecting and absorbing sources of illumination, the V strikes one as perhaps the most visible historical example of Thomas Pynchon's postmodern reading lesson. Victory, Valor, Victim, or, simply, Vietnam, the possible permutations are endless. Both unwanted reminder and collective resolution, the memorial stands as the kind of associative figure found in a tale by Hawthorne or Melville, its plenitude of symbolic possibilities unlimited, the power of its blackness within personal consciousness undeniable. Within the seams of the black stones are found messages to the dead written daily by families, friends, and surviving veterans—a strange and poignant form of communication that indicates that the war is far from dead history. We have not put Vietnam behind us, the messages suggest, nor can we, for in regard to both national and individual sensibility, its status as story is open and unresolved.

The suggestion of Pynchon's V is not stretching an analogy, for within its unresolved story elements and abundant symbolic possibilities, the war as lived history had a distinctly postmodernist composition. Narrative strands led everywhere and nowhere, intertwined and separated as official mythologies not only succeeded but also contradicted themselves. Journalistic consistency was difficult, if not impossible, to find, the stories in print and on television, especially after Tet in 1968, offering competing versions of the truth. The stories by reporters who relied on the daily official briefings on the war's progress—the "five o'clock follies," as they were called by the journalists—correlated less and less with the dispatches filed from the jungles, rice paddies, and fire bases where the fighting took place. As Time, Newsweek, and the major dailies displayed radical shifts of specific criticisms and overall editorial policies, the official summaries and the corrective journalistic ones became more opposed, more contradictory, and couched in an ever-expanding cloud of mutual mistrust. The effect was the most disorienting kind of imagism, a proliferation of fragments, horrific glimpses, and ambiguous synopses that suggested the war to be Crane's half-organic, half-technological beast fueled by its own inexhaustible power for contradiction and multiple costume change.

Much of the trouble concerning both official truth and journalistic clarity resulted from the war's not being a single narrative but a number of successive and simultaneous wars within a war, a loose collection of political, ideological, and military vignettes that would not conform easily to the form of the collective mythic novel in which previous American wars resided. If generals, politicians, activists, journalists, and the public at large desperately sought in the events internal congruity and traditional connections, the war consistently resisted such processing and maintained its position as a cultural disturbance of a new kind, the end point, at least in terms of genuine collective believability, of a number of long-standing components of national myth. The war simply would not support the weight of the competing readings placed on it, and the cracks and fissures in the immediate tension-ridden narrative spoke to a great number of writers of a deeper cultural rending, the visible separation of the indigenous impulses of idealism and pragmatism that in previous wars had seemed one balanced organism and the most typically American unitary response to national crisis.

Traditional historical methodology was tested immediately by the war, for even asserting a starting point for the historical narrative proved difficult, if not impossible. The convenient increment of 1965 to 1973 as the period of active military involvement is suspect and unstable, for in 1950 the Truman administration contributed $10 million to the French war effort against the Vietminh, a figure that reached $1 billion, or approximately 80 percent of the French bill, in 1954 when the debacle of Dien Bien Phu occurred and the Geneva Accords were cast. If the American involvement is dubbed the Second Indochina War, such a designation illuminates a certain historical continuity but shrouds the earlier American complicity and support. September 1945 might seem a reliable date, for when Ho Chi Minh's appeals to the United States for support of the newly declared Democratic Republic of Vietnam fell on deaf ears and the French returned to Hanoi to resume colonial status after the defeat of Japan, America's failure to uphold Franklin Roosevelt's declaration that "France has milked it for one hundred years. The people of

Indochina are entitled to something better than that" was the first step toward a wider involvement that would consume American resources and resolve for the next thirty years. Such a starting point, however, is only a historical repetition of Nguyen Ai Quoc, alias Ho Chi Minh, appealing for help in fostering self-determination in Indochina to Woodrow Wilson at Versailles in 1919.

To speak of the Vietnam War as a unity is a disarming of historical gloss, for at least four distinct phases of American involvement are discernible after the French defeat in 1954: 1954 to 1961, the period of the creation and support of the instant regime of Ngo Dinh Diem and covert operations in both the North and the South; 1961 to 1965, the post–Bay of Pigs phase, during which 17,000 American advisers assumed their role with the South Vietnamese Army (ARVN) and the beginning of the endless military juntas that followed Diem's assassination; 1965 to 1968, the beginning of America's full combat role, during which troop increments steadily increased and official reports of success were offered confidently and were generally well accepted by both the media and the American people; and 1968 to 1973, the post–Tet offensive period of home-front disillusionment, reversed media reaction, the Cambodian invasion, Vietnamization, and the death dance of the Paris talks.

These are, of course, broad cross-cuts across the narrative fabric, and more specific increments might be defensible, but the discovery of at least four distinct phases serves not only to indicate the chimerical, processive nature of the war, but also to pose necessary questions to the prospective historical novelist: Which war or wars do you hope to represent? What stage of confidence, commitment, disillusionment, or vitriolic debate influenced your narrative choice? Will your novel purport to be an inclusive interpretive statement, or will it define itself as a partial reading? Is a full statement possible?

The sequential nature of the war raised narrative problems for the novelists, but so did the existence of a unique historical simultaneity. While the United States forces were conducting full military operations in Vietnam, they were also an army of occupation experiencing and engendering the kind of cultural clash and confusion that offered stories at least as significant as those offered by the military operations. If World War II writing presents distinct groupings of combat and occupation books, the Vietnam novelist was faced with the task of representing not only the nature of the fighting, but also the larger cultural and political developments and machinations that surrounded and finally dwarfed it. In regard to both the political and the psychological aspects, the relationship between the United States and South Vietnam was that of parent of child, ally to ally, and mistrusted benefactor to recalcitrant client. The American soldier was encouraged to understand the conflict as his war, "their" war, and a shared endeavor, an impossible situation in regard to either collective commitment or individual orientation.

The most perceptive of the Vietnam writers dealt heavily with the "bomb them and feed them" surrealism of the American project, and Frank Ross's notion of the American soldier as assailant–victim[1] takes on new tragic dimensions. If American innocence, a core feature in all of American war writing, is once again central in the Vietnam works, it is present in a historical laboratory that renders some revolutionarily new test results. From Crane and Bierce onward, there has been a pronounced tendency in the American war novel to present the final form of the inexperienced initiate of the battlefield *Bildungsroman* more as the victim of war than as its deadly agent. Vietnam, however, forced a remixing of the proportional make-up of the assailant–victim equation. The fullest and most self-conscious works redefine the American complexes of innocence and experience, guilt and expiation, taking into account not only the price paid by the Vietnamese in human life, material waste, and cultural fragmentation, but also the admission that any assertion of American victimization or loss must be accompanied by a recognition of the national capacity for excess and destruction. In *The March of Folly: From Troy to Vietnam*, Barbara Tuchman summarizes the collective reappraisal when she states, "For many, confidence in the righteousness of their country gave way to cynicism. Who since Vietnam would venture to say of America in simple belief that she was 'the last best hope on earth'? What America lost in Vietnam was, to put it in one word, virtue" (374). If, as Tuchman asserts, America lost virtue in Vietnam, it might also be argued that it was one not worth keeping, an untested conception of natural goodness that consistently revealed itself in a post–World War II evangelical strain, an ideological voice articulating a national text that was both jeremiad and prophetic history.

The finest of the literary point men of Vietnam share a key narrative project—to re-create fully and imaginatively how the American soldier became both agent and victim of the narrow interpretive spectrum by which the conflict was illuminated. From the official American standpoint, the war was always an immediate military and political project for which it was presumed the tools could be powerful and easily provided, but few in number. Innate faith in the power of improvisation and technical know-how was the trump card of national myth, but it was an impoverished notion. At no time during the war were the historical and cultural roots of the conflict sufficiently examined amid the various bombing campaigns, troop build-ups, aid programs, and diplomatic missions. The failure of brute force and sheer numbers to subdue what was considered an inferior, ill-organized, and badly supported adversary produced frustration and manic determination to use more of the same. Fresh perspectives were foreign to American policy; the main line of established approaches seemed to preclude necessary detour and additional, panoramic vista.

The failure of American leadership to respond to the historical and cultural origins of the war produced the most tragic bulldozing effect in Vietnam for both the peasant population and the Americans who operated the official machinery. If the villagers were buffeted continually by the shifting practices of Saigon and Washington, America itself seemed like a blind giant thrashing angrily in the wilderness, an ideological Polyphemus arguing that no man could defeat it while never comprehending the full nature of its self-inflicted wound. In *Fire in the Lake: The Vietnamese and the Americans in Vietnam*, Frances FitzGerald identifies the nature of that blindness as she traces a larger national tendency:

> Americans ignore history, for to them everything has always seemed new under the sun. The national myth is that of creativity and progress, of a steady climbing upward into power and prosperity, both for the individual and for the country as a whole. Americans see history as a straight line and themselves standing at the cutting edge of it as representatives for all mankind. They believe in the future as if it were a religion; they believe that there is nothing they cannot accomplish, that solutions wait somewhere for all problems like brides. (9)

If from 1858 through 1954, French colonialism was the repetition in miniature of two millennia of Chinese intervention and exploitation, the presence of the United States, one that seemed interminable to most Americans, was to the Vietnamese no more than a minor scene in a national drama of epic scale. If American negotiators and military leaders were confounded constantly by the patience and intractability of the enemy, those qualities had much deeper roots and a more circuitous narrative than they ever imagined. Faith in the quick fix and failure to read Vietnamese cultural history, however, would prove fatal to the desire to avoid a quagmire.

American military planners often were amazed at the return of transplanted peasants to the villages and paddies that had been cleared as free-fire zones, those areas swept of "friendlies" so that any living thing remaining could be construed to be the enemy and therefore fired on. The strategic-hamlet program, a plan designed to root out the Vietcong infrastructure by relocating villagers into protected areas far from their ancestral homes, not only produced a massive refugee population, but also was the very policy to erode the nominal loyalty that most non-urban Vietnamese held for the Saigon government. American notions of instant social reorganization informed by monolithic strategic thinking helped to foster cultural dislocation and historical upheaval that had greater long-range effects than even the persistent bombing campaigns. As the puzzled American soldiers who searched or swept the villages were met with passive or angry stares, they were redefining national innocence in a most disastrous way. Victims of the official failure to read history and often unable to distinguish friend from foe, they became too often agents of the most telling forms of human and technological retribution.

Beyond questions of guilt and innocence in relation to unread cultural history, the Vietnam War novelist had another major issue to confront. The creation of a credible protagonist to become the center of the familiar battlefield education could be both an aesthetic and an ethical problem, for notions of fair odds, moral imperatives, and admirable struggle inherent in established definitions of heroism were tested severely by the national experience in Vietnam. The early crusade metaphors of the Kennedy–Green Beret period were stretched to the breaking point for the general public by 1968 and significantly sooner for the astute critic. As the darker aspects of the war became public knowledge, not only by Daniel Ellsberg's disclosures, but also via a new adversary journalism, the prospect of offering fiction or memoir that would connect readily with mainstream American war writing seemed an impossible endeavor for anyone but a dehistoricized romance writer or a peddler of visceral pulp fiction that would capitalize on the more regrettable and cartoon-like aspects of national mythology.

American soldiers, while failing to produce the confidently predicted victory, seemed to have all the advantages. For many Americans, the early romance of the daring but sympathetic Special Forces adviser was replaced with discomforting images of the big guy kicking the little one about, intimations that simultaneously shot tremors through national myth and appeared to sound the death knell for the old-fashioned war novel. Outlining the specific historical difficulties involved in refurbishing the American "good-guy" syndrome, Stanley Karnow notes that

> . . . American soldiers went into action in Vietnam with the gigantic weight of American industry behind them. Never before in history was so much strength amassed in such a small corner of the globe against an opponent apparently so inconsequential. If Ho Chi Minh had described his war with the French as a struggle between "grasshoppers and elephants," he was now a microbe facing a leviathan. (435)

Karnow's metaphors are telling, for they not only place the unprecedented American firepower and technology in historical scale, but also challenge figuratively the novelist to channel the heroic initiation and quest toward new categories of personal knowledge and collective ritual or to abandon shopworn conventions for new forms. What many Vietnam War writers discovered was that conventions such as the personal initiation and the platoon as ideological and social refracting device could be recycled but that a new degree of self-consciousness was necessary for their use. Because the historical readings and collective sensibility promulgated by the war were radically new on many levels, the older narrative patterns that were employed successfully not only become conduits for the interpretation of immediate history, but often seem in aggregate a metacommentary on the tradition of the American war novel itself, a self-conscious exploration and revision of previous aesthetic projects. The most intriguing aspect of the best works on the war is how familiar story patterns and narrative conventions are resuscitated for the rendering of new or revised definitions of innocence and experience, guilt and expiation.

An appropriate subtitle for the national experience in Vietnam is the one that Kurt Vonnegut attached to *Slaughterhouse-Five*, his absurdist moral treatment of the Dresden fire bombing of World War II. A children's crusade, the Vietnam War was fought by disproportionate numbers of the poor, the minorities, and the uneducated, soldiers whose grasp of history, politics, and culture was intuitive rather than formal. As the lived experience of the war forced an exchange of crusade metaphors for the figurative language of mere survival, as public opinion soured and adversary journalism entrenched itself opposite official glosses, an authentic subculture, one with its own language, rituals, politics, and social practices, emerged in the jungles and paddies of Vietnam. If the media and the managers were engaged in increasingly hard-bitten debates, the soldiers in the field constituted a third position, which argued with persistent vehemence that neither public voice was telling it correctly. That subculture and that voice are the heart of the finest Vietnam War writing and the prime argument for the books to be appraised as the most valuable kind of compensatory history, for as the emissary of American will and idea in Vietnam, it was the foot soldier whose testimony, imaginatively and symbolically rendered by the literary point man, would be the most telling historical text.

The cultural responsibility of the Vietnam point man as historical witness was not only to represent the actions, language, and sensibility that lay largely buried during the war and its immediate aftermath, however, but also to suggest how the experience—the personal transformation of the soldier from FNG ("fucking new guy") or "cherry" to "short-timer," which is the core narrative the war's true interior history—deforms and reshapes the American self-image. If there is a common bond among the thematic, modal, and stylistic strategies of the writers, it is the unwavering commitment to resurrect and to speak to what Michael Herr refers to as the war's secret history, to be accessible conduits for a radically new American sensibility.

The soldiers who fought the war were what Shad Meshad appropriately calls "warrior-teenagers" (202). The average American soldier of World War II was twenty-seven, but the typical combat veteran of Vietnam was in his late teens; a grunt in his late twenties would invariably be granted the nickname "Pop." Forty percent of the casualties were received by blacks and Hispanics, and a disproportionate number of official reprimands, brig confinements, and dishonorable discharges were given to soldiers of those same ethnic groups. Within the novels and memoirs is present not only racial tension as a prime theme, but also the delineation of an intuitive political consciousness among many soldiers—white, black, and Hispanic—who found Vietnam to be a short course in economics and political science as well as military tactics. Gloria Emerson sketches one of many Vietnam history lessons when she states,

> Vietnam illuminated nothing quite so clearly as the American caste system. Watching who was fighting the war was to be aware of a caste system that is almost ironclad. It was the working class who got caught and who died. They were the surplus. They were the children we could afford to lose, the acceptable casualties. ("Vietnam Veterans Speak" 182)

Emerson's message and tone were commonplace in both the experience of the soldiers and the works of their spokesmen, for Vietnam writing as protest fiction is the identification of a number of enemies on several levels of magnitude, the least of which are not the cultural imperatives and supporting national mythology that catalyzed the skewed historical quest of the American fighting man.

The protest impulse within the books, however, if pronounced, does not in most cases assume an overtly polemical or didactic posture. The most significant addition to the tradition of American war writing in the Vietnam works is the coexistence of the rigorous representation of specific horrors and surrounding causes and the conclusion, often implicit, that the lessons learned will not affect finally the institutions, policies, and mythologies they expose so graphically and tragically. There is a curious inertia in the works, a tendency toward imaginative entropy that threatens even the most self-conscious and controlled, a protest that, unlike the World War I paradigm, announces itself continually as darkly ironic illustration rather than effective social catalyst. The warnings of Melville and the shock of Dos Passos are replaced by the implicit conclusion that the trick is not to change the world but to survive it. Unlike Heller's Yossarian and Hemingway's Frederic Henry, however, the Vietnam protagonist finds the prospect of the separate peace impossible, the likelihood of physical, psychological, or spiritual disengagement a dangerous myth.

The prime historical message within the new literature of Vietnam resides finally in how terminally its heroes are transformed by the experience, in how complete seems the discrepancy between necessary personal explanation and inevitable violent agency. Most often, the protagonist is not merely affected or altered by the history he helps to write; he is spiritually and emotionally annihilated by it, reshaped internally so that his new state becomes a dark joke that only the initiated can share. Within all its aesthetic restructurings, behind its many necessary transformations of the conventions of a specific literary tradition, there is in even the most powerful writing something that language cannot reach or explicate, an experience that words point toward but that only the reader's own creative energies can begin to trace. The imaginative products of the newest point men are necessarily incomplete, inherently unstable, and deeply challenging, texts that do not invite imaginative, creative readership but demand it with the shared claim that what is in hand is new and volatile material bearing an ancient and deadly message. Graphic realism, psychological horror, poetic meditation—the literature of Vietnam in mode and theme offers itself as both the apparent terminus of a tradition and a fulfilled historical prophecy of what mythic excess had always threatened to produce. The best works have the feel of the worst dream becoming real, but they also bear within them a puzzling riddle for collective memory, one discoverable in many permutations throughout the novels and memoirs but concentrated best perhaps in a Lurp's small narrative to Michael Herr in *Dispatches:*

> . . . what a story he told me, as one-pointed and resonant as any war story I ever heard, it took me a year to understand it:

> "Patrol went up the mountain. One man came back. He died before he could tell us what happened."

> I waited for the rest, but it seemed not to be that kind of story; when I asked him what had happened he just looked like he felt sorry for me, fucked if he'd waste time telling stories to anyone dumb as I was. (4–5)

The bitter minimalist tale of Herr's Lurp contains the seed of the larger narrative challenge that the Vietnam War posed to its imaginative recorder—and to those readers who follow in the point man's footsteps. Treading on new mythic ground, both writer and reader require the standard field equipment that has always been part of a larger tradition: the ability and sympathy to consider new data that threaten deeply rooted stories; and the understanding that a credible public memory may originate not in painless fabulation but in a hazardous but necessary imaginative journey into the dark interior regions of the soldier's personal experience.

What follows is an examination of the principal thematic elements and modal strategies of some of the finest Vietnam prose narratives. Although I discuss many works along the way, my own narrative design is deliberately selective and qualitative: each chapter is a discussion of a particular aesthetic strategy shared by a number of writers and a close examination of what I consider to be the two most resonant, challenging, or fully realized examples of that narrative type. The paired texts are intended to speak, then, not only for the lived experience they so powerfully re-create, but also for the other imaginative archivists who share their specific historical project, who are fellow members of their particular aesthetic platoon. David Halberstam and John Del Vecchio demonstrate how realistic narrative could be made adaptable for a war seemingly resistant to that mode. Tim O'Brien and Philip Caputo poignantly explore the connection of new history to classical categories in the personal memoir, while Gustav Hasford and Charles Durden provide a new artistic report on the uses of black humor. Michael Herr and Tim O'Brien perform dazzling alchemistic operations within a revised American romanticism, and Stephen Wright and Ward Just, with radically different tones and styles, explore the status of American memory after the veteran has rejoined "the World."

This study is, perhaps, an example of the literary desert-island question—"If you could take any ten Vietnam books . . . ?"—and students and scholars will perhaps make substitutions based on different critical criteria or unbridled personal enthusiasm. Necessary debate notwithstanding, all the writers discussed here, briefly or extensively, are the necessary FNGs who, as they enter new American terrain, pass a line of ghostly short-timers that includes Cooper and Melville, Crane and Hemingway, Jones and Mailer, Heller and Pynchon. Walking point, they share the interior artistic resolution, the deciphered historical riddle, for, as Michael Herr reveals, "War stories aren't really anything more than stories about people anyway." Right foot after left, they succeed because they must.

1

THE CAMERA'S EYE

When he first came to the country, he had been told the Vietnamese were not like Americans, they died silently, but it was wrong, they died like everyone else.

ONE VERY HOT DAY

What causes war? The situation here is perfect for study. I've brought with me all my knowledge of philosophy. It is dusty and tarnished but it is here, in me. And here are all the elements of war about me. Here are all the major races of mankind, representatives from every socio-economic group, from every government-politico force, all clashing. And the language groups: English, French, Vietnamese, American technologese, Spanish. Here a democracy upholds a dictatorship in the name of freedom while a dictatorial governing group infiltrates five percent of its nation's population to a different country in the name of nationalism. The answer to the question must be here, waiting to be discovered.

THE 13TH VALLEY

Indicating that art does indeed continue to imitate life, significant writing on the Vietnam War has suffered from some of the same historical misconceptions as the war itself. For many, American involvement in Vietnam seemed to begin when the first Marines waded ashore at Da Nang in 1965, and, unfortunately, for many readers the chronology of important appraisals of the war begins perhaps in 1977 with two memoirs, Michael Herr's *Dispatches* and Philip Caputo's *A*

Rumor of War; in fiction, the date may be 1978, the year in which Tim O'Brien's Going After Cacciato began to garner both critical acclaim and wide readership. In 1980, Joseph Tetlow noted that "for reasons lodged in the flow of history and culture, critics are not reviewing the Vietnam War novels and the American businessmen who have taken over the publishing houses have been printing them only reluctantly" (36). Although three Vietnam War novels, Going After Cacciato, Robert Stone's Dog Soldiers, and Larry Heinemann's Paco's Story have won National Book Awards, many works have found limited readership or have become casualties within an increasingly "cost-effective" publishing environment.[1]

There is once again a great burgeoning of interest in the war, a demand finally for a comprehensive, readable history of events and their larger significance. Wearied from following the war for years and subjected to a continual flow of interpretations, what Herr has called the "jargon stream," most readers seemed uninterested in any further renderings, true, invented, or otherwise. The return of the last American troops was followed by a collective, decade-long breath, a turning away from the realities and lessons of the war, but the body of writers who have been busy re-creating, analyzing, and interpreting the war is finding a wider, more receptive audience: multipart written histories and television documentaries and retrospectives are proliferating; photo and oral histories, personal memoirs, and new fiction have grown exponentially since 1977. Present world tensions, especially in Central America and in the Middle East, and an alarming revival of militaristic thinking certainly account for much of the interest; the moss-covered conclusion "No more Vietnams" is being revived in private thoughts and revised in many public arenas.

What the rapidly expanding body of Vietnam War writing makes available is a multiplicity of perspectives and approaches, a fuller spectrum for what Philip D. Beidler has called the necessary project of "sense-making." Beidler praises those novelists who recognize that the war itself was a puzzling mixture of new developments and pre-existing myths and who undertake the search for appropriate forms for its rendering, texts that are combinations of reportage and invention, blends of fidelity to the experience of the war and the imaginative use of facts that will connect the war and its immense associative power to an existing body of myth and history.[2]

A persistent theme in many Vietnam works is that the war was radically different from all previous American conflicts, that unfa-

miliar geography, constantly shifting official pronouncements, absence
of discernible objectives, and decaying support at home, especially
after Tet in 1968, produced a historical event that no one, from successive residents of the Oval Office to the soldier in the field, could
decipher, let alone render intelligently to a wide, confused audience.
Beneath the accruing layers of Vietnam War discourse lay Herr's notion of a secret history, the troublesome suggestion that no one could
or would perform the necessary kind of archaeology. Many of the
early writings have been denigrated for their failure to do more than
offer graphic realism. Pearl K. Bell has noted that many of the early
books are characterized by "obsessive minuteness of detail" but concludes that such an approach is an understandable reaction to the
"incomprehensible peculiarities of Vietnam" (75, 77). Bernard Bergonzi also has observed "an impulse toward total documentary realism in the early fiction," but, echoing Beidler, he describes the appropriate novelistic strategy, the necessary point of departure from verbal
photography, to be "the right blend of history and imagination"
(84). Extending the critical debate, Peter McInerney has observed
that such a blend of fact and fiction is a common assumption in the
tradition of American war writing. In his appraisal of Vietnam War
novels, he reminds the reader of the shared belief in the power of
fiction to render what straightforward historical reporting cannot and
describes the Vietnam War as "a breakdown and transformation of
the historical imagination itself," but, departing from Herr, he argues
finally that "the secret history of true books about Vietnam is that
there is none for that war" (187, 203).

What such assessments suggest is that the task of the Vietnam
War writer is to free himself from what Mailer calls "the clearly demarcated limits of historical inquiry" and to extend imaginatively the
war where he must; only then will larger historical and cultural connections become visible. The task of the writer remains what it has
always been: to use every means at his disposal to offer a self-sustaining congruent whole, a text that both illuminates the specific historical events from the admittedly limited perspective of a single imagination and sheds light on the possible placement of those events within
a larger field of belief and imagining. Such a venture carries within it
finally the recognition that Vietnam War history and Vietnam War
myth occupy the same imaginative terrain; when the history of the
war is defined as the network of beliefs, interpretations, and self-

contained statements prompted by events, notions of secret histories evaporate. The record for examination becomes not the events themselves, forever lost to notions of value-free objectivity, but the accumulation of readings and renderings that compose an expanding, contextual body of writing. Rather than freeing the novelist from responsibility to historical facts, however, the enlarged definition of history redefines and complicates the writer's task, allowing him to merge with facts whatever meaningful reverberations and associations the facts prompt. McInerney is quite right when he asserts that there is no secret history of the war; when the Vietnam War novelist begins to explore the accumulative, associative imprinting process within both personal and collective imagination, he becomes a historical being. Joseph Tetlow has offered a reasonable definition of the writer's responsibility: "Critics, at least, continue to expect war novels to interpret and evaluate and fault them when they do not. This may be unfair to the novelists. There it is, as the grunts said; Nam isn't over" (34).

There has been vigorous debate among critics on the merits and failings of both early and more recent offerings. In 1979, Martin Napersteck concluded, "Vietnam has not yet produced a novel equal to Stephen Crane's *Red Badge of Courage*, Ernest Hemingway's *Farewell to Arms*, or Norman Mailer's *Naked and the Dead*; Vietnam has not yet produced a novel likely to be regarded as a masterpiece" (37). Peter Marin darkened the critical canvas further with the assessment that the majority of novels are "the work of distraught and alienated men who are unable to locate any sort of vision or binding values" and that the novelists overall are "lacking in both tragic dimension and the capacity to perceive the Vietnamese as anything more than stick figures in an American dream" (43). In response to both Napersteck's and Marin's charges, Beidler and James C. Wilson have offered positive overall assessments of the corpus of novels and memoirs, with many early, forgotten works receiving overdue recognition, and as the war itself is undergoing a more studied collective reassessment, so are its representations in art of both early and more recent vintage. Public memory is living through a painful maturation process on both levels, a discernible movement toward more considerate and complex reading skills.

Attempting in *Dispatches* to date the wreckage of the American historical project in Vietnam, Michael Herr suggests,

Maybe it was already over for us in Indochina when Alden Pyle's
body washed up under the bridge at Dakao, his lungs all full of
mud; maybe it caved in with Dien Bien Phu. But the first happened in a novel, and while the second happened on the ground
it happened to the French, and Washington gave it no more substance than if Graham Greene had made it up too. (49)

The shadow cast over the entire American corpus of Vietnam works
by Greene's 1955 work (first published in the United States in 1956)
is indeed a large one, for the mixtures of fact and imagination, minute observation and historical connection, reportage and prophecy set
an early standard for fiction of that war and placed before American
writers a workable model of the contemporary historical novel of ex-
traordinarily high levels of vision and control. In his dedication to the
novel, Greene asserts, "This is a story and not a piece of history, and
I hope that as a story about a few imaginary characters it will pass for
both of you one hot Saigon evening." One senses throughout his
presentation of Alden Pyle's romantic quest for a "Third Force" in
Vietnam that Greene's description of and humility toward his narrative are disposable commodities, for in The Quiet American, he
succeeded in offering a symbolic prophecy of the next eighteen years
of American commitment in Indochina, a cultural adventure whose
hubris concerning political and social-engineering principles could be
read finally as the most tragic but preventable discrepancy between
means and ends.

   Gloria Emerson has remarked of Greene that "he had always understood what was going to happen there, and in that small and
quiet novel, told us nearly everything" ("Our Man in Antibes" 45);
even in the light of the most self-conscious American offerings—Going After Cacciato and The 13th Valley, for example—Greene's effort remains a valuable touchstone. Its central value continues to be
its melding of experience and invention in such a way that the immediate story elements and the larger historical statements attain a
synchrony not often achieved in later works. As a text accessible to
the kind of double vision that the best of Vietnam War writing fos-
ters, The Quiet American has elicited from Gordon O. Taylor the
suggestion that the novel "is as likely to be cited as 'evidence' by
historians and reporters as to be lauded as exemplary by literary critics" (294), an insight that reasserts the twin projects of the historical novelist of the Vietnam War: the coupled necessities of re-
creating and interpreting, the construction of a particular story or

stories that overlap freely into vast historical and cultural waters, a binary operation that Greene's work achieves admirably.

If Emerson is not entirely accurate in suggesting that Greene told us "nearly everything," she does speak directly to the fact that Greene's textual loom is one on which future novelists would test the intricacy, consistency, and overall design of their individual Vietnam tapestries. Although a reading of Greene's delineation of the 1946 to 1954 French–Vietminh conflict is an eerie experience in regard to the replicating and enlarging of its key elements during the American involvement, The Quiet American is most important as a variety of textual challenge. Greene argues successfully by example that re-creation and interpretation are not only unopposed but naturally conjoined processes in the self-conscious historical novel, that the widening circles set in motion by the interplay of Fowler, the cynical, dissipated, but realistic European sensibility, and Pyle, the romantic but expedient American one, concerning both the "Third Force" and Phuong, the symbolic Vietnamese mistress, are the desired by-products of the well-crafted story he tells. By refusing to sacrifice the focus of the larger historical portrait for the sharp imaging of the details within it, Greene demonstrated that, no matter how sophisticated the apparatus of the realistic narrative, the success or failure of the camera's eye has to do most with the controlling human artist behind it. Never confusing personal vision with the well-ground lens, Greene revealed that the adroit manipulation of the realistic mode of the historical novel is more a matter of selective composition and interpretation than it is of comprehensive, unreflective recording.

Despite Greene's lesson in the art of composition, many American writers attempted to use the realistic mode much like a neutral camera equipped with both zoom and wide-angle lenses, to offer minute re-creation and sweeping photographic mural. Certainly, the nature of the war seemed to encourage recourse to such aesthetic strategies, to recommend that the writer give in to the impulse toward documentary realism while forgetting that even the most carefully rendered texture of realism demands selection, arrangement, and, finally, deeper judgment. Many of the books speak powerfully and convincingly on the level of immediate experience, but as they assemble the daily horrors and boredoms of the tour of duty in Vietnam, they often seem to abdicate the tasks of larger historical vision and cultural connection to the reader or critic sifting through the particular images on the page. They offer scenes of battle, racial tension, drug use, and spiritual despair in a wealth of detail, often repeating or compounding the specificity in attempts to deny the necessary historical closure, but such portraiture declares itself as limited documents of the war, time-bound images whose power to affect on the emotional level is undeniable but whose attempt to sort out, to clarify, and to connect is dwarfed by the process of graphic recreation. There is in such works a kind of despairing faithfulness to facts and an unverbalized, collective denial of both the power and the responsibility of imagination. From a certain perspective, it might be argued that interpretation and connection are not the primary duties of the novelist, that the telling of an internally congruent, well-crafted story precedes all other concerns, but Greene's and the finest American versions of the war indicate that much more was necessary and possible.

Books of such immediate emotional power and graphic impact as James Webb's *Fields of Fire* and Larry Heinemann's *Close Quarters* take the reader into the heart of the war experience but refrain from larger connections as they itemize the human sacrifice. Webb offers a triumvirate of protagonists—Hodges, the officer of warrior lineage; Snake, the mean-streets-educated volunteer and natural killer; and Goodrich, the ambivalent, morally questioning conscript—to explore the ethical uncertainties and violent inevitabilities, but beyond a close delineation of the effects of the war on his three-cornered sensibility, he offers few aesthetic judgments on the significance of the human sacrifice to the culture that produced it. Heinemann, through the developing friendship of the two protagonists, Dosier and Quinn, resides uneasily in a brand of high-energy prose that seems at times both excessive and evasive, the often moving portrayal of male bonding under unusual circumstances offering itself finally as a well-intended but insufficient historical closure. Robert Roth's *Sand in the Wind* and Steven Phillip Smith's *American Boys* are panoramic in intention and effect, but by offering the reader a spectrum of characterization and theme and failing to discriminate or to interpret within the bands, both seem stuffed but obscure murals, a legacy of horrible effects graven in stone and trapped in time.

Greene's model of the historical novel as a variety of realistic parable was not lost on the writers overall, however. Joe Haldeman's *War Year* is a spare, almost stripped, evocation of one soldier's tour of duty. It contains no extraordinary incidents, no gratuitous details, and succeeds, in part at least, because of its lack of Cinemascope pretensions. But Haldeman's narrative seems finally too hermetically personal, too faithfully autobiographical, and too unwilling to probe for the connection of its protagonist's experience to the larger, collective one. Joe Farmer's initiation seems both typical and inconclusive, a finely etched portrait that demands an interpretive postscript.[3] Jack Fuller's recent *Fragments* is a more fully realized realistic parable, a book that seeks both personal and natural closure; his well-intentioned protagonist, Neumann, whose salvational impulse produces the most deadly results for himself and the Vietnamese, seems very much a variation of Alden Pyle looking to his predecessor over the ruins of the American commitment. Tom Mayer's *The Weary Falcon*, a collection of five vignettes that make up a loose, impressionistic Vietnam narrative, speaks with controlled irony and careful selection of detail. His story "A Birth in the Delta" says more of the overall American experience than do many large novels whose effects confuse graphic portraiture with historical statement. And William Pelfrey's *The Big* V is a fine example of how traditional realism may be recycled in a self-conscious, combinative way. By placing the familiar American battlefield *Bildungsroman*—in this case, that of Henry Winsted, a clear descendant of Crane's hero—within a context of media and Hollywood myth and military legend, Pelfrey demonstrates how his particular war both fostered and deflated new forms of personal and collective American romanticism. Winsted is both a well-delineated representative of his war and a necessary connection to the tradition stretching back to De Forest, Bierce, and Crane. His perspective toward his personal initiation conveys well the new American attitude of deep cynicism, guilt, and loss. He describes the rite of passage as "the full trinity of war. . . . Kill a dink, see an American killed, mourn for him with the colonel and chaplain before the plastic tape recorder" (79), an evocation in miniature of the hardened irony that characterizes the most significant Vietnam works of the realistic mode.

Two American works stand as full-fledged responses to the challenge of Graham Greene. They are an intriguing study in contrasts. One, a work from the early stages of the war, seems a direct descendant of the economical, associative narrative of *The Quiet American* and, like its predecessor, offers the tightly constructed synchrony of minute observation and large historical and cultural resonance; the other, a sprawling, often quirky delineation of the war's late stages, takes both the battlefield initiation and the platoon as historical laboratory to new heights of self-consciousness and aesthetic exploration. Together, they reenunciate the hard-won lesson first taught by Greene in 1955: that the finely ground lens by itself is inert crystal, the mere potential for either the blurred or the high-resolution image. As contradictory practitioners of the realistic mode, David Halberstam and John M. Del Vecchio prove once again that it is the artist behind the recording device who makes all the difference.

At the conclusion of David Halberstam's *One Very Hot Day*, the unlikely American protagonist, Captain Beaupre—old, out of shape, exhausted from his personal walk in the sun, and surveying the dead and wounded among the ARVN force he has helped guide into a Vietcong ambush—offers an epiphany of an apparently anticlimactic nature: "He had finally seen the enemy for the first time; all those months in Vietnam and he had finally seen one. They make a lot of noise for such small people, he thought" (227). Such an insight hardly seems the stuff of piercing historical observation or satisfactory cultural connection, but Halberstam, seasoned *New York Times* correspondent, author of the Vietnam analysis *The Making of a Quagmire*, and prime actor in the new adversary reportage, knew that in 1967 his novel was an attempt to write a different kind of Vietnam account, a minutely rendered story of one advisory mission that was for him a necessary form of compensatory history.

Although initially well received by the critics and public when it was published—it was reviewed favorably on the first page of the *New York Times Book Review* and was a Literary Guild book of the month—it did not sell well and was out of print until 1984. In the Afterword for the new edition, Halberstam explains why he decided to write on Vietnam in a form other than journalism, stating that "there was a part of me which wanted to tell something more, what for lack of a better description, the war felt like on a given day. I wanted to portray the frustrations, and the emptiness of the war" (228). His self-appraisal, however, accounts for only half of the book's value, for while he carefully re-creates and interprets the advisory period through the particulars of a single mission, Halberstam creates a fiction that, like Greene's, speaks prophetically of the larger commitment still to come. *One Very Hot Day* demonstrates that something beyond photorealism was called for in Vietnam War fiction and that, despite the fragmented, layered nature of the conflict in regard to its political, social, and military aspects, a small book of carefully chosen details, self-conscious arrangement, and sufficient associative power could do in a reduced frame what many panoramic attempts would fail to achieve.

The novel was praised initially as a piece of finely rendered but traditional realism, a work with immediate significance and effective presentation of its particular story, but it was not considered generally to be the historically and culturally resonant document it has proved to be. The larger historical project at the novel's core was most often disregarded amid the laudatory appraisals of Halberstam's journalistic acumen; viewed more as skillful, specific reportage than as far-reaching historical analysis, *One Very Hot Day* was the subject of limiting if favorable criticism. One critic in particular chose to read the book through a critical monocle. Assessing the work in the *Saturday Review*, Seymour Epstein concluded in 1968,

> What Mr. Halberstam does not make clear is the issue itself: what are we doing in Vietnam? That, one might say with complete justification, is not the job of the novelist. The job, or the art, of the novelist is to be true to his people and his theme. These do not necessarily involve issues or solutions. But to deny that a historical context exists is like denying the noonday traffic on Fifth Avenue. (87)

Epstein would soon have his original question severely complicated, for his review appeared a mere two weeks before the Tet offensive, but his complaint of a lack of historical context misses both the form and the substance of Halberstam's fictional project. In the most astute early appraisal of the novel, Wilfrid Sheed, in the *New York Times Book Review*, observed that Halberstam's specific story is "clearly a parable" (1) and that the novel overall "has an immediate educational function" (45), a recognition of the book's claim to be read as history. Moving well beyond Epstein's limiting vision, Sheed found metaphorically the novel's true ambition, suggesting that "he believes the war's defects are intrinsic and that in showing us round the malformed embryo, he is also showing us the shape of things to come" (1).

Like Epstein, Sheed offered his assessment at the very historical moment when the management of the war, the official explanations, and general public opinion were all to be tested, revised, and placed under a number of new pressures. Although Halberstam's novel was read at the time as the most immediate variety of adversary journalism—it was called, like Greene's assessment, anti-American in some quarters—as the war recedes in time and broadens within greater critical perspective, One Very Hot Day can be assessed most properly as a variant of prophetic history as the novel, the same finely realized synchrony of particular story and larger association for which Greene provided the prototype in 1955. Halberstam, while using the traditional realistic narrative for concerns beyond the creation of three-dimensional character, powerful event, and textured setting, demonstrated that traditional forms of American war writing could be resuscitated for a new national experience but that their implementation demanded unusual dexterity and purpose.

Captain Beaupre, tired, recalcitrant, resentful of his role and of the Vietnamese he advises, is the most unlikely hero in the corpus of American works on the war. A veteran of World War II, a line crosser in the Korean conflict, he is a protagonist out of time and out of joint with the new technology, the political and social confusion, and the nature and conduct of guerrilla warfare. Beloved by neither the ambitious young American advisers, to whom he supplies almost total contrast, nor the Vietnamese officers with whom he begrudgingly shares responsibility, Beaupre is that imprisoned military professional of the twentieth century, the career man on the down side of romantic exploits who finds his insertion into the widening Vietnam conflict the most unexpected and undesirable development possible. Afraid of helicopters, openly sarcastic toward his indifferent, ineffectual allies, he seems to trace a most ludicrous figure through the paddies and villages he reluctantly and repeatedly searches for an enemy he would prefer not to find. He appears on the basis of his surface features to be an inversion of both the battlefield initiate of mainstream American war writing and the chivalric frontiersman of national myth. In regard to the historical lesson of One Very Hot Day, however, he is more than the buffoon of American good will who sneaks water on missions and who loses his pistol in the stagnant water of the rice paddies; he is Halberstam's Vietnam eiron who performs a number of thematic and structural functions.

The title of the novel is a bit of a misnomer, for Halberstam, via flashback and multiple perspective, assembles about his particular mission a number of very hot days, not only those of the American advisory force in Vietnam, but also, through Beaupre's remembrances, comparisons of the experience of this guerrilla war with that of the more straightforward and comprehensible events of World War II and Korea. Beaupre performs two functions simultaneously throughout the mission. He analyzes ironically and personally the nature of his historical moment, but he also serves as a historical conduit through which a much wider range of American myth and sensibility is allowed to flow into the immediate fictional terrain.

Halberstam's first chapter, the prelude to the mission, is a minor tour de force of well-chiseled historical and cultural analysis. Philip Beidler, offering the best late appraisal of the novel, has encapsulated Halberstam's project overall as "America considered in terms of a whole nexus of recurrent mythic symbologies" (33), a suggestion that is illustrated in detail in the novel's systematically constructed opening sequence of images. The American contingent of the book, the "Eighth Infantry Division U.S. Advisory Group. Best There Is," is garrisoned in the province of My Tho in a decrepit but heavily fortified structure called the Seminary, a former residence of French clerics and now the farthest western outpost of the American incursion. Both Alamo and French colonial wreckage, the Seminary offers its visitors a sign on which a grinning American face is accompanied by an undeciphered acronym, WETSU, an inscription that is shorthand to the fortification's residents for We Eat This Shit Up, an ironic form of expression for warriors who control only the ground they stand on. The immediate effect of Halberstam's image is of historical recurrence—the American repetition of French mistakes—and the ignoring of that very history lesson as a confident process of Americanization is lacquered over the ruins of the first Indochina war.

The re-creation of American myth on foreign soil and within a misunderstood culture is amplified by Halberstam's account of the "Us-against-Them" American-Vietnamese volleyball game promoted by the American commanding officer. American confidence is asserted and deflated as the deferential Vietnamese team "made a quick work of the Americans" (3), who, "prepared to be good winners" (3), are forced to fall back into inter-American engagements at the net as "the Colonel, resilient as ever, had bounced back and reinstituted the American game" (4). Of course, the sequence of American overreaching and retreat into a falsely sequestered and ungiving national posture would be the historical pattern not only during Halberstam's advisory period, but also within the post-1965 full-combat role that loomed on the horizon. The American-Vietnamese volleyball match and the uneasy barbecue that follows in Halberstam's opening sequence are small comic symbols of much more serious cultural misunderstandings, patterns of mutual mistrust that would become historical promontories as the terrain of the war shifted and expanded. As more men and materiel flowed into Vietnam, the price for mutual misreadings would prove to be much greater than temporary loss of face.

Before the evening briefing for the mission, a movie is shown to the American advisers. Most often, they would see the Hollywood iconography "of Elvis Presley in Hawaii, or Doris Day in bed with someone, her pajamas unwrinkled, and her hair all in place" (4), but on this evening, they are offered *The Guns of Navarone*, with Gregory Peck and his team of saboteurs attempting to infiltrate a Nazi island fortress and silence a technological marvel, a pair of huge, radar-controlled guns. The advisory group cheers for Peck and company until someone makes the unwelcome observation that "Peck was a Cong, and from then on the complexion of the picture changed sharply, and the loyalty to Peck ended abruptly, the hearts did not beat so fast when the Germans came near" (5). The collective realization is that the American experience in Vietnam has already prompted an inversion of a number of components of popular myth, that the daily treks within the rice paddies and villages have stood the persistent good-guy syndrome on its head. After the last reel, in which Peck's guerrillas succeed against overwhelming technological odds and escape, Beaupre is "annoyed to find that Vietnam took the pleasure even out of Gregory Peck killing Germans" (6). The erosion of myth and its replacement by a newly historicized American sensibility is Halberstam's history lesson. As acronyms, volleyballs, and celluloid images congeal in the concentrated prelude, the larger lessons of the approaching mission are ominously and ironically foreshadowed, and before a single step is walked during Halberstam's fateful hot day, the needed historical, cultural, and mythic context is carefully assembled and analyzed.

The briefing itself is a further thematic concentration. After a brief scene in which Beaupre and the unit chaplain speak "somewhat nostalgically about Korea" (7), Halberstam delineates both generational and racial tension among the advisers. Beaupre and his kind stand in sharp opposition to the new breed of Alden Pyles: "Their physiques alone told much of the story of the changing army: the young ones, lean and hard and anxious to go, the older ones, in two wars already, showing some of the softness of the long years of peace and peacetime army diet, flabby around the middle" (8). Throughout the narrative, Beaupre is placed in opposition to Lieutenant Anderson, "a chosen young man" with "a carefully muffled ambition" (55), an eager West Point product who hopes to use his advisory experience as a means to join the new heliborne force, the very technology that produces cold shivers in Beaupre.

The best adviser in terms of cultural connection is Captain William Redfern, "Big William," a huge southern black who is revered almost religiously by the Vietnamese Rangers under his charge. But Halberstam is careful in the novel to identify the incipient problems within the cultural relationship that Redfern and his disciples encapsulate:

> Each morning he would greet them: "Good morning, Vietnamese," he would say, and they would answer in a chant he taught them, "Good morning, Big William." "How they hanging, Vietnamese?" he would ask and they would answer, their voices thin like school children, "They hanging fine, Big William." (12)

When Redfern is killed by the Vietcong during the mission, the Rangers fall apart, a study in miniature of the dark side of the Americanization of Vietnamese concerns and responsibilities. A meaningful symbol of the ongoing tendency to encourage self-motivation while undermining it with a continual flow of American language, ritual, and culture that would be deferentially imitated or appropriated but that would consistently erode any incipient South Vietnamese national identity or commitment, Redfern and the Rangers are readable, ironic iconography of the unique tensions of independence and compliance that characterized Saigon–Washington dalliance throughout the conflict. When Vietnamization was tested once and for all in 1975 and the ARVN forces broke so quickly and completely that even the enemy was taken by surprise, Halberstam and his early readers may have heard the echoes of the daily chant at the Seminary. Redfern is a troublesome presence among his white peers as well. Finding Big William's enthusiasm and boastfulness off-putting, one adviser suggests, "I've seen them all, and he ain't the best, they don't have a best, but maybe he's the worst, they got that" (11). As both historical continuity and ethnic melting pot, the

American mission is rife with tensions, cultural fault lines that Halberstam is quick to locate and to probe.

Both Vietnamese intelligence gathering and combat proficiency are denigrated by the Americans during the briefing sequence. Delineating Big William's unique success with the Rangers, Halberstam offers, "the Rangers always bewildered the Americans. They were supposed to be elite troops like the Marines and the Airborne, but they were not particularly effective and had regularly disappointed the Americans" (13). A question concerning the veracity of the Vietnamese information that prompted the mission garners derisive laughter, and Beaupre discovers that he is to work in tandem with Captain Dang, "who was considered the worst of the Vietnamese officers" (13). If tensions exist within the American advisory group, even greater political and cultural fissures are evident in the uneasy cooperation of supposed allies. It must be recognized, however, that Halberstam's prelude overall is devoted exclusively and deliberately to the American point of view, with the cultural apparatus it attempted to implant in Vietnam to create an image of its own visage. A series of historically resonant omens, the first chapter is also an intentionally imbalanced cultural perspective, one that meets its match in the studied Vietnamese response that Halberstam offers as the joint mission spreads out into the countryside in search of the elusive enemy. Near the end of the chapter, it is suggested that "the VC kept agents inside the Seminary simply to gauge when they were getting up" (16), an unverified but disturbing complication that foreshadows greater manifestations of enemy omniscience and determination. Like the series of small, connected historical metaphors that precedes it, the final suggestion of enemies in the home camp looks backward ironically to the unread French military lesson and forward prophetically to the larger war that would offer new villains at every turn.

Once the walk in the sun, a three-pronged search of local villages and the surrounding area, is under way, Halberstam makes it clear that the officers involved, the Americans Beaupre and Anderson (Redfern and his Rangers are a heliborne reserve force) and the Vietnamese Captain Dang and Lieutenant Thuong, are a microcosm of cultural and political tensions. The goals of the mission seem less the discovery and destruction of the enemy than the preservation of the delicate symbiotic balance between cultures. Deference, civility, cooperation, and saving face are the chess pieces within the tactical game played out in the paddies and within the villages. The prize overall becomes avoidance of enemy contact and intercultural friction, preservation of a modicum of order and discipline, and personal and group survival on a mission that is clearly a repetition of many that preceded it and a presage of many that will follow it. Placing this day's events into a larger context, Beaupre muses, "Every day the circles get bigger and emptier. Walk them one day, erase them the next" (119).

Anderson, although still the most committed of the four, has suffered a severe lessening of enthusiasm for the American involvement in general and the repetitive, often fruitless, missions in particular. When he had arrived in Vietnam full of secular missionary zeal, he had come with a number of preconceived salvational views that his early impressions of the geography, people, and culture seemed to bear out. A 1960s variant of the American impulse that Leo Marx addresses, Anderson had observed, "this country is in Technicolor. He had never forgotten how green it looked and that sense of life which it had seemed to reflect, it was a giant garden" (60), but if Anderson's original intentions had been to become part of the armed, rotored machine within it, his time in-country has altered the shining vision: "He had come with high expectations to Vietnam, and he had been disappointed since arrival: disappointed with the war, the Vietnamese themselves, with the Colonel, and disappointed with Beaupre" (55).

By the time of this particular walk in the sun, Anderson has entrenched himself in a determined, personal professionalism, one without the expansive, hopeful overtures to the Vietnamese, the confident attempts to form meaningful cultural connection. Politeness, watchfulness, and rigid cooperation have replaced the grander teleology. The reality of his specific duties has produced the sea change; ignoble, uncoordinated, often embarrassing to both sides, but, beyond all else, tedious, the war has caused Anderson's clean vision to become transmuted into the commonplace observation, "When they tell you about the war, the one thing they never say is how slow it is" (66). Philip Beidler has said of *One Very Hot Day* that what is striking about the work is how Halberstam transformed the "utter, soul-killing ordinariness" of the war into a vision that has the "archetypal quality of nightmare" (59). Anderson's transformation is one American end product of that process; Vietnam, no romantic quest for the upwardly mobile hard-charger, alternates consistently in its potential to surprise and to benumb, and before the full American troop commitment to Saigon occurs, Anderson stands as an emblem of ideological erosion and national entropy. Moving quickly beyond the romanticism of Robin Moore's *The Green Berets* and other such Cold Warrior visions, he is an early intimation of the larger historical accident looking for a place to happen.

Captain Dang, diffident, proud, and cowardly, combines the worst aspects of self-preservation and self-promotion. Approaching this and other missions as dramatic performances in which the illusions of professionalism and tangible success are manipulated to prompt good reviews from higher authority, he is also the catalyst for tensions within the Vietnamese forces and between the allies. Careless and hard-headed, he is an albatross when real trouble appears. Resistant to American advice unless made in a conciliatory way and callous to the real dangers in which he places his undisciplined, indifferent troops, he is a counterweight to the very aspects of order and safety that, despite their varying commitments and attitudes toward the war, the other officers seek to foster. Willing to sacrifice lives to achieve transient cosmetic victory, Dang is careful to keep his own interests, military and political, safely out of the line of fire. Reflecting on a previous instance of Dang's dangerous duplicity, Lieutenant Thuong recalls the captain's expedient masking of his identity when a quiet mission became suddenly hot: "Dang taking off his officer's pips. If you are going to wear the pips in the great halls of Saigon, he thought, you must wear them in the U Minh forest" (142).

One of the persistent problems within the American corpus of Vietnam works is the failure often to connect aspects of American tragedy to the larger Vietnamese one, to re-create imaginatively the cultural and political points of view to which American vectors of frustration, confusion, anger, and guilt pointed. The creation of three-dimensional Vietnamese characters who offer the necessary, understandable historical counterpoint is a rare achievement in many of the works, the resorting to images of a mysterious, unseen enemy or a passive, untrustworthy, unreadable peasantry being the most common, regrettable aesthetic strategy. Halberstam's success with Dang is a real, if limited, one, but his gradual unfolding of Lieutenant Thuong's attitudes, frustrations, and insights through the day's journey is one of the major victories of *One Very Hot Day*. If Beaupre is both conduit and prism for immediate and recent American history, Thuong is a similar structural device for the consideration of a variety of Vietnamese concerns. His musings on Beaupre and Anderson and on the American presence overall constitute the rebuttal in a two-way historical debate; as he completes the symmetry of Halberstam's narrative structure, he illuminates and addresses a number of dangerously hermetic American assertions.

Like Beaupre, Thuong is older than his peers and is displaced in both a personal and a cultural sense. A northerner in the South, a Buddhist among Catholics, he performs his duties with little hope of reward or advancement and with the same tenuous commitment and pointed criticism he finds so reprehensible in the slow-moving, caustic American. Both skeptical and admiring of the enemy he seeks alongside his American counterparts, he summarizes the first war, "The Vietminh side was as cruel as the French, and lacked only the corruption of the French" (139), and assesses self-consciously his position in the new one against the Vietcong: "It was simply that he knew he was too cynical for the passion and commitment their life took. To gain religion in Vietnam, he thought, you must start very young; to retain it, he thought, you have to be very lucky" (139).

Uneasy in his own cultural and historical disjunction, Thuong is an emblem of the mixture of traditional and new historical impulses that made South Vietnamese loyalty and order so difficult to promulgate or to maintain among either the military or the buffeted peasantry. Responding to Beaupre's assertion that the bunched-up, dangerously targetable troops are his people, Thuong replies, "So are the Vietcong" (34). And confronting the early evangelical confidence of Anderson:

"You came to save us, you Americans," he said.

"Not to save, to help," Anderson said.

"No, save, save is the better word, but I am afraid, Lieutenant, that you will find that we are not an easy people to save." (172)

A disillusioned professional with an unstable commitment to the power bloc he represents, Thuong is a most valuable voice when he reflects on the new American presence. Stepping on a *punji* stick early in the long walk, he attempts to ignore the injury and observes with embarrassment that "the recruits were slapped in the face for doing it; and the Americans gave themselves medals, the heart of purple for doing it" (35). He notes that the new breed of advisers "were brave, professional, and competent, but they were curiously without passion" (50). When the Americans had come, he had been hopeful, for Americans "did not, after all, lose wars" (47); but having worked with several indifferent, careless, or cruel men before the new prototype of Anderson arrived, Thuong now fights side by side with envoys from a nation he finds "at the very least a fallible people" (48). Thuong, however, saves his most severe appraisal for Beaupre, the man out of synch with the new wave of faceless Andersons. Perceiving the clumsy, lamenting American as both an imitation soldier and a real danger, he offers a merciless abstract of his ally: "the worst, sloppy, careless, indifferent to the troops, contemptuous of the Vietnamese, and worse, he was sure he sensed Beaupre's fear" (50). But Halberstam makes clear that Thuong is also criticizing his own double image, a figure who, beyond frayed commitment and physical infirmity, salvages from the day the only variety of personal or collective victory this war will allow. When the ambush occurs, both characters are forced to attenuate and to modify their specific arguments from opposite sides of the cultural gap they have willingly and energetically created. Despite their criticisms, Thuong's "great truth" seems their common bond, the distillation of all complaints into the simple observation, "living, more important than anything else" (80). In the most ironic way, Thuong and Beaupre, the most skeptical of the leaders, emerge as the two heroic impulses of the book, redefinitions of personal and national commitment from both Vietnamese and American points of view.

As eiron, Beaupre is offered as a grouping of unsoldierly, ignoble characteristics, the inversion of the classic hero in almost every respect. But if the romanticism of the Hollywood war film and the would-be warrior is exposed and deflated by Vietnam, Halberstam's complaining, perspiring veteran of three wars completes the history lesson that replaces older, unsupportable mythic components. Trapped within his simultaneous roles as diplomat, good-will ambassador, coach, and combatant, Beaupre is both the culmination and the device for study of an entire spectrum of post–World War II American ideological and evangelical impulses. Emblem of willing self-entrapment and delusion, he is the historical test that analyzes ironically and bitterly its own data; both conclusion and warning, he supplies a tracing of the larger national narrative that has placed him in the new war and seeks desperately a life line with which to extricate himself from it. As he redefines personal heroism within a particular set of unprecedented historical circumstances, he slowly sheds his self-serving, unlikable surface and reveals himself to be an early representation of the most typical American Vietnam War novel protagonist, a figure who—combining self-centeredness and pragmatic group cooperation, acute survival instincts and deflations of mythic vainglory, and philosophical fatalism and personally regenerating comic irony—may be designated as the participant-resister, the most recognizable updating of an American tradition leading back to Cooper's vanishing frontier.

The Vietnam participant-resister, as a heightening and modifiying of tendencies at the core of the American tradition of war writing, is a new but familiar variant of the assailant–victim, who is the conduit and target for the most violent aspects of national policy. Beaupre, a world policeman seeking a pension and a prisoner of the deadliest American historical impulses, is a study in the widening gap between innocence and pragmatism. The enemy of any romantic or mythic projection within history that denies or cloaks what the advisory missions make readable, he is the historicized warrior who demands realism and a strange form of professionalism as he probes the limits of his prison.

A terminus of eye-fooling national projections and secular evangelism, Beaupre finds new enemies at every juncture: hubris-filled commanding officers; ambitious, romantic peers; unmotivated, vulnerable allies; new technology; the geography; the heat. Capable of neither separate peace nor liberating victory, he finds the war not a linear struggle but the most dangerous tape loop, a cyclical game that rewards personal and group survival only with a spirit-sapping repetition of its key elements and patterns. An evolving historical sensibility, Beaupre "had not distrusted people in World War II. . . . It had been simpler there, even in Germany where you hated everyone, but once you entered the villages, you were not loved and kissed, you were not ambushed or tricked or betrayed" (132). His "distrust had begun in Korea," but "compared to this country, Korea was simple: here you began with distrust, you assumed it about everything, even things you thought you knew" (133). Beaupre's heightened historical paranoia is perhaps the primary characteristic of the participant–resister; cultural hormonal imbalance and a hub of a wheel of smaller practices and attitudes, it is the most visible manifestation of the individual's perception of himself as both inmate and marionette, as recipient and purveyor of the by-products of the mythic impulse.

Beaupre's criticisms of the Vietnamese, unlike those of the racist, confident advisers of Thuong's memory, have their origin in his evolving historical perspective, in the recognition of the ludicrous cyclical patterns of the nonvictory of immediate history and of the new war itself as part of a larger twentieth-century pattern of war as a permanent institution. When Beaupre speaks of widening circles, he places himself in the smallest circumference within a set of revolving historical diagrams. Within that circle, he confesses his new-found philosophy: "When he realized he was not winning his war, he had begun to cheat. . . . So far his luck had been good" (33); but Beaupre's tired knowledge does not extend to abdicating notions of personal and group responsibility and protection. Although he perceives the Vietnamese troops as "miniature soldiers, armed Boy Scouts" (27), his angry appeals to the Vietnamese officers to keep the men spread out and watchful stem from his knowledge of what a well-placed shell or grenade may do to a knotted formation. Beneath his sweating, asymmetrical form resides a germ of redefined heroism, the American variant of Thuong's "great truth" as sole value.

Beaupre's distrust of his allies is coupled with a grudging admiration for the enemy he seeks but never sees. Vietnam is a haunted forest of omniscient, teasing spirits, and Beaupre at times seems an updated Hawthorne figure whose imaginary conversations with his personal devils provide another form of historical meditation. Placing himself figuratively on the other side of the mission with the contingent that seems to establish all the patterns and to set all the rules, Beaupre dreams:

> He wondered, not for the first time, what it would be like to be an adviser to the VC. All the advisers thought about it. Just for a week, he thought, even if it meant wearing black pajamas and walking all night. Not so much grinning, he thought, he was sure the VC were sterner and never grinned, their weapons would be clean. Dang would be on the other side. There was a quality of luxury to his thoughts. (189)

But Beaupre is aware that such fantasies are only momentary succor within the no-exit drama in which he finds himself. The reality of his war, the alternating shades of debilitating tedium and unexpected violence, affords the time for imaginative projections but warns constantly of the price of too much individual or collective detachment.

Like Joseph Heller's Yossarian, a precursor of the Vietnam participant–resister from an earlier, more comprehensible war, Beaupre will have no commerce with assertions that his victimization is part of larger problems. He personalizes the conflict at all times, discovers instantly the discrepancies between means and ends, and is ever-vigilant against the real dangers, the ones that arise most often not from the unseen enemy but within the allied forces and the supposedly neutral villages. More diplomatic courier and solver of cultural riddles than warrior, he is the hero who concludes, "Some war, he thought, smile at all the peasants, be good, be nice. The Ipana War. What did you do in that Vietnam War? Killed three VC, and kissed 346 peasants" (69). Finding the historical stretch from Korea to Vietnam too great for his tired frame, Beaupre discovers in the confident technology of the new war some of his greatest adversaries. Having none of Anderson's admiration or career goals in regard to American engineering principles, he detects in the machine metaphors of early 1960s hubris a personal threat and a grand cabal:

> He wondered if he could tell him all: that it was not just helicopters, that it was everything new about this war; helicopters, spotter dogs which were guaranteed to find VC but were driven insane by the heat and bit Americans instead, water purification people, psywar people, civilians in military clothes, military in civilian clothes, words which said one thing and always meant another, all these things, and particularly helicopters, nowhere to hide in a helicopter, you try to get your ass down in a helicopter and it's still in the same place, exposed, worse, elevated for them, nowhere to run, nowhere to hide, all too modern for him.

> "Because it was designed so they can see you better than you can see them. Check it out, you'll find it was Communists who invented the helicopter," he said. (73)

Surrounded by enemies on every level, Beaupre survives the day only by improvisation and instinctive behavior, an instantaneous shedding of the eiron's garb. When the force is decimated by a well-prepared ambush, he and Thuong rouse the petrified Vietnamese troops and manage to save a remnant of them through individual initiative and coercion, but theirs is the most qualified kind of victory. Having finally fought the "small people" who populate both his dreams and his waking hours, Beaupre notices that "already the Viets were lollygagging again, laughing and talking, even the ones carrying the dead" (226) and attains finally only the pedestrian tragic knowledge that "the VC were getting close" (227), the realization that he may yet be liberated from his personal historical treadmill in the most unacceptable but predictable way.

Halberstam states in the Afterword to the 1984 edition that he wanted his book only to be "small and true" (230). As a worthy heir to Greene's associative parable, the novel fulfills his hopes and stands as one example of a Vietnam fiction that escapes the traps of photo-realism and historicizes a celluloid war.

And of all these things the Albino whale was the symbol. Wonder ye then at the fiery hunt?

HERMAN MELVILLE

When John Del Vecchio's The 13th Valley[4] was published in 1982, William Plummer of Newsweek struck the proper chord for many reviewers when he described the book as "a big, lumbering, rhetorically uncombed war novel in the tradition of The Naked and the Dead" (71). Falling in step, Neil Baldwin described the nearly 600 pages of text as "a complex, ironic, dense mixture of fierce firefight action, nighttime philosophy bull sessions and, as always, tense hours of waiting for something to happen" (36). Other reviewers have praised the novel for its experiential veracity, its rendering of the feel of ground combat. But such assessments would seem to relegate The 13th Valley to the status of Vietnam photograph, a regression to the traps and limitations of documentary realism. Pearl K. Bell, commenting on an earlier novel, Winston Groom's Better Times Than These, a work frequently cited for the inappropriateness of its style, argued that "the conventions and devices of naturalistic fiction will surely defeat any novelist trying to fit the savagery and humiliation of Vietnam into a shopworn frame" (75). The early reviews indicated that The 13th Valley, despite praise for its experiential immediacy, might be read as a late, overly full verbal snapshot in an already stuffed Vietnam album.

Plummer, however, offered a more penetrating assessment in his review. Admitting that The 13th Valley impressed him as a great

American book, he suggested that the novel could be compared with another "rhetorically uncombed" work, *Moby-Dick*. Plummer failed to develop his suggestion, but his comment reaches the core of Del Vecchio's venture. Beneath the Maileresque skin of *The 13th Valley* beats a Melvillean heart, and the bone and marrow of this puzzling Vietnam epic are the same tensions of man and nature, knowledge and innocence, and history and language that Ahab's vengeful hunt entails. If Halberstam's associative historical parable is an effective small species of Vietnam writing, Del Vecchio has rendered the war's first true leviathan.

The novel is a curious mix of facts and fictions. In 1970, the 101st Airborne Division did conduct an operation in the Khe Ta Laou area, but in his Author's Note, Del Vecchio reveals that the specific unit he describes is "entirely fictitious." He confesses, "The combat assault by Company A to the peak of Hill 848 occurred as described, as did many of the events included, although the story here is a composite of events from several operations." As he severs secure connections between real and imagined, Del Vecchio announces, "This is a novel. The characters and their backgrounds are imaginary. In no way are they meant to depict, nor are they based upon, any soldiers, past or present, of the 101st." What Del Vecchio unveils with such obviously opposed statements is the imaginative use of real events for larger purposes, the intention to place the particular actions he describes into a larger frame of association and interpretation. Del Vecchio's description of the attack is a collage of truth and invention; because the reader cannot tell which events are created and which are re-created, the narrative becomes both photograph and symbol, both history and myth meeting in circles of association that move outward from the events described into widening rings of speculation and connection. What Del Vecchio quests for in *The 13th Valley* is not another surface of the war but its essence, a center that, like the core of Melville's universe, reveals itself to be a tangled ball of multiple readings and elusive epistemological strands, an intricate interweaving of points of view about the same object of inquiry.

Like Melville's figure-laden sea, Del Vecchio's valley is in ambiguous relation to man. Much more than an evocative setting, it is a presence, a primordial power that absorbs technological onslaught and historical inquiry with the same unspeaking ease. Del Vecchio's Prologue is a rich description of the valley's "stable symbiotic balance," an equilibrium of abundant life forms and processes that may be an emblem of human society or that may constitute its own oblivious order standing mutely indifferent to the human demands and questions put to it. The Prologue establishes the novel's prime symbols—the spider, the web, the ancient teak tree—which accumulate associative power as Del Vecchio's narrative gains momentum, the possible correspondences widening and deepening as the images recur and recombine. The actions of the human combatants seem to be mirrored in nature:

> Around the spider, vestiges of tunnels and prey traps encapsulate dried crusted exoskeletons. The spider perceives its home through simple clear read eyes and through a sensory bristle of exceedingly fine red hairs. At one time the home was good, food was plentiful. The spider had never needed to extend its world beyond the limits of the cavern.

But the apparently readable symbols and obvious portents, Del Vecchio makes clear, are possibly only the imaginative projections of human arrogance, the application to nature of a false lexicon. The Prologue ends with a general description of the valley that poses one of the novel's key inquiries:

> The Khe Ta Laou river valley is difficult to enter, hard to traverse. For a long time it had remained isolated. Life in the valley is highly organized and each plant and animal form aids and is dependent upon the entire system. The equilibrium is sharply structured—a state, perhaps, which invited disruption.

Bracketed between natural order and man-made violence is Del Vecchio's key question: Is war to be understood as a predictable, natural development, an evolutionary, biologically determined phenomenon, or is it an arbitrary, culturally produced violation and destruction of the order in which it festers? About this large Melvillean inquiry are arranged as many responses as Del Vecchio can muster, and the reader is asked to determine if the many voices speaking, heard in the aggregate, offer meaningful counterpoint or hopeless cacophony. What looms constantly within the intricate historical inquiry of *The 13th Valley* is an interpretive Janus at the door of secret history, its opposed faces those of relativism and nihilism.

"It don't mean nothin" is the epistemological challenge that is both the credo and the conclusion of many members of Del Vecchio's

Alpha Company, and as the reverberating assertion gains nihilistic power through the novel—as snipers, leeches, physical exhaustion, and psychological attrition take their toll on Del Vecchio's "boonie-rats"—the search for reasonable interpretations of the particular assault and of the larger war intensifies and grows more problematic. The mission in the Khe Ta Laou is symbolic of the entire American presence in Vietnam. For the mission's designers, the valley is the congruence and validation of a number of broad, unexamined assumptions; for the soldiers in the field, it is a historical black hole absorbing into itself all attempts to explain, radiating nothing. Like the jungle it attempts to penetrate, Alpha's mission, and the American enterprise overall, is a terrain offering perhaps only limited vision, eye-fooling illusions, and deadly surprises. Beneath its more obvious *Naked and the Dead* components, the novel reveals itself to be the darkest of Vietnam dark romances.

Del Vecchio arranges his rings of historical readings around a triadic nucleus of characters: Rufus Brooks, the black, Berkeley-educated commanding officer of Alpha who lives through and believes in the power of language to provide full explanations; Sergeant Daniel Egan, a natural warrior who survives through "healthy animal paranoia" (19) and who believes in war as its own justification; and James V. "Cherry" Chelini, a battlefield apprentice who undergoes a tortuous, ambiguous initiation. Employing *Moby-Dick's* narrative pattern of alternating sections of action and of meditation, Del Vecchio blends his three principal voices with a number of smaller ones in vigorous debate on the valley, the war, and history itself. Brooks and Egan are alternative ways of approaching the valley, the poles of Del Vecchio's interpretive spectrum: Brooks, through preestablished mental categories and the application of the lacquer of language on experience; Egan, through an updated primitivism, an intuitive, pre-verbal connection with his immediate physical circumstances. Whereas Brooks cultivates ideas, spins elaborate linguistic structures, posits a "semantic determinant theory of war," and writes the grand, synthetic gloss, Egan deals in specific objects and actions, cultivates his powers of kinesthesis and night vision, and combines technical expertise and highly developed survival skills to approximate the deadly stealth he sees in his adversary. Brooks enfolds the war in words; Egan burrows through it in the most elemental way.

Highly competent as both a field officer and a synthetic thinker, Brooks finds in Alpha Company a professional responsibility and a tool for intellectual inquiry. He approaches his boonierats as a society writ small—a Vietnam rendering of Melville's whaling ship as world—an advanced seminar in human conflict that engages in high-level discussion as deftly as it destroys enemy tunnel complexes. Brooks welcomes the addition of new "specialists" to Alpha, men with specific educational background or expertise who can offer fresh perspectives to his already copious theorizing. His experts include El Paso, a Chicano radio operator with a background in law and with extensive knowledge of Vietnamese history; Minh, a Vietnamese scout who provides both Oriental philosophy and a broad Vietnamese cultural perspective; Doc, a black medic from Harlem whose specialty is the "Americanization" of Vietnam and the subsequent breakdown of its social structure; Silvers, a Jewish soldier who is the conduit for current events and *Newsweek* analysis; Whiteboy, an ethnocentric weapons master who refers lovingly to his M-60 machine gun as "Lit'le Boy"; Jax, a militant black from rural Mississippi whose specialties are race relations and economic theory. And the list goes on. In each specialist, Del Vecchio combines a limited cultural perspective with a specific interpretive strategy, a mode of thought, or an approach to language. Natural groupings and categories emerge within the think tank. Egan and Whiteboy are the exemplars of an instinctive phenomenology; Doc and Minh intersect as sociological impulses; Brooks's and Silvers's semantic strategies provide another combination. Throughout the think-tank sections, voices combine and recombine, sometimes in identifiable binary oppositions or complements, often as larger, unstable interpretive structures.

Within *The 13th Valley*, Del Vecchio offers Brooks's magnum opus, a battlefield dissertation called "An Inquiry into Personal, Racial, and International Conflict" that is a patchwork of Brooks's own theories and of the input of his specialists. Asserting that "*we think ourselves into war. The antecedents are in our minds*" (506), Brooks argues that the presence or absence of conflict in a given culture is determined largely by its language structures, that the way to end war is to restructure the violent lexicons that make it inevitable. Like his specialists, however, Brooks offers a limited reading; his synthesis is shaped by his general cultural orientation (Western) and by a specific cultural perspective (black). As he builds his theory, he also suffers psychologically from a breakup with his wife that affects both the nature and the intensity of his search. In his desperate attempts to harmonize the immediate and the personal with the abstract and the universal, Brooks bears more than passing resemblance to Ahab and his cosmic overreaching; his quest to delineate the intricate web of action and language, to correlate general history with specific mythic structures, is a tragicomic undertaking, for Brooks is both a crippled leader searching for personal and universal validations and a Casaubon in jungle fatigues writing a key to all Vietnam mythologies.

Critical to the overall design of *The 13th Valley* is the interplay between the various "gams" of the think-tank sequences and the encounters of Alpha with both an elusive enemy and an ambiguous nature. The discussions are stylized, and the reader may well conclude that they probably would not occur in these particular forms in a combat zone. Joe Klein has objected to Del Vecchio's narrative strategy, arguing that "the bull sessions only dilute the narrative" and concluding that "Mr. Del Vecchio thrashes about in the whys and wherefores of Vietnam, unable to make moral or intellectual sense of the very real sacrifices that were made" (16). But his assessments miss the true nature of Del Vecchio's interpretive method in the novel. *The 13th Valley* carries within it Peter McInerney's denial of a secret history, but the book also cautions that any attempt to write a single true history or a final statement will be only a reductive failure. Brooks's attempt to etch his statement in stone is a skewed quest, a text that is as privileged and inconclusive as any single reading of the whiteness of the whale. Del Vecchio's "bull sessions" are as important to his overall design as Melville's technical and philosophical tangents are to his. Del Vecchio's apparent failure to offer a final meaning is simply the refusal to seal off inquiry, a reasonable, comprehensive reply to the ironic double negative "It don't mean nothin." *The 13th Valley* is a sniper-infested cathedral without a copestone, an acknowledgment that the appraisal of complex human action and thought requires effort, patience, and a number of tools. Like the voyage of the *Pequod*, Alpha's search for the mysterious North Vietnamese Army headquarters is both an examination of events through time and the arresting of time to reveal the layers of discourse that reside and compete in any given historical moment. Del Vecchio's greatest achievement in *The 13th Valley* is his making visible in a fictive frame what Michel Foucault calls the discursive formations that describe the massive application and coercive use of power and ideology.[5] *The 13th Valley* places the Vietnam War into a larger historical-cultural context than any other novel in the realistic mode has done.

Philip Beidler has argued that Vietnam War fiction overall demonstrates the self-conscious use of "an existing set of novelistic strategies" (141), the refurbishing and rearrangement of traditional modes in "a new ground of desperate, ironic affiliation" ("Truth-Telling" 156). In *The 13th Valley*, the "shopworn frame" of naturalistic writing is recycled and used for new purposes; placed in close proximity to both a network of powerful, elusive metaphors and an indeterminate epistemology, it learns to speak a new, combinative language. Egan seems to be Mailer's Sergeant Croft revisited, the tested veteran and pure war lover who asserts, "The only justification you need for Nam is we're doin it" (490), the trained killer who recalls the Tet offensive with nostalgic enthusiasm. Speaking to the novice Chelini on the personal merits of warfare, he offers unequivocal counsel:

> "War," Egan said forming his lips into a trumpet and sensuously blowing the word at Cherry. "They send you to the far corners of the earth. You hear the blasts of artillery and bombs. You get weapons, helicopters. You can call all heaven down, all hell up, with your radio. War. It's wonderful. It don't make a gnat's ass difference who the enemy is. Every man, once in his life, should go to WAR." (146)

But Egan reveals himself to be as much an inversion of Croft as he is his reflection. For Croft's murderous jealousy, Del Vecchio substitutes a civilizing impulse that, like Brooks's semantic theory, is an attempt to order chaos and to assert humanity in the face of its opposite. In a memorable scene, Egan transforms C-rations into a jungle vichyssoise and beef béarnaise, astonishing Cherry with his culinary improvisation. And when a fellow soldier cuts off the ear of a dead North Vietnamese, Egan flies into a rage, defending both personal principles of decorum and prescribed rules of engagement. Capable of eloquence and of detailed intellectual analysis in the think-tank sessions, both killer and erstwhile saint, Egan is a hybrid character, a unique Vietnam frontiersman standing midway between Cooper and Mailer and partaking of both.

Zalin Grant has traced the shifts in interpretation regarding the behavior of the American soldier in Vietnam and has argued that "bad American–good Vietnamese" Manichaeism gave way to "the concept of the veteran as a victim of the war's madness" (23, 24). Del Vecchio argues effectively through Egan, Brooks, and a number of other characters that, despite the high levels of cultural confusion and historical ambiguity inherent in the war, simplistic portraiture of the American soldier in Vietnam as either a debased purveyor of atrocity or an uncomprehending victim is inaccurate, ineffective fictional strategy. Del Vecchio offers a representative cross section of human responses, a spectrum of action that complements the interpretive one with which it alternates. In its use of multiple perspectives on two levels, *The 13th Valley* deflates or revises a number of dangerously reductive readings of the war.

Like Brooks's synthesis, Egan's pronouncements on war incorporate the idea of traceable antecedents, but his orientation toward man and history stands in opposition to Brooks's language structures:

> His direct experiences were close and easy to grasp, to drop him into a channel which flowed back, inhibited but deep and straight for a million years to a million years of data. And his enemy, Egan thought, conceived without words, knew, they too would bring the collective lessons of tens of millions of men from thousands of years of fighting, of fighting North against South, brother against brother, the same pattern from antiquity to post-Geneva, the enemy with a mind-set developed by tens of billions of man-years of war all brought to the battle for the Khe Ta Laou. And the land, Egan thought. No experience needed. That he knew for sure, felt for sure. (162–63)

Egan's argument for a collective, experiential memory shaped by natural, universal processes is the counterswing to Brooks's thesis, but between these two interpretations reside many others. Economic, political, racial, biological, psychological, and merely personal models of the war compete for consideration, and, like the apparent metaphorical correspondences within nature, the implicit connections between the spun threads of human thought seem alternately artificial and organic. At first glance, Del Vecchio's rendering of character seems merely another example of the familiar ethnic melting pot, an overt refurbishing of the time-machine strategy à la Mailer à la Dos Passos, but, again, Del Vecchio is employing a traditional element of war fiction for new purposes within the larger design. Each character is a unit of discourse in the polyglot framework of the novel, a small book within a larger one, a compounding feature in a confusion of languages. The characters are lexical bridges between the manifold center of the valley and the specific, limited cultural perspectives from which the bridges originate. Making the respective lexicons readable as a powerful magnifying glass enlarges the print face of a miniature dictionary, *The 13th Valley* transforms the traditional small-unit naturalism of American war writing into a self-conscious interpretive experiment of high eclecticism. A true history of the war incorporates the vantage points of both Harlem and Hue, includes the perspectives of both theories of brain physiology and Taoist philosophy. In his presentation of the abundance and limits of reading, Del Vecchio opens his design to charges of hopeless relativity, the creation of an interpretive mandala that has written among its many colors the message "It don't mean nothin." But, like Melville, Del Vecchio offers his answer to the puzzle of the One and the Many not in his substance, but in his method. As he separates his layers of discourse to illuminate the manifold nature of Vietnam War history, he substitutes for the assertion of final, reductive statements the delineation of an ongoing process.

Responding to the assessment of the Vietnam War as a radically different kind of conflict, Del Vecchio offers both a yes and a no. The boonierats of *The 13th Valley* are both a closed society and an extension and combination of the larger cultural components from which they spring. There is a constant tension in the novel between shared experience—Egan asserts, "We got a separate culture out here. And in some respects it's better" (405)—and a desperate attempt by each character to place the war within a larger, illuminating field of experience and belief. Despite the eclectic nature of Alpha's constituency, the soldiers speak a common language, one that is in constant counterpoint with the heterogeneous cultural lexicons. Alfred Kazin has described the master tongue of the American soldier in Vietnam as "a male language original in its profanity, exhaustion, and suspicion of the next man. It was sad-funny, mostly black jive, theatrical in its outrage. It was as seeming smart in overkill as the unprecedented American firepower" (120). Like the war it rails against, the dialogue of *The 13th Valley* is a combination of tradition and invention, of mythic residue and coinage, of crisis-forged idiom and technological acronym, a frozen historical dialect that in printed form may strike future generations as so much supercharged hieroglyph. Shortly after Alpha has been helicoptered to the Khe Ta Laou, Silvers, a Jew, and Jax, a southern black, converse:

> "I'm up for a 180-day drop. They cuttin back the size of the armed forces. They're goina let me out the same day as you. You can ride

on my lap all the way back to the World if they don't have enough
room for ya on my Freedom Bird."

"Get serious, Man. I knows what comin down. Got the word from
the Man himself. Sho did. Right from the head honcho. No Leons
ever leave. They jest fade away."

"No way, Jax. If them fuckin REMF clerkjerks mess with the kid's
drop I'm callin in TAC Air on their AOs." (164)

The glossary that Del Vecchio provides for the explication of such
interchanges is more than window dressing; it offers yet another lexicon, an additional key to the tangled nature of Vietnam War discourse. Like Melville's "Etymology" and "Extracts" sections, the
glossary both illuminates and complicates and might be read as its
own novel in miniature, a tale telling itself by the sheer associative
power and incongruity of its key terms.

Del Vecchio plays against the main narrative with other devices
and strategies. Following the combat chapters are summaries of the
day's activities written in military officialese. Flat, clipped abstracts,
they fail even to suggest the texture and depth of the human activity
and thought that precede them. Called *Significant Activities* reports,
an irony-laden designation, they offer summaries of troop movements,
statistics of soldiers killed or wounded or weapons captured, or other
data. Combined with an elaborate set of topographic maps, they
speak finally of the failure of such apparently value-free histories to
be more than opaque surfaces. Like the straightforward chronology
of important dates and events that follows the last chapter, such
aids bring into high relief the density of the main narrative as they
reveal their historical limitations. Along with reductive readings of
the war, Del Vecchio dispenses with body counts as well.

One primary component of the narrative has not yet been discussed: the curious, indeterminate battlefield initiation of Cherry
Chelini. The first sentence of the novel is a lengthy variation of
Ishmael's initial exhortation: "From that day on they called him
Cherry and from the night of that day and on he thought of himself
as Cherry" (1). Like his nineteenth-century counterpart, Cherry begins his education as a fumbling outsider in a subculture of rigid
social patterns, rituals, and language, a society that is both projection
and deformation of major elements of American myth. Like Ishmael,
he finds a teacher who combines technical expertise with a close
relationship with nature. Egan, the updated primitive, guides the

twentieth-century model of middle-class innocence through a world that demands constant vigilance and intense cooperation. Beyond tracing the classical line from experience to knowledge, however, Cherry is both the tabula rasa on which the multiple readings of his peers are written and the principal medium for Del Vecchio's testing of the relationship between thought and action.

The Old Fox, the Yahweh-like brigade commander of the Khe Ta Laou operation, speaks of the valley assault as "a historic mission" (69) and a "rendevouz with destiny" (70); Del Vecchio's white whale is the mysterious NVA headquarters, the discovery and destruction of which will vindicate symbolically the American presence in Vietnam. To the upper levels of command, the headquarters is the great overlooked secret, a lock to be turned with the keys of human sacrifice and massive firepower, the expenditure of which will validate an official reading of the war that is arrogantly asserted. Conducted in late 1970, when media suspicions are high and popular support has dissipated, the assault is a post–My Lai refusal to accept ambiguity, a demand that history write itself in terms taken from an abbreviated interpretive lexicon. During the staging operations for the assault, the Old Fox explains the mission to Brooks in metaphorical terms, referring to the enemy as a cancer to be expunged from a diseased body; and as Alpha prepares to embark, another officer exhorts the men to fight "for the Glory of the Infantry" (151), a rallying cry from other times and other wars. As Alpha is lifted by helicopter to the object of the official glosses, however, convenient, unexamined figures of speech and pro patria football cheers are lost in the wash of the spinning rotor blades.

Within the Khe Ta Laou, Cherry receives jarring history lessons on the true relation of theory to practice as Alpha becomes the pen and ink for the official writing of a symbolic closure of the Vietnam War. Entangled within the interpretive strands of both the official explanations and the limited perspectives of his peers, Cherry discovers that both individual initiation and communal ritual are reduced to simple survival, that self-preservation and a tenuous but necessary group solidarity are the only readable texts. Whereas the synthetic probing of Brooks holds sway in the nighttime discussions, the elemental phenomenology of Egan becomes the true path through the dense jungle terrain; within the Khe Ta Laou, action and meditation cannot achieve meaningful counterpoint. As Cherry witnesses and perpetrates scenes of increasing horror and waste, he adopts the jungle dictum "It don't mean nothin," the true signifier of the break between larger inquiries into the meaning of the war and the effects of the valley on individual sensibility. But Del Vecchio's war of attrition between thought and action moves beyond both despair and relativity. If there is a general lesson imparted in *The 13th Valley*, it is that traditional notions of human heroism, cruelty, cowardice, and responsibility were not inapplicable to or canceled out by the heightened ambiguity of the Vietnam War; rather, they were reconstituted, reinterpreted, and, finally, intensified. In Del Vecchio's Vietnam, concepts of good and evil are not obliterated by the problems of reading; they are instead enlarged and redefined in a new historical crucible. Through Cherry's problem of reading and his subsequent actions, Del Vecchio attempts to pass through the wandering rocks of relativity and despair and to reply reasonably to the riddle of One meaning/No meaning.

It should be noted that Del Vecchio's soldiers in the field are the most self-conscious and sophisticated in the history of American war fiction, a condition that may explain why individual protest and disengagement occur only on a theoretical level within the think-tank debates. In the jungle, there are no Frederic Henrys, John Andrewses, or Yossarians, no separate peaces in a physical sense. The members of Alpha are contemplative men who demonstrate another of Brooks's axioms: "Every man has the capacity for very complex thought" (34). What is discernible in the novel is an examined, hybrid response to war, a mixture of the moral outrage of World War I fiction and the world-weary sophistication and matter-of-factness of World War II novels. The boonierats speak continually of the necessary changes in, or the radical restructuring of, the culture back home in "the World," the soldier's designation for all that is not Vietnam. But felt by all is the necessary deferment of individual protest, the practice of specific historical theories, until the immediate problems of collective survival can be solved. Like the natural setting, time is a presence in *The 13th Valley*; the short-timers of Alpha, those soldiers near the end of their one-year tours of duty, carry a heightened response to the ambiguity and threat of the valley; many contend that secret history will not remain so when they return home.

As he tests through Cherry individual and collective theories of warfare within the historical laboratory of the valley assault, Del Vecchio refrains from offering a stable closure for his apprentice's ritual by fire. Like Crane's Henry Fleming, Cherry is an undifferentiated

grouping of responses; experiencing moments of bravado and cowardice, group identification and furious isolation, savagery and mercy, he
is capable of both finding the jungle "very beautiful" (157) and
using it to create a deadly mechanical ambush. He is the experience
of Vietnam distilled in a single sensibility, a walking emblem of the
phenomenology of war, and it is through him that Del Vecchio establishes most firmly the relationship between the Vietnam War
and all wars. Both a new development and a classic condition, he is
a character frozen in a specific historical moment and the recurring
figure in American war fiction who Wayne Charles Miller calls the
"idealized common man" (18). What Del Vecchio finally discovers
within his historical mandala is not a secret history but some very old
lessons. It is possible to believe one thing and to do another; it is
likely that in situations of high stress and moral ambiguity, some
men will behave responsibly and others, savagely; it is possible to
feel greatly for people one moment and to kill them the next. What
is most remarkable about Del Vecchio's achievement is how he rests
his unwieldy forum of historical inquiry on the twin pillars of human
stamina and frailty and makes the edifice stand.

The 13th Valley extends Vietnam War realism into new realms.
Incorporating and reshaping the dark romancing of Melville, the
individual, internalized protest of Cummings, the walk-in-the-sun
worldliness of Mailer, and the gallows humor of Heller and Vonnegut, the novel is both a fully realized model of Beidler's "desperate,
ironic affiliation" and a jungle-warfare manual of John Barth's literature of replenishment, a compendium of traditional forms combined
for new purposes. If the Vietnam War itself was a strange blend of
new historical developments and a great amount of mythic flotsam
and jetsam, so The 13th Valley simultaneously breaks new ground
and provides a readable map of its ancestral lands. By refusing to seal
off inquiry or to provide a secure closure to his multilayered quest,
Del Vecchio offers both a comprehensive corrective to reductive re-
creations and an admission that no single appraisal can be complete.

Appropriately, the novel concludes on more than one level of
ambiguity. A huge cache of NVA supplies is discovered within an
underground tunnel complex and is destroyed, an apparent validation of a mission that remains a tragicomic endeavor within the historical context that Del Vecchio presents. Cherry suffers what is at
least temporary insanity during the climactic fire fight on the knoll,

torturing his wounded instructor, Egan, unintentionally while claiming to save him as he toys with a huge spider, Egan's prime phobia, that is moving near his fallen comrade. Whether Cherry's dementia—he has moved well beyond Egan's internal checks, envisioning himself as a "Man-God"—is a permanent falling over the edge or a transient affliction is a question left unanswered, a symbolic gesture suggesting the deeper, unknown effects of Vietnam on American consciousness. Even the huge teak tree topping the knoll, the crowning emblem of Del Vecchio's "stable symbiotic balance" within the valley, assumes problematic status. Blown off the knoll so that helicopters may evacuate the wounded, the tree remains standing in the river below, a final challenge to those attempting to decipher the nature of this war, all war.

Following the evacuation of the survivors of the climactic battle, a roll call of Alpha Company is conducted, a rite that is for Del Vecchio a final comment on both the secret history of the Vietnam War and its easy assessment in fiction:

The theater was silent.

"Hey, Jax, El Paso." Cherry nudged El Paso. "How come they didn't call out Egan? or Doc? or the L-T?"

No one answered. Cherry turned to Thomaston. The new company commander looked at him coldly and said, "Haven't you heard? They listed them as MIAs."

"Well fuck," Cherry smiled. He was happy they were not listed among the known dead. In me, he thought. He laughed. "Fuck it. Don't mean . . ."

Thomaston cut him off, "Don't say it Soldier." (589)

Left bobbing in the currents of both personal response and large historical inquiry, the reader finds *The 13th Valley* to be a different kind of life buoy, one that carries within its beveled structure the only history lesson either memory or imagination may find acceptable. Offering the reader the most challenging and symbolically resonant work within the realistic mode, Del Vecchio transforms a familiar set of conventions. Substituting the organicism of historical inquiry for the false stasis of the faded photograph, he also demonstrates that, for all its orphans, Vietnam isn't over.

2

THE MEMOIR AS "WISE ENDURANCE"

Can the foot soldier teach anything important about war, merely for having been there? I think not. He can tell war stories.

IF I DIE IN A COMBAT ZONE

The book, a gift from my sister, took me a long way from Vietnam, to the peaceful hills of Wales, to the rocky Welsh coasts where herons flew. I liked "Fern Hill" and "Poem in October," but I could not read "And Death Shall Have No Dominion." I didn't know much about Dylan Thomas's life, but I guessed that he had never been in a war. No one who had seen war could ever doubt that death had dominion.

A RUMOR OF WAR

When William Bradford reported in *Of Plymouth Plantation* the first great clash of indigenous aspects of American idealism and pragmatism in the new City on the Hill, he also engraved for later practitioners of the memoir the central inscription that American renditions of self, society, and history would most often employ and refine. Although ostensibly a collective history rather than a personal memoir, *Of Plymouth Plantation* remains a most valuable tract for the sound and sense of Bradford himself, an evolving sensibility recording the intrusion of historical contingency and the deflation of Puritan myth. Bradford's voice, a modulated but changing historical complaint and confession, would find an accompanying chorus in the memoir and autobiography of later American writers. Woolman in the *Journal*, Crèvecoeur in the *Letters*, Franklin in the *Autobiography*, Thoreau in *Week* and *Walden*, Adams in the *Education*—all would follow Bradford's lead in the offering of the meeting of spiritual confession and worldly contingency as a particularly native form of personal history.

Although the techniques, emphases, and conclusions are a study in aesthetic and thematic disagreement—Thoreau's metaphorical, meditative narrator and Franklin's enterprising, "virtuous" speaking voice would seem unlikely bedfellows—the prime pattern of the shaping of American historical consciousness in terms of both natural and social pressures is the one in which the specific narrative models of disparate memorialists have been cast. The American memoir is characterized more by wrenching personal development—the violent meeting of unexamined assumption and persistent historical lesson—than by smooth, progressive evolution. As story, it is most often a chain of hard-won epiphanies rather than a serene, symmetrical historical graph. Woolman's crisis-forged social consciousness, Thoreau's rough-hewn metaphorical leaps, and Adams's despairing replacement of spiritual metaphor with the figure of technology are all examples of the sort of historical bargain and exchange that is endemic in the American memoir.

As the memorialist traces the successive shifts in personal spiritual and social evolution, he becomes a newly historicized sensibility, one who most often offers advice or corrective to the very shaping collective mythology and historical practice that nurtured him during the maturation process. The American memorialist is the former child calling the parent to studied reappraisal or entirely new historical projects. Thoreau ventures out from Concord and returns with the outline of a new national economy; Woolman transmutes inner light into a radically different social protocol; and Franklin extrapolates confidently from personal projects of self-development to visions of national engineering. The American memorialist offers individual, often painfully gained historical knowledge as catalytic agent, as political manifesto, as spiritual guideline; the small story becomes both precedent and signpost for larger historical narrative.

Because of its ambitions beyond the evocation of personal history, the American memoir is most often a self-conscious literary performance and a rhetorical strategy that would prompt not only a thoughtful, but also a felt reaction to its illustrative poetics. The narrative is an example for general living or specific action; the carefully manipulated historical speaker is an individual philosophical or spiritual dynamic, a figure who would have his example, like a stone tossed into the center of Walden Pond, trace its rings of widening significance and influence to the larger circumference of American social, political, and economic concerns. Value-free objectivity or documentary faithfulness to facts are hardly issues in the most significant American memoir. Rather, the necessary project of the re-creation in narrative of personal history becomes the discovery and implementation of the appropriate aesthetic and rhetorical strategies that will produce the desired associative growth in small history, the embryonic link between individual and group behavior and belief. The narrative, then, becomes an identification and artistic representation of not only what is normative within past and present personal history, but also what might be possible in future collective narrative. If the finest American memoirs are not finished blueprints for society, they are invariably dramatic monologues with a variety of implicit and explicit demands. Woolman, Thoreau, Franklin, and Adams offer small addresses on the State of the Union as they modulate their historical voices; whether quiet meditation or confident oratory, the American memoir announces that the poetic principle and the aesthetic response are the appropriate and necessary first steps toward meaningful group activity and social transformation.

If the Vietnam War novel both extends and revises aspects of traditional American war writing, so the memoir of that war plants and harvests new varieties of personal narrative in the rich earth of its ancestral lands. The prime pattern of the shaped, evolving historical sensibility remains intact. Like the novel, the memoir is most often both a rite of initiation and a historical–mythical barter and exchange. But also like the fiction, the Vietnam memoir is likely to offer historical lessons that seem more hermetically personal and less optimistic, hard-edged data that are delivered in many cases with little hope or suggestion of how they may be transformed into meaningful group dynamics. A broad cross section of the memoir reveals several books of effects, sealed personal histories that cry to be read as illustration but that often fail to speak to their own reports. Others, thrashing angrily about in the immediate effects of war, hesitate to take advantage of the historical suggestions that reside within the folds of pointed, eloquent rage. They too often rest uncomfortably in one wavelength of a larger cultural spectrum. As the best of the realistic novels demonstrate, the re-creation of and the habitation within immediate history is but half the battle.

Gloria Emerson's *Winners and Losers* and Ron Kovic's *Born on the Fourth of July* are unrelentingly bitter onslaughts against American interests and practices in Vietnam. Emerson ably itemizes the many levels of victimization, personal and collective, wrought by the war but often seems to leap furiously beyond her implicit inductive method, interpreting vigorously along the surface of the war's effects but refraining from excavating within the mythic bedrock below the most visible, regrettable historical outcroppings. Her anger, however justified and well-documented, too often becomes its own subject, the more intriguing and telling associations of her episodic narrative allowed to remain buried cultural ore. Ron Kovic's personal tract is perhaps the most singularly powerful vision of the war experience among the memoirs. His climactic battle as a disabled veteran takes place not in the rice paddies or the jungles but at the 1972 Republican National Convention in Miami, where he screams his historical analysis to the war's current managers on the stage and is caught on national television as both symbol and agent of the war's refusal to recede easily into collective mythos. Like Emerson's analysis, Kovic's personal pilgrimage to Miami and his careful delineation of the callous and deliberately forgetful treatment of veterans is a historical vector of pure rage, but it is one that calls for placement within a wider grid of cultural origins and collective analysis, movement beyond telling portraits of individual victimization into larger areas of national appraisal and connection. Emerson's and Kovic's sensibilities, polemically white-hot, extend the American memoir into new, more volatile regions, but they are voices that require a larger historical context for their full articulation.

Like the novel, the Vietnam memoir is rife with books of effects, careful re-creations of statement and event that refrain from necessary historical or cultural gloss. Frederick Downs's *The Killing Zone*, a matter-of-fact narrative of a platoon leader's experience, and Robert Mason's *Chickenhawk*, one of the few full statements by a helicopter pilot, are telling records in terms of experiential veracity. Offering their historical lessons by examples both are studies in the ambivalence of professionalism and disaffection that characterizes so much of Vietnam War writing. Downs, physically crippled by the war and the symbolic target of monolithic criticism on his return,

and Mason, suffering psychologically and professionally from his experience, offer themselves to the burgeoning casualty list but refrain from attempting to state explicitly how that list should be both
read and implemented in a collective way. Powerful illustrations,
moving personal testimony, they wait for connection and explication
by voices outside their narratives; like many of the novelists, they
encourage rather than provide judgment.

As a new and problematic form of collective appraisal, the oral
history of the Vietnam War demands a modified critical perspective
for its appreciation and assessment. Similar in effect to the novels
and personal memoirs that rely on the strategy of implicit historical
and cultural analysis within powerful, graphic portraiture, the oral
histories add to that pattern an impressionistic, contextual challenge
to their readership. Less continuous narratives than chains of personal abstracts and insights, works such as *Nam*, *Everything We
Had*, and *Bloods* have undeniable accumulative impact, but critical
questions concerning the selection and arrangement of the voices
speaking are warranted and inevitable. The collective testimony in
the works would seem to be the raw, unfiltered stuff of true history,
the sort of first-person comprehensiveness that any single interpreting
or re-creating imagination may only artificially emulate. The problem
of a single voice manipulating, shading, and falsely codifying disparate experiences would seem to be alleviated by the presentation
of a broad, often contradictory and tension-ridden fair sample. But
the offering of the American experience in Vietnam as an impressionistic collage of images raises questions of connection and interpretation.

*Nam: The Vietnam War in the Words of the Soldiers Who
Fought There*, edited by Mark Baker, contains well over a hundred
anonymous voices offering confessions, charges, and thumbnail assessments. On the basis of immediate sensory impact, it is unrivaled
among the memoirs as a gallery of jarring glimpses into American
practice and victimization at their most basic and personal levels.
Despite its achievement as an emotional sledgehammer, however,
the book assumes rather than indicates its overall historical lesson
and cultural appraisal. The collection offers speakers who hated the
war, who found degrees of fulfillment and achievement in it, who
salvaged some aspect of humanity, who emerged from it as permanent victims, who found release for their darkest inclinations. Baker's
choice to offer an anonymous spectrum often raises more ques-

tions than it answers. As a single narrative, despite its eclectic composition, it seems more demonstration than judgment, a text directed at both heart and solar plexus. It is good to be moved, to be shocked from complacency and willed forgetfulness, to have a document that is deliberate compensation for the gloss of body count. But the quick impressions create the desire for more depth and connection, to know simply and specifically the people speaking and their larger untold narratives.

Al Santoli arranges thirty-three identified speakers in *Everything We Had: An Oral History of the Vietnam War by Thirty-Three American Soldiers Who Fought It* and Wallace Terry, twenty voices in *Bloods: An Oral History of the Vietnam War by Black Veterans,* the latter work a valuable collective testimony of the black soldier's heightened disaffection and victimization in Vietnam. Because they are identified in time, place, and role and because their narratives are less abbreviated than those of *Nam,* there is a greater sense of depth and story in both works, a feeling of more fully developed personal epiphany and considered response. Overall, however, the same advantages and problems inherent in a series of impressionistic, linked narratives as single document manifest themselves. Santoli is to be credited for having assembled a broad range of personalities; officers, enlisted men, combatants, support people, and medical staff offer a wider field for analysis. But the links among the individual tales are tenuous, and the unwritten assumption that oral history constitutes a form of interpretation and judgment is not validated by this or other such collections. Berry's *Bloods* presents the very real problems that the black soldier faced in regard to specific racist policies, de facto and otherwise, and general commitment and loyalties. His assemblage of speakers attacks successfully a number of stereotypes and speaks to a variety of psychological and political pressures felt acutely by combatants of color, but too often the collective narrative describes effects rather than causes, those larger implicit relationships of ideology, power, and economics that produced the conflict overall and the unique position of the black soldier within it. *Bloods* is a valuable addition to the memoir, but it would be a greater piece of history had it traced and judged the larger grid of relationships in which its specific issues reside. The inequitable aspects of American practice in Vietnam are most visible in the testimony of the black soldier, the prime victim along with the Hispanic soldier of the caste system that Gloria Emerson addresses. But *Bloods* often leaves its rage disconnected from the next level of response. Again, there is the assumption that the mere compilation and arrangement of voices in historical chorus constitute by themselves interpretation. The power and integrity of such works are unquestioned, but it is the evocative strategy of portraiture that is most evident, not the synthetic rigor of the comprehensive analysis or the imaginative, associative cultural apprehension. The oral histories are data as necessary, compensatory complication of collective appraisals, but they are uncorrelated data. They demand rather than supply a new level of historical commentary.

Michael Herr's *Dispatches* has been such an influential work since its appearance in 1977 and the subject of so much lavish praise that it seems to have been with us for decades. Herr's approach, so experimental, quirky, and poetic that it has helped to define an entire school of journalism, will be dealt with in a later discussion along with Tim O'Brien's *Going After Cacciato* as forms of a new American historical romanticism, but two other personal narratives of note, O'Brien's *If I Die in a Combat Zone* and Philip Caputo's *A Rumor of War*, represent another dominant impulse in the Vietnam memoir—the offering of individual confession and historical lesson in terms of comparison of immediate history with classical models of heroism, ethics, and proper action. Both works assume implicitly the status of the personal narrative as a test of powerful myth and as a necessary compensatory history. They not only compare and contrast, re-create and judge, but also successfully take the reader outward on a personal voyage and return homeward with collective news. As O'Brien and Caputo look forward to meaningful national appraisal, they cast a glance backward to Bradford and the initial collision of idealism and contingency and add new chapters to the literature of American spiritual transformation. *If I Die in a Combat Zone* and *A Rumor of War* not only are contemporary examples of violent American personal epiphany, but also carry within their classical frames the energy of the catalytic agent, the heavy demand of the chastened warrior. In the most painful way possible, they extend and redefine a long-standing narrative pattern: the meeting of world and spirit as national report, the offering of the personal dark night of the soul as notes for collective reading and plans for broader restructuring. Like the best novels of the realistic mode, the memoir nods to its ancestors as it announces its new agenda.

In an interview published in 1984, Tim O'Brien, summarizing the critical reception that his *If I Die in a Combat Zone* had received, stated that "a book which I published and intended to be a straight autobiography or war memoir is now called a novel by everyone, and everyone writes about it as a novel" (Schroeder 136). In the same discussion, O'Brien categorized his own work, a gloss that is only a half-truth: "The power of *If I Die* is the same sort that one gets from a book like Ron Kovic's. It's just there as a document. It's not art. I didn't know what literature was" (148). If he did not know, he was moving certainly toward a personal definition, for in the memoir O'Brien shapes the data of his personal history into a narrative that looks suspiciously like a self-conscious aesthetic strategy. Standing at quite a distance from straightforward reportage of statement and event, the work extends the personal initiation into a studied exploration of how reliable history and emphasized artistic effect may be not only conjoined but also announced as one and the same. *If I Die in a Combat Zone* is the illumination of immediate history by the testing of universal or classical propositions within a narrative that is as much invention as presentation, as much revision of an entire grid of beliefs as evocation of one nexus within it. The memoir both produces ripples in the chronological line on which it moves and shifts the strata of contemporary mythic elements in which it uneasily resides.

To illuminate immediate history by invoking a tradition, to offer his personal passage in Vietnam as a contemporary testing of both classical and Christian propositions of bravery, sacrifice, charity, and proper action, O'Brien undertakes a complicated personal quest. Throughout his narrative, he seeks not only established philosophical, spiritual, or literary standards by which to define himself, but also a stable narrative within immediate history that will describe his part in America's newest historical performance. Encountering a story that seems something other than pure tragedy or epic, comedy or romance, he begins the work with an emblematic chapter called "Days," a vignette of what is most typical in the banal, antiheroic realities of life in the Vietnam bush. Asserting that neither classical standard nor universal story is discoverable, he offers a senseless attack on a village as symbolic action of a new historical genre. "Things happened, things came to an end. There was no sense of developing drama. All that remained was debris, four smouldering holes in the dirt, a few fires that would burn themselves out" (17). Having offered the new wasteland of Vietnam as the ravaged, leveled frame of action and belief, O'Brien begins to beat ceaselessly into the past in a search for personal definition.

O'Brien begins the search in the chapter called "Pro Patria" in a sortie into the near past that presents war as generational linkage and mythic bonding. His speaker is both a shaping and a shaped figure, one who would write his personal history in response to acceptable patterns of thought and action. A seeker, he sifts through philosophical and theological advice, political debate, and moral imperatives, but his earliest influence as a boy in rural Minnesota is the evocative power of the war story, the symbology of the small-town reminiscence as lesson and prelude. World War II is a presence with the power of folklore; he tells the reader, "I grew out of one war. . . . My bawling came with the first throaty note of a new army in spawning" (20). Embryonic warrior, he is shaped by language and ritual, and, like Joyce's young Dedalus, his apprehension of national myth precedes real understanding. As a boy, O'Brien finds the historical shadow of recent American wars a mixture of ominous and comforting aspects. History offers a personal link—"I rubbed my fingers across my father's war decorations, stole a tiny battle star off one of them and carried it in my pocket" (21)—but as he plays war games, the shading of historical knowledge takes on a different hue: "Growing up, I learned about another war, a peninsular war in Korea, a gray war fought by the town's Lutherans and Baptists" (23). Like a young Thoreau of the plains, he takes long walks near Lake Okabena and ponders Tillich's argument for God as both transcendent and immanent. A complex of uncorrelated data and untested influences, he contemplates the myth-laden grayness of his town and imagines a Deity inhabiting and informing its patterns and practices, concluding, "Jesus . . . I hope not. Maybe I'm an atheist" (24).

Drafted in 1968, O'Brien, looking for no war at all but a just one if need be, becomes the most ambivalent, reluctant warrior. Considering flight from America as the right action in response to an unjust war, he tests his emotions and beliefs against Plato's *Crito*. Recalling Socrates's refusal to leave Athens despite the threat of execution, he begins to separate personal trepidation from general objection, con-

cluding, "He had not chosen Sparta or Crete. And, I reminded myself, I hadn't thought much about Canada until that summer" (27).
Despite his philosophical and political doubts, he allows himself to
be inducted not from any firm internal resolution, but because "in
the end, it was less reason and more gravity that was the final influence" (27). Exchanging classical resolve for the story elements of
Christian myth, he describes his last evening with his family as "a
cautious sort of Last Supper" (27), an assertion of his position within
immediate history as victim and assailant. He is a conscripted warrior
whose only early truth among his literary analogues is that "I was not
soldier material, that was certain" (30).

During basic training at Fort Lewis, Washington, O'Brien describes himself as the sensitive elitist, an updated John Andrews
whose relation to other recruits vacillates between antipathy and contempt. Referring to his barracks mates as "the savages," he initially
finds within his experiences with his peers of the mindless discipline
and enforced martial mythology only the realization that "in that
jungle of robots there could be no hope of finding friendship; no one
could understand the brutality of the place" (40). But like many of
the historically inviolate assertions that O'Brien is forced to temper
or discard, this one is complicated by the discovery of a fellow seeker,
a draftee called Erik who becomes sounding board, teacher, and structural device for O'Brien's moral evolution through the narrative.
Struggling no less than O'Brien in attempting to separate personal
fear from broader philosophical and political resolve, Erik admits,
"I'm really afraid that all the hard, sober arguments I have against
this war are nothing but an intellectual adjustment to my horror at
the thought of bleeding to death in some rice paddy" (44). As the
two friends examine a modernist historical lesson from World War I,
Erik suggests that Pound offered judgments in "Hugh Selwyn Mau-
berley" that are more than applicable to their predicament, that it is
not philosophy or ideology that accounts for their acceptance of the
call but "fear of society's censure" (45). No less adept than O'Brien
in pressuring immediate history with literary analogy, he concludes,
"We came to Fort Lewis afraid to admit we are not Achilles" (45).

Searching throughout his training for an acceptable model to resolve his internal debate, O'Brien considers heroes. He remembers
that Socrates was said to be a brave soldier, but, questioning the com-
pleteness of the historical record in regard to the philosopher's reasons for fighting, muses, "Plato may have missed something" (53).

Contemplating figures such as Audie Murphy, Sergeant York, and T. E. Lawrence, he finds the opaque surface of myth rather than knowledge. He requests a conference with the camp chaplain and is reminded by the warrior-priest that "Peter the Hermit raised an army, led the men himself, and they marched a thousand miles to win back the holy city. . . . He believed" (64). Questioning whether or not Vietnam is the appropriate set of historical circumstances for the chaplain's recycled crusade metaphors, O'Brien is told that "you've read too many books, the wrong ones" (64) and that his only necessity is "Faith, that does it" (63). The basic-training sequence culminates in a small voyage by O'Brien that precedes the larger one to Vietnam. Having carefully researched and planned a flight to Sweden, he makes it only as far as Seattle, where his first tactical defeat is his failure to pick up a sorority girl at the University of Washington in a scene more reminiscent of Holden Caulfield than Odysseus. Failing to discover the courage to rescind his military contract, he concludes, "I simply couldn't bring myself to flee. Family, the home town, friends, history, tradition, fear, confusion, exile: I could not run. . . . I was a coward" (73). O'Brien arrives in Vietnam an acutely eloquent, introspective variant of the new participant–resister, one whose desperate search for acceptable standards and models would now be conducted within the most deadly aspects of revised American historical theory and practice.

O'Brien's search for meaning takes the form of a sort of mythic deductive reasoning. If his tradition has provided him with apparently universal models and standards, ethical and moral imperatives for thought and action, then Vietnam is the most recent repetition and validation of the entire network of collective beliefs. Atypical of most soldiers in Vietnam, he is not only the individual participant–resister, but also the self-appointed cultural emissary. A reviewer in the *New Republic* remarked of O'Brien that although he is "no ordinary draftee" in terms of the great amount of literary and philosophical content he brings to immediate history, "he was typical of other GIs in his desire not to be a hero" (30). Certainly, O'Brien's narrative has a more overt literary and philosophical texture than most of the memoirs, but his failure to find historical analogues for his general propositions is finally emblematic of the more personal, less allusive lessons gained by the majority of combatants. His cracked syllogisms speak eloquently for the soldiers whose sense of a failed tradition was often merely despairing, intuitive, and silently endured.

O'Brien discovers that none of his peers is interested in the kind of questioning he undertakes. The officers controlling the war engage in a kind of myth-enfolded pragmatism, the application of firepower and unexamined assumption with equal quotients of brute force; the grunts with whom he shares the danger and the tedium in the jungle and villages play an unreflective game of hide and seek. The goal is less the discovery and destruction of the enemy—"We ignored the Viet Cong" (104)—than mere survival until the great American support system can resupply the ambivalent warriors: "We took our oranges and sacks of cold Coke for granted like haircuts and bullets. There could be no war without them" (105). O'Brien reaches back to Greece to describe a platoon leader known as Mad Mark, who seems to be "the perfect guardian for the Platonic Republic" (85). But O'Brien's desired connection proves to be unstable. Mixing his philosophers freely, he asserts of the platoon leader, "like Aristotle, Mad Mark believed in and practiced the virtue of moderation; he did what was necessary in war . . . he did no more and no less" (86). Shortly after this passage, O'Brien recounts an incident at a village called Tri Binh 4; after Mad Mark returns from a night patrol with the ear of a dead Vietcong he has personally removed as a trophy, he calls in gun ships to attack the village. The sequence ends with O'Brien's unit itemizing and practicing the new moderation the following morning: "Little fires burned in some of the huts. Dead animals lay about. There were no people. We searched Tri Binh 4, then burned most of it down" (88).

In the field, O'Brien finds not only antitheses of traditional heroic impulses, but also the deflation of the myth of the soldiers' bond. Comradeship in Vietnam proves to be an unstable cooperative relationship, trust and dependence always balanced by a necessary psychological distance. The new language patterns of the war are more than regrettable euphemism and convenient defusing of real practice. They extend to the revision of social organization in the bush, the preservation of psychic space for mutual protection: "the platoon's squad leaders were named Ready Whip, Nestle's Quick, and Shake and Bake. And when two of them—Tom and Arnold—were killed two months later, the tragedy was somehow lessened and depersonalized by telling ourselves that ol' Ready Whip and Quick got themselves wasted by the slopes" (84). Finding heroes and friends in short supply, O'Brien corresponds with Erik, who, in a noncombat role, supplies questions and intimations to O'Brien that help to shape

the new historical report. Both voices search for literary images that
will somehow capture and clarify the immediate data, and Erik suggests that lines from Frost—"truly / brutally / we are the mercenaries
of a green and wet forest" (107)—and the opening quatrain from
Eliot's The Waste Land ring true; but O'Brien, closer to the war's
core, finds more alien figures necessary, observing that the barren
landing zone he presently inhabits is "like the planet Mars. The
place was desolate, hostile, utterly and vastly boring" (107).

As O'Brien's deductive project bears less fruit, as the universal
and the particular describe themselves as opposed faces across a widening fissure, the internal search takes him to more discomforting
comparisons and intimations. Recalling the war writing of Ernest
Hemingway and Ernie Pyle, O'Brien, the apprentice writer of personal narrative, locates the disjunction between their historical posture and his own. He imagines himself writing the ultimate war memoir: "I would write about the army. Expose the brutality and injustice
and stupidity and arrogance of wars and men who fought them. . . .
I would have another crusade" (96). But he finds the reality of his
complicity in Vietnam his dominant theme, his acceptance of his
part a telling influence on his romantic self-righteousness:

> The men in war novels and stories and reportage seem to come off
> the typewriter as men resigned to bullets and brawn. Hemingway's
> soldiers especially. They are cynics. Not quite nihilists, of course,
> for that would doom them in the reader's eye. But what about the
> people who are persuaded that their battle is not only futile but
> also dead wrong? What about the conscripted Nazi? (97)

O'Brien's unwanted historical epiphany—the exchange of visions
of romantic victimization for the admission of violent agency—marks
If I Die in a Combat Zone as a new direction in the American war
memoir and as an emblem of the principal moral shift in Vietnam
writing overall. O'Brien's deductive method produces not the validation but the inversion of many of his mythic propositions, both classical and Christian, and the work itself, the realized counterstatement to the type of memoir he posits within the narrative, traces its
narrator's advancement to a new historical position as it presents the
quiet meditation as cultural indictment. O'Brien's historical victory
lies in his defeat before the feet of myth, his inability to correlate
traditional precept with new data becoming finally his shining mo-

ment. As trope and allusion fail to support lived referents, O'Brien's search for workable definitions of courage becomes increasingly tension-ridden; the reality of Vietnamese tragedy overtakes notions of an American one in the narrative as a synchronous process with O'Brien's passage from tenuous martyrdom to confessed complicity. As he sheds his protective sheath of universal propositions, he reveals himself as an embryonic moral impulse, one who returns to his tradition with a restatement of the necessity of historicized vision. What lends O'Brien's effort a certain nobility is his very inability to assert finally that quality of his war.

As O'Brien continues to search for acceptable definitions of courage and proper action, he discovers in himself and his peers a capacity for malice, indifference, and revenge that his Western tradition and his specific American cultural nurturing had kept restrained within a Pandora's box of collective storytelling. When a dangerously gung-ho officer is killed, O'Brien and his fellow grunts find their proper tone in macabre reference to popular American mythology: "A lieutenant led us in song, a catchy, happy, celebrating song: Ding-dong, the wicked witch is dead. We sang in good harmony. It sounded like a choir" (114).

O'Brien and his unit adopt a new historical stance as their shared tradition rends itself to reveal its darker underpinnings. Their senses, physical and psychic, heightened to define a new phenomenological sensitivity, they become a collective receiving set acutely aware of and adaptive to the dangers presented by the enemy and the land. Learning that they are to operate within the Pinkville area and the villages of My Lai, O'Brien describes their reading as a primitive, tribal collective act: "Even before the headlines and before the names of Calley and Medina took their place in history, Pinkville was a feared and special place on earth" (118). Plagued by snipers, heat, and fatigue, watching peers wounded or destroyed by the inevitable mines and booby traps, they discover an impulse that had always resided deep within the belly of bright collective myth but that now has an unrestricted course of action:

> In the next days it took little provocation for us to flick the flint of our Zippo lighters. Thatched roofs take the flame quickly, and on bad days the hamlets of Pinkville burned, taking our revenge in fire. It was good to walk from Pinkville and to see fire behind Alpha Company. It was good, just as pure hate is good. (121)

In a chapter called "Step Lightly," a darkly ironic description of the many varieties of mines and booby traps that made the land the foot soldier's greatest enemy, O'Brien even finds the capacity to reward imaginatively those Americans who would rationalize the conditions of his history lesson as unfortunate but necessary facts of war: "to those patriots I will recommend a postwar vacation to this land. . . . Certainly there will be a mine or two still in the earth. Alpha Company did not detonate all of them" (130). As blooded participant–resisters, O'Brien and his peers become emblematic of the dominant Vietnam double bind: the entrapment between the clear and present dangers from the enemy and the very land they walk on and the awareness, a painful mixture of rage and guilt, that the new lessons of history have disenfranchised them from the confident historiography of collective memory. O'Brien, by testing his tradition within the violent, bracketed terrain of American theory and practice in Vietnam, is shaped, along with many of his peers, as the afflicted warrior, an Odysseus who returns to find too many deceitful suitors in a home whose proportions and overall design seem grotesquely altered.

An important aesthetic strategy in *If I Die in a Combat Zone* is O'Brien's use of what may be called inverted parable, brief illustrations of the effects of American practice and attitude in Vietnam. Taking the form and tone of biblical moral lessons, O'Brien's parables offer substance that vigorously upends that primary textual association. Although not as overtly distinct from the main narrative as the pointed, italicized interchapters of Hemingway's *In Our Time*, O'Brien's series of scenes provides the same kind of counterpoint to his own pilgrim's progress. The first parable, "The Man at the Well," presents an aged, blind villager who is showering tired American soldiers. A young American, with no motive beyond malice, throws a carton of milk that strikes the man in the face. As O'Brien describes, "The carton burst. Milk sprayed into the old man's cataracts. . . . He was motionless, and finally he smiled" (103). This initial image of violent agency is extended in the next parable, "Mori," the attempt of a few American soldiers to save a wounded female NVA soldier one of them has shot. When she dies before a dust-off helicopter can arrive, a medic suggests, "Damn, she is pretty. It's a crime. We could have shot an ugly old man instead" (117). The mixed mode of charity and cruelty receives its coda as O'Brien relates, "She lay curled up on the floor of the helicopter, then the bird roared and went into the air. Soon the pilot radioed down and asked what we were doing, making him risk his neck for the sake of a dead woman" (117).

O'Brien offers his most telling mixture of classical and Christian allusion in the parable called "Centurion," a scene of three enemy suspects who are gagged and tied to trees by their American captors. O'Brien describes that as evening came, "the guard started, the ritual came alive from our pagan past—Thucydides and Polybius and Julius Caesar, tales of encampment, tales of night terror—the long silent stare into an opaque shell of shadows and dark" (132). Aware that he is now standing opposite his tradition's most powerful iconography, O'Brien completes the transformation from literary victim to historical agent with his confession that the prisoners are "hanging to their saplings like the men at Golgotha" (133). Such striking mythic inversion intensifies and complicates his dilemma, for as the parables become emblems of how Vietnam is rewriting a number of prime narratives, O'Brien finds himself forced to exchange the cross for the sword, to abandon the pure pose of the American sacrifice for the heavy role of afflicter.

His personal quest attains its most elaborate connections in the key chapter called "Wise Endurance," a careful exploration of personal courage and proper action in an unjust war. O'Brien locates in Plato a definition that, although difficult to practice personally or to discover in his fellow grunts, becomes a centering proposition within even this war. Recalling that in the dialogue *Laches*, the philosopher argued that courage is both an understanding of specific historical circumstance and an acting based on that considered judgment—a "wise endurance"—O'Brien concludes that bravado without temperance, justice, and wisdom cannot be called courage: "Which is why I know few brave men. Either they are stupid and do not know what is right. Or they know what is right and cannot bring themselves to do it. . . . It takes a special man" (141).

This adherence to personal standards within bad circumstances is the only value O'Brien extracts, but it is a volatile truth for him. Not only is his earlier intimation of cowardice as consent to serve intensified by *Laches*, but he finds his peers indifferent to this line of questioning. He asserts that "most soldiers in Alpha Company did not think about human courage" (141). He finds a dearth of historical models for the proposition he desires most to apply to Vietnam: "when the time in my life came to replace fictional heroes with real ones, the candidates were sparse" (144). He discovers in his company's commanding officer the only complement to his own inquiry, a man, experienced and wise, who seems to be a historically realized example of O'Brien's most admired figures, "Alan Ladd of *Shane*, Captain Vere, Humphrey Bogart as the proprietor of Cafe de' Americain, Frederic Henry" (142). O'Brien channels all his historically inapplicable idealism into Captain Johansen and creates him a figure who becomes the exception who defines the rule. In a meditation following Johansen's departure, O'Brien brings into high relief the lived emotional quality of Vietnam by painting its opposite:

> . . . losing him was like the Trojans losing Hector. He gave some amount of reason to fight. Certainly there were never any political reasons. The war, like Hector's own war, was silly and stupid. Troy was besieged for the sake of a pretty woman. And Helen, for God's sake, was a woman most of the grubby, warted Trojans could never have. Vietnam was under siege in pursuit of a pretty, tantalizing, promiscuous, particularly American brand of government and style. And most of Alpha Company would have preferred a likeable whore to self-determination. So Captain Johansen helped to mitigate and melt the silliness, showing the grace and poise a man can have under the worst of circumstances, a wrong war. We clung to him. (145)

Such a passage, beyond being a small validation of his universal proposition, points finally to the larger report, the assessment of the war as a turning point in American mythic sensibility. O'Brien's discovery of one personal oasis of value describes more strongly the arid historical terrain in which it rests and heightens rather than defuses his internal contradictions. O'Brien rejects Hemingway's dictum, arguing that "grace under pressure means you can confront things gracefully or squeeze out of them gracefully. . . . Grace under pressure is not courage" (146). Moving hard toward historical knowledge of an acceptable kind, O'Brien's epiphany is a reaction to his own desperate fabulations: "It is more difficult, however, to think of yourself in those ways. As the eternal Hector, dying gallantly. It is impossible. That's the problem. Knowing yourself, you can't make it real for yourself. It's sad when you learn you're not much of a hero" (146). O'Brien's role as a participant–resister in Vietnam provides him with a new standard of heroism. Stripped finally of classical, literary, and Hollywood touchstones, he defines his war as tragedy without Aristotelian magnitude: "You promise, almost moving your lips, to do better next time; that by itself is a kind of courage" (147).

The remainder of O'Brien's personal narrative is the final shaping of the new knowledge, the collective lesson written by the passage from myth to history. Johansen's replacement is also his opposite in O'Brien's hierarchy of values, an ROTC officer named Smith, who "looked like a grown-up Spanky of 'Our Gang' " (148). Hector's antithesis, he is a study in rash endurance, a leader whose bravado and incompetence produce many casualties and who can proclaim joyously to O'Brien after being slightly scratched in his initial combat, "My first big operation, and I get a Purple Heart. Gonna be a long year, Timmy. But wow, I've lost a lot of men today" (155). Soldiers do not die heroically or meaningfully before O'Brien's eyes, but stupidly and horribly: "The next day we blew up tunnels and bomb shelters. A piece of clay came down and hit a man, slicing off his nose, and he drowned to death in his own blood. He had been eating ham and eggs out of a can" (159–60). Now closer in tone to Bierce or Vonnegut than to Homer, O'Brien can only observe, "All the courage in August was the kind you dredge up when you awaken in the morning, knowing it will be a hard day. Horace's old do-or-die aphorism—'Dulce et decorum est pro patria mori'—was just an epitaph for the insane" (174).

In the penultimate chapter, "Courage Is a Certain Kind of Preserving," O'Brien offers his final clash of established standard and new historical data. Achieving every grunt's wish, he is assigned a rear-area job as a battalion typist and meets a figure called Major Callicles, "a last but defiant champion of single-minded, hard-boiled militarism" (189) whose real enemies in Vietnam are neither guerrilla nor booby trap, but "moustaches, prostitution, pot, and sideburns" (189). A walking emblem of the overall American presence, he is an agent of order who battles symptoms rather than causes and who would avoid the unsettling history lessons residing just below the surface of the anachronistic decorum he furiously promulgates. Callicles, however, is pursued by historical furies. An afflicted sensibility who has "stuffed the burden of My Lai into his own soul" (189), he works desperately to explain the massacre at My Lai 4 in a way that will extend rather than blunt collective memory. Like the Old Fox of The 13th Valley, he would disperse by deflection, rationalization, and force of will the most demanding historical assertions of his war, and his failure to do so, an amplification of O'Brien's own falling from mythic grace, is a rending of all the euphemism, hair splitting, and deliberate denial that support the overall mission. Charged with securing and preparing My Lai 4 for the investigation, Callicles attempts to explain Calley's actions within the context of a war zone, but in the village itself, "his eyes shifted from detail to detail, searching out stability in his world; other times he glared into dead space" (193). After the investigation is concluded, he returns to his battle against minor infractions and real or imagined malcontents, but he has merely put off rather than buried the persistent ghost of My Lai. The Callicles episode culminates with the officer taking O'Brien out on a needless two-man ambush, a symbolic attempt at individual and collective salvage that ends with a drunken Callicles falling asleep in the rain. Asserting finally that "all it takes is guts—right, O'Brien?" (201), the internally fractured warrior is rebuked officially, "and the next day he was given two hours to leave LZ Gator for good" (201). Incapable of holding the pieces of a shattered vision together any longer, he is removed from the historical field.

O'Brien's own departure from Vietnam is offered with the tone and gestures of a chastened historical messenger. The bearer of a narrative that has shed its allusive skin for a new historical texture, O'Brien examines what he has lost and gained and offers a singular farewell: "It's the earth you want to say good-bye to. The soldiers never knew you. You never knew the Vietnamese people" (203). Although he no longer reaches for dusty analogues to bear his message, he concludes with an abstract of his insights that carries its own impact. Thinking back to the old men telling war stories in his Minnesota town, he adds one more tale that, like the memoir overall, assesses a new American experience, only to place it within a larger realm of experience:

> You add things up. You lost a friend to the war, and you gained a friend. You compromised one principle and fulfilled another. You learned, as old men tell it in front of the courthouse, that war is not all bad; it may not make a man out of you, but it teaches you that manhood is not something to scoff; some stories of valor are true; dead bodies are heavy, and it's better not to touch them; fear is paralysis, but it is better to be afraid than to move out to die, all limbs functioning and heart thumping and charging and having your chest torn open for all the work; you have to pick the times

not to be afraid, but when you are afraid you must hide it to save respect and reputation. You learned that the old men had lives of their own and that they valued them enough to try not to lose them; anyone can die in a war if he tries. (204)

Like the narrative voice controlling it, *If I Die in a Combat Zone* recedes into memory not as a reconciled text but as a historicized tension of opposites, an assertion in form, substance, and tone of classical connection that consistently undermines its own needs and desires. As O'Brien joins inevitably the chorus of veteran archivists before his Minnesota courthouse, he also attempts to make his individual voice heard and to suggest new readings for old American folk tales. For standing between Hector and a new army in spawning, he knows certainly that all boys love to hear war stories.

Tim O'Brien is not the only Vietnam memorialist to forge a version of immediate history by testing his war against universal propositions of courage and proper action. Philip Caputo's *A Rumor of War*, a work published four years after O'Brien's meditative narrative, has garnered more attention and acclaim and, with Michael Herr's *Dispatches*, is a touchstone in the renaissance of serious consideration of the war and its textual representations. The tone and style of O'Brien's and Caputo's works are remarkably similar. Intensely personal and allusive, broodingly and brutally honest, both works conduct tests of preexisting myth as forms of confession, means to offer individual guilt and expiation as small models for collective peripeteia and catharsis. Neither work claims to be more than one person's story; both achieve a synchrony of individual and national tragic knowledge rare in either the novel or the personal narrative of the war. Like O'Brien, Caputo creates a carefully modulated narrative voice that describes implicitly its own development as American symbolic action of the most significant kind.

In his Prologue, Caputo contends that his tract "does not pretend to be history" (xiii) and that it "is not a work of the imagination" (xx); echoing O'Brien, Caputo defines his endeavor as "simply a story about war" (xiii), a personal, faithful account of one man's initiation. But, like *If I Die in a Combat Zone*, *A Rumor of War* is both a true work of the imagination and a valuable compensatory history, a memoir whose very literariness—its crafted, minute rendering of its speaker's rite of passage—is the pathway to its historical significance. More important than Caputo's insistence on the accuracy of his narrative is the quality of the voice speaking, the inner rhythms of the confessor who makes his transformation a painful emblem of national experience. Caputo speaks in classical tones, insisting that his book is as much about all wars as it is about this one. His Vietnam is a discrete set of historical circumstances, but it is also an exemplar of configurations of human thought and action that he perceives as constant. What pervades A Rumor of War, and finally dominates it, is the progressive discarding of both romantic myth and historical difference to reveal a few eternally recurring truths. Caputo's Vietnam is less a military or political struggle than it is an American tragedy in which knowledge is gained only by a kind of collective death, the passing of long-supported notions of national goodness, invulnerability, and power. A Rumor of War is as much a handbook of historical limits as it is a record of cultural excesses. As it connects American experience to a larger human pattern of self-betrayal and loss, it signifies, through its speaker, the end of an indigenous, confident warrior mythos.[1]

Caputo's narrative voice in the Prologue is a problematic one, for a reader encounters Vietnam as a field of action, feeling, and belief disconnected from the continuity of tradition and culture. The heart of A Rumor of War is, like O'Brien's core project, a moral exploration, an attempt to find a center of meaning in a war that seems most often manically repetitive, powerfully centrifugal, and deeply absurd. Finding the keynote of his war to be "absolute savagery" (xix), Caputo isolates many factors as catalysts for loss of control, excess, atrocity: the nature of guerrilla warfare, the inability to distinguish enemy from civilian, the strategy of attrition, the geography, and the climate. Assessing the experience as the deadliest combination of civil war, revolution, and jungle warfare, he asserts, "Twenty years of terrorism and fratricide had obliterated most reference points from the country's moral map long before we arrived" (xviii). Caputo's incubator for the nurturing of a new historical consciousness is described as a near-void of traditional controls and cultural signposts. Near the conclusion of the Prologue, he offers a passage that seems like Hobbes's Leviathan revisited: "It was the dawn of creation in the Indochina bush, an ethical as well as a geographical wilderness. Out there, lacking restraints, sanctioned to kill, confronted by a hostile country and a relentless enemy, we sank into a brutish state" (xx). The ability or willingness to accept the passage is the hub of reader response to the narrative, for it serves as an abstract, in tone and substance, of the moral drift of the book. Caputo's delineation of darkness proves to be as absolute and formative as Conrad's, the difference being that Caputo returns as the custodian of his own memoir and chronicler of his own evil and penance. Both Kurtz and Marlowe, Caputo offers a three-stage descent into a personal underworld that both intensifies and reshapes the quest for wise endurance.

The first large section of the narrative, "The Splendid Little War," presents a figure who is the antithesis of O'Brien's apprentice in *If I Die in a Combat Zone*. No reluctant warrior, Caputo leaps to become a valorous knight for Kennedy's Camelot. Describing himself as "a restless boy caught between suburban boredom and rural desolation" (5), Caputo seeks to escape the stultifying comfort of American middle-class existence and to have "a chance to live heroically" (5). Shaped by the mystique of the warrior cult, weaned on Hollywood heroics, he categorizes his decision to enlist in the Marine Corps as "an act of rebellion" (7). Untroubled by or unaware of the tempestuous philosophical, political, and ethical debates already swirling about his war, he seeks combat as "the ultimate adventure" (6), an idealized state in a historical frame of his own imagining. Like O'Brien, Caputo is the bearer of a classical impulse, but his is the call of the arena rather than the podium, the enthusiasm of the would-be gladiator rather than the fine philosophical shadings of the youthful sophist. His preconception of the Vietcong— "the new barbarians who menaced the far-flung interests of the new Rome" (16)—describes him as a revised version of Wharton's Troy Belknap, a willing, unhistoricized crusader who leans naturally toward Vietnam as "a place where I might find a bit of dangerous adventure" (17).

Initially, the mythic impulse Caputo brings to basic training is validated. He thrives in the "monastic isolation" (8), and he appraises the Marine Corps as the true nurturing ground for his romantic fantasies:

> It was a society unto itself, demanding total commitment to its doctrines and values, rather like one of those quasi-religious military orders of ancient times, the Teutonic Knights or the Theban Band. We were novitiates, and the rigorous training, administered

by high priests called drill instructors, was to be our ordeal of
initiation. (8)

Caputo's presentation of himself as callow romanticist is complicated,
however, by intimations of resistance to his warrior fancies within
the corps. Driven by his self-propelled vainglory and his primal fear
of failure—"That awful word—*unsat*—haunted me" (10)—he takes
to the physical and mental torture, the long hours of drilling and
field exercises, but as Caputo begins to speak retrospectively of his
own persona in the opening section, he offers an implicit dialogue
between the post-Vietnam voice and the uninitiated one. Caputo
consistently presents two figures in the memoir: the warrior in the
process of historical transformation and the finished product, a carefully controlled narrative voice that presents evidence and finally
passes judgment on his former persona. The reader confronts a
double image, a chastened Caputo chronicling the passage of an immature but developing one, one dramatic monologue in constant tension with the other. Offering his thoughts, feelings, and actions in the
historical context in which they occurred, he also provides a wrenching, often polemical gloss of their significance. As Caputo offers the
original data and refracts them through his new perceptions, the
reader is encouraged to judge both speakers, the romantic warrior
but also the transformed confessor of the original sins.

As Caputo presents his early enthusiasms for the martial rituals,
he assesses them from his new position of hard-won historical knowledge. Speaking of the field problems of basic training that seemed
so real at the time, he surmises, "We couldn't know then that they
bore about as much similarity to the real thing as shadow-boxing
does to street-fighting" (15). The narrative movement of *A Rumor
of War* is the closing of the gap between the romantic voice and
the educated one, the completed transformation signaled by the
final disappearance of the mythic warrior to leave only the historical
speaker. Caputo does not apologize for or rationalize his early figure;
he merely presents his untested assumptions and shows how they
were inexorably stripped away. Even before Caputo journeys to Vietnam, the Hollywood façade begins to drop; Caputo asserts, "I
wanted the sort of thing I had seen in *Guadalcanal Diary* and *Retreat, Hell* and a score of other movies. Instead of romance, I got
the methodology of war" (14). And a fellow romanticist encapsu-
lates Caputo's first historical shift when he notes, "You know . . .

the trouble with war is that there isn't any background music" (15).

Caputo goes to Vietnam at the very moment the American involvement is metamorphosing from the advisory period of Green
Beret romanticism to a full combat role, the war of attrition that
would grind on for the next eight years. Landing at Da Nang in
March 1965 with the 9th Marine Expeditionary Brigade, the first
American fighting unit to enter the country, Caputo and his peers
are both the recipients of two decades of conflict and the authors of
a new chapter of American foreign intervention. Told they are the
best prepared, best equipped warriors in history, the Marines land
with a combination of confidence in their newly acquired skills and
technology and eagerness to write history in the most visible, telling
way. What they discover on arrival, however, is the immediate deflation of Hollywood myth and traditional military strategy and a
study in heroic anticlimax. The landing at Da Nang proves to be
comic rather than romantic. Caputo relates that one of the unit's
platoons, after charging up the beach to encounter the smiling mayor
of Da Nang and a battalion of schoolgirls who bestow flowers on
the fledgling crusaders, takes its first objective with little opposition:
"Garlanded like ancient heroes, they then marched off to seize Hill
327, which turned out to be occupied only by rock apes—gorillas instead of guerrillas, as the joke went—who did not contest the intrusion of their upright and heavily armed cousins" (50).

In *American Literature and the Experience of Vietnam*, Philip
Beidler has described Caputo's progress throughout the narrative as
an "evolution of consciousness" (155), a fair assessment of the narrator's transformation from willing warrior to new historian, but the
prime value of *A Rumor of War* is perhaps Caputo's presentation of
the entire spectrum of feelings and attitudes he experiences as that
evolution occurs, the honest probing of what he refers to as the
war's "ambivalent realities" (xvi). Recounting his first combat assault into a landing zone, he isolates the tension of opposites that
would always exist for him, even when bitterness, disaffection, and
rage overtake the original heroic impulse:

> After I came home from the war, I was often asked how it felt,
> going into combat for the first time. I never answered truthfully,
> afraid that people would think of me as some sort of war-lover.
> The truth is, I felt happy. The nervousness had left me the mo-
> ment I got into the helicopter, and I felt happier than I ever had.
> (76)

William Styron has remarked of Caputo that "he is never less than honest, sometimes unrelentingly so, about his feelings concerning the thrill of warfare and the intoxication of combat" (3). The tension between Caputo's attraction to war as a primal experience and his growing alienation, guilt, and criticism of his historically realized example is the moral center of the work, a test of both his and the reader's ability to correlate sentimental Platonism—the impulse to be the ideal guardian in the imagined Republic—with a violent archive of increasingly disturbing data.

Caputo learns that it is possible to become literally high on war, that combat provides its practitioner with both a heightened sense of awareness and subsequent withdrawal symptoms. He can, despite his growing aversion to certain aspects of the war, remain affected by others, the experience of artillery, for example:

> It was a sight that would move me always, even after I became disillusioned with the war: the sight of heavy guns in action. . . . The Cordillera looked especially beautiful at that hour, and, in the clear air, close enough to touch. . . . The explosions of the first shells echoed and reechoed through the mountains; just as their reverberating roar began to fade, there was another burst and another series of echoes, and still another, until all we heard was a rumbling, solemn and unbroken. . . . The scene charmed me: the dim valley, the hill and the gray puffs blossoming above it, and, towering above it all, that great mountain with its mysterious name. (74)

He is moved by the physical beauty of Vietnam, stirred by the sight and sounds of men in battle, by cooperation under intense circumstances, by his own ability to lead and to persevere. But the classical urn on which Caputo's figures are painted stands in the shadow of immediate history, the specific aspects of this war that threaten always to erase any positive appreciation of personal valor or collective achievement.

When Caputo's company suffers its first casualty, his depiction of the effect on the men of that death is a moving assertion of value within travail: "One-Three was a corps in the old sense of the word, a body, and Sullivan's death represented a small part of it. The corps would go on living and functioning without him, but it was aware of having lost something irreplaceable" (155). But such appreciations in A Rumor of War coexist at all times with other lessons of immediate history, the images and practices that consistently thwart or undermine Caputo's classical impulse. He recalls of his platoon's first fire fight, "Perhaps it had been heroic for Lemmon's platoon, but for the rest of us, it amounted to a degrading manhunt; pulling bodies out of the mud had left us feeling ashamed of ourselves, more like ghouls than soldiers" (121–22). During this first stage of his Vietnam experience, Caputo retains the capacity for remorse for the dead, for disgust at atrocities, even for sympathy for the enemy, but the seeds of personal transformation have already been planted in the heat and the grime of jungle warfare. He notes, listening to heavy artillery pound enemy positions, his feelings that "the shelling seemed, well, unfair" (110), but he adds, retrospectively, "But this was early in the war; later I would be able to see enemy soldiers incinerated by napalm and feel quite happy about it" (110).

As Caputo and his men learn to distrust the passive faces in the villages, to respect and to hate an elusive enemy and a merciless climate, to live grudgingly with the constant threat of sudden maiming or death, he says that "a callus began to grow around our hearts, a kind of emotional flak jacket that blunted the blows and stings of pity" (90). He perceives, moreover, that the change in himself and in his men has two faces, one of felt victimization, but one also of the most deplorable form of violent agency. "An arrogance tempered their ingrained American idealism" (129), says Caputo of his men and, implicitly, of himself. He discovers Vietnam to be a historical field on which the most deeply buried hates and prejudices find their venting; he beholds a national visage as foreign and foreboding as the Vietnamese mountains that both attract and repel his gaze. Near the end of "The Splendid Little War," Caputo struggles to understand how a seemingly good soldier in his unit could matter-of-factly slice off the ear of a dead enemy soldier as a trophy, and a veteran of an earlier American conflict, a sergeant who has seen soldiers sight their rifles by shooting at Korean farmers, supplies the missing historical gloss: "Before you leave here, sir, you're going to learn that one of the most brutal things in the world is your average nineteen-year-old American boy" (129). The suggestion needs time to gestate in Caputo, but before he leaves Vietnam, he learns to accept the aphorism not only as a cultural generalization, but also as a personal accusation.

Theodore Solotaroff has said of *A Rumor of War* that "the ultimate effect of the book is to make the personal and the public responsibility merge into a nightmare of horror and waste experienced humanly by Caputo and inhumanly by the politicians and generals" (21). The next stage of Caputo's education, the middle portion of the narrative called "The Officer in Charge of the Dead," is a presentation of his experience, and knowledge gained, as an assistant staff officer, a position that emphasizes the disjunction of response and attitude between the soldier in the field and the managers of the war.[2] No longer a functioning part of the figurative body he describes when Sullivan dies, he becomes a casualty-reporting officer and gains a historical perspective that erodes steadily the few salvational human values he discovered amid the mixture of horrors and intoxications of his first combat experience. Immediately after Sullivan's elegy, Caputo contrasts that level of feeling with his new duties as "death's bookkeeper," the reporting of casualties that offers its prime metaphor as the keeping of "an accurate scoreboard," the tallying of the gain and loss of America's deadliest continuing athletic contest. His duties offer "the beneficial effect of cauterizing whatever silly, abstract, romantic ideas I still had about war" (157), but the price exacted from him for new knowledge is a high one. He becomes familiar with the sight and smell of the dead on a day-to-day basis, but he learns to speak a new language as well, a quantitative, euphemistic idiom that sterilizes linguistically the shattered data of the war's key processes and allows the manipulators of those processes to sleep less uncomfortably. Acquiring his own skill for word games, Caputo says that

> the phrase for dismemberment, one of my very favorite phrases, was "traumatic amputation." . . . *Traumatic* was precise, for losing a limb is definitely traumatic, but *amputation*, it seemed to me, suggested a surgical operation. I observed, however, that the human body does not break apart cleanly in an explosion. It tends to shatter into irregular and often unrecognizable pieces, so "traumatic fragmentation" would have been a more accurate term and would have preserved the euphemistic tone the military favored. (158)

When Caputo's commanding officer orders the retrieval and display of four blasted Vietcong corpses as a public-relations gesture for a visiting general, Caputo can only record the death of some old personal truths: "Man's body is the Temple of the Holy Spirit; man is created in the image and likeness of God; have respect for the dead. Well, the four temples in that trailer had undergone considerable demolition, and it was hard to believe a Holy Spirit had ever resided in them" (170). If the thesis of heroism that Caputo discovers in the field allows little in the way of a classical gloss, the antithesis of life as a casualty officer is purely ignoble, a state of consciousness governed by the repetition and numbers, the grinding down of individual human value and collective tragic impulse. The psychological and emotional pressures of his position produce a discrepancy between physical and spiritual calendars: "Chronologically, my age had advanced three months, emotionally about three decades. I was somewhere in my middle fifties, that depressing period when a man's friends begin dying off and each death reminds him of the nearness of his own" (182). Confessing hate for the scoreboard, the endless rows of figures that mock the significance of individual sacrifice and personal loss, he volunteers for a line company from a mixture of feelings. Boredom, guilt, and the heightened reality of combat contribute to his decision, but so do the fear of madness—"I had begun to see almost everyone as they would look in death, including myself" (219)—and, most powerfully, the necessity to strike back at one agent of the daily statistics: "I did not hate the enemy for their politics, but for murdering Simpson, for executing that boy whose body had been found in the river, for blasting the life out of Walt Levy. Revenge was one of the reasons I volunteered for a line company. I wanted the chance to kill somebody" (219).

Threatened not only with physical death but also with the loss of his deepest philosophical and spiritual beliefs, Caputo succumbs, as do the men under his command, to "combat madness," the opposed face of intense comradeship in an unheroic war, the transmuting of official practice into personal retribution. The final section of the memoir, "In Death's Grey Land," is an exploration of the moral entropy and ethical fragmentation that result when such a transformation occurs. Stripped of meaningful political or military explanations, reduced to a primal historical arena in which collective visions of life and death become the combat alchemy for private directives of love and hate, the war, as Caputo presents it in the synthesis of his historical movement, is a variety of social behaviorism, an explanation of atrocity as a cause-and-effect relationship governed by an intricate, unique set of external circumstances, and a plea for the recognition of the power of dark influence and the inefficacy of personal checks or internal conscience to resist it. It is this argument, one that reaches its climax in Caputo's ordering the deaths of two Vietcong suspects and the subsequent trial of him and his men, that is the essential moral challenge of the book, the delineation of the fine line of individual resolve and helplessness that has been the catalyst for critical debate on the value and message of Caputo's narrative.

James C. Wilson has argued that A Rumor of War, through Caputo's careful arrangement of influences for the inevitability of retribution and atrocity, "denies the very possibility of moral responsibility" (63), that Caputo's delineation of "combat madness" falsely and conveniently disregards the real power of responsible people to maintain control under stressful conditions. Philip Beidler, however, amplifying Caputo's assertion of Vietnam as an "ethical wilderness," has described his field of action as one in which "there is no philosophy, there are no morals, there are no meanings, except as the war creates them from moment to moment in its own imponderable terms" (American Literature 156). But such a nodding critical gesture casts away too quickly and completely the very real connection, with its accompanying pain and guilt, between Vietnam as a revised field of act and feeling and the cultural influences that were tested within it. What Caputo offers throughout "In Death's Grey Land" is not the mere presentation of the influence of new historical circumstances but the desperate attempt to correlate the fresh, disturbing data with old myth and belief. Like O'Brien, Caputo itemizes the wreckage of the heroic impulse on personal and collective levels, but neither he nor his peers can afford or accept the tempting denial of personal responsibility. The third movement of A Rumor of War is not a self-serving plea for acceptance of a "war made me do it" thesis, but a careful record of transgression, guilt, and the hope of expiation. It is, in short, personal confession as symbolic history, the positioning of individual frailty as the emblem of national tragedy.

What Caputo emphasizes is the failure of personal checks and principles, not the impossibility of them. He argues graphically and convincingly for an understanding of the factors that produce the angry burning of villages, the unusually cruel interrogation of prisoners, and, finally, the murder of enemy suspects, but he does not attempt to deny complicity or to avoid judgment. On the contrary, he asks only that individual sins be understood as well as metaphors of national transgressions. The chain of horrors he witnesses and perpetrates, Caputo argues, is normative and predictable within the form of history that his country is helping to write. Once the overall structure and tone are cast, certain plot lines will appear out of necessity.

When Caputo returns to the field, he finds a war that has escalated in its cruelty and deadly repetitiveness and has produced a collective perception antithetical to his original vision: "In the patriotic fervor of the Kennedy years, we had asked, 'What can we do for our country?' and our country answered, 'Kill VC.' That was the strategy, the best our military minds could come up with: organized butchery" (218). Caputo and his platoon discover a state beyond normal human cares and fears, a psychological terrain in which even one's own death or the deaths of others fail to be significant. At one point, Caputo reads the book of nature in Vietnam and finds in the Cordillera at night a new connection between world and spirit: "It was absolutely black. It was a void, and, staring at it, I felt I was looking into the sun's opposite, the source and center of all the darkness in the world" (225).

Complicating an old philosophical question, what Caputo conjures in "In Death's Grey Land" may be called evil and the absence of good: darkness as violent agency, darkness as missing standards and controls. When he orders a village immolated with white-phosphorus rockets, he illustrates the new states of feeling by confessing, "I did not feel a sense of vengeance any more than I felt remorse or regret. I did not even feel angry. Listening to the shouts and watching the people running out of the burning homes. I did not feel anything at all" (270). He and his men fight only to endure, but even the prospect of death somehow fails to achieve noble resonance. Finding only energy loss where the heroic impulse had once resided, he admits, "I had ceased to fear death because I had ceased to care about it. Certainly I had no illusions that my death, if it came, would be a sacrifice. It would merely be a death, and not a good one either" (247). Discovering the ascent from the rung of mere mortal to that of glorified warrior an impossible climb, Caputo describes a different kind of movement for himself and his men on the historical ladder: "I was a beetle. We were all beetles, scratching for survival in the wilderness" (247). Such a recognition leads Caputo finally to a moment of exultation quite removed from the kind he hoped his adventurous quest would provide: "Walking down the trail, I could not remember having felt an emotion more sublime or liberating than that of my own death" (248). No longer the garlanded heroes

of Da Nang, Caputo and his men carry themselves figuratively atop
their own shields.

If the hollow center of his historical moment is the crypt of
the warrior mythos, it also manifests itself as a redefined power of
blackness, the chimerical capacity of nonfeeling to transform itself
instantly into its most destructive other. Caputo and his platoon are
numbed beyond caring by the nature of their war, but the anesthe-
tizing quality alternates regularly with the exercise of the deepest
retributive instincts, the compulsion to transform Vietnam into a
distinctly American nightmare with the combined power of vindictiveness and modern technology. The proscribed strategies of the
deadly war of attrition and the alternation of debilitating boredom
and unexpected violence foster a collective psychological shift into
a dark state of consciousness: "We slid over the edge. That was what
it was like every time we moved off the outpost and into the enemy-
controlled territory beyond, like sliding over the edge" (239). Caputo
traces carefully how traditional values provide for a time a tenuous
restraint; recalling his desire to slap a village woman, his "first violence fantasy" (242), he performs the act in his mind but refrains
from real assault because of "that inner system of moral checks called
conscience. That was still operating" (242). When his platoon en-
joys clear-cut success, the joy—the sense of payback—is great. During
one skirmish, Caputo, overcome by Hollywood myth and real bravado, walks in clear sight of the enemy, hurling epithets out of a
movie script: "I was John Wayne in Sands of Iwo Jima, I was Aldo
Ray in Battle Cry. No I was a young, somewhat immature officer
flying on an overdose of adrenalin because I had just won a close-
quarters fight without suffering a single casualty" (255). The unbridled satisfaction in victory is coupled with the deepest self-preservation instincts and the strongest hatred possible, feelings that bracket
off his immediate responsibilities from any notion of a larger interpretive context: "It was just an icy, abiding fury; a hatred for
everything in existence except . . . those men of mine, any one of
whom was better than all the men who had sent them to war" (268).
Without a context of meaning, political or philosophical, in which
to explain or to reconcile specific actions and feelings, Caputo argues,
a war becomes a purely personal matter, a reduction of official euphemism to a few persistent emotions.

A key moment in the narrative occurs when Caputo's platoon
finally loses control and irrationally burns the village of Ha Na to

the ground, an act that Caputo describes as "the sudden disintegration of my platoon from a group of disciplined soldiers into an incendiary mob" (288). The aftermath of the outburst, as strangely calm as the action was incoherently destructive, produces a most disquieting reflection in Caputo: "It had been a catharsis, a purging of months of fear, frustration, and tension" (288). But he also admits, "It was not only the senseless obliteration of Ha Na that disturbed me but the dark, destructive emotions I had felt throughout the battle" (289). Finally, a kind of split vision ensues for Caputo and his men, the admission of guilt for their actions and the simultaneous sense of helplessness before the compulsion to destroy. He captures the contradiction when he offers, "Strangest of all had been the sensation of watching myself in a movie. One part of me was doing something while the other part watched from a distance, shocked by the things it saw, powerless to stop them from happening" (289). Any moral judgment that a reader might make, Caputo argues, must take stock of these seemingly opposed conclusions and emotions: the admission of wrongdoing; the catharsis of violence; the experience of shame; the assertion of powerful influence. Demanding in the narrative a recognition of the undeniable relationship between specific incident and general practice, Caputo does not offer easy or even consistent explanations for Ha Na, but neither will he accept the historical whitewashing of atrocity as a regrettable American aberration. Re-creating Ha Na as a small study in excess, he offers it also as a readable example of a tragic status quo.

The destruction of Ha Na, an incident that seems to be the climax of the narrative, is only a prelude to Caputo's final moral crisis. His decision to send a team into a village that is off-limits to capture two Vietcong suspects is one that illustrates in the most deadly way "the wide gulf that divides the facts from the truth" (312) on both personal and national levels. His time as a casualty officer has given him a close-up view of the discrepancy between official versions of the war and the reality behind statistics and euphemism. Now, as an individual historical wedge for that very discrepancy, he becomes not recorder but agent for the moral ambiguity of body count. With his words, Caputo orders his men to capture the two men and to kill them only if necessary, but he realizes that his true directive resides beneath the official orders: "In my heart, I hoped Allen would find some excuse for killing them, and Allen read my heart. He smiled and I smiled back, and we both knew in that moment what was going to happen . . . blood was to be shed" (300). When the wrong man is killed, he and his men are tried for murder, and on one level Caputo knows that the charges are warranted: "There was murder in my heart, and, in some way, through tone of voice, a gesture, or a stress on *kill* rather than *capture*, I had transmitted my inner violence to the men" (309). He reaches the unavoidable conclusion that "something evil had been in me that night" (309).

But Caputo's re-creation in the final sections of the memoir goes beyond the necessity of personal confession. He argues as well for understanding of the relationship between individual moral failure and the unique historical circumstances in which it festers. He has transgressed, but he also asserts that his sin has occurred in a war in which a commanding officer can offer an extra ration of beer to the unit that produces the largest mound of bodies. About his trial and that of his men, he asserts that "the fact that we had been charged in the first place was absurd. They had taught us to kill, and now they were going to court-martial us for killing" (305). Coupled with the painful admission of loss of personal control is the strong argument for the absence or ambiguity of moral limits on a larger level, the identification of the essential problem of readability of the American historical narrative in which he is more a spear carrier than an Achilles. He asserts of himself and the other men prosecuted that they are both scapegoats and the most unwanted reminders of the war's true nature: "If such cruelty existed in ordinary men like us, then it logically existed in the others, and they would have to face the truth that they, too, harbored a capacity for evil. But no one wanted to make that recognition. No one wanted to confront his devil" (313). The manifestation of evil in *A Rumor of War* is, finally, neither purely innate nor culturally or historically conditioned, but a binary relationship between individual capacities and limits and unique lived experience and influence. The failure of the military tribunal—and of the war's managers and much of the American people—to correlate the small with the large is Caputo's greatest complaint, the assertion that individual sacrifice and death are trivialized or unrecognized within a convenient national amnesia.

The figure speaking in the closing passages of *The Rumor of War* is a chastened and isolated one, a retrospective voice, like O'Brien's, that emerges from the trial stripped of much of the classical impulse but whose new historical knowledge carries within it the assertion of human value and the demand for honesty amid the debris of exploded myth. No longer the romantic adventurer living or dying with the praise or criticism of his superiors, Caputo can only stand opposite his judges as they fail during the prosecution to read the larger historical text and assert within himself, "I would not break. I would endure and accept whatever happened with grace. For enduring seemed to me an act of penance, an inadequate one to be sure, but I felt the need to atone in some way for the deaths I had caused" (315). And even before his tour is over, Caputo's inner transformation allows him to sign the new American peace treaty of the participant–resister: "The war simply wasn't my show any longer. I had declared a truce between me and the Viet Cong, signed a personal armistice, and all I asked for now was a chance to live for myself on my own terms" (315). When his physical escape finally does come, long after spiritual transformation and disengagement have taken place, he can offer only the small signature, "None of us was a hero. . . . We had survived, and that was our only victory" (320).

When, in the Epilogue, Caputo returns to Vietnam as a reporter to cover the last days of the war, he finds operating within him still the same odd mixture of emotions, the "ambivalent feelings" that his first tour had prompted. Leaving Saigon at the moment when North Vietnamese forces are closing on the southern capital, he admits, "Regardless of the outcome, I wanted to see it end. At the same time, a part of me did not want to see it end in a North Vietnamese victory. . . . Those men had died for no reason" (325). It is finally the very diminishment of significance, personal and historical, that is the greatest wound. When Caputo departs by helicopter for the last time to a ship in the South China Sea, he meets a young Marine from his old unit, the 9th Expeditionary Brigade of the splendid little war, now eons removed. As the ship embarks for the United States, the young soldier looks at a Vietnam already relegated to historical memory and suggests, "Well, that's one country we don't have to give billions of dollars to anymore" (328), an unreflective comment that both points toward the likely collective reading of future history and frames Caputo's definition of wise endurance. He joins O'Brien and many other questers as he speaks at memoir's end in tones less dramatic and more somber. Hearing the next day of the fall of Saigon, he can report only, "We took the news quietly. It was over" (328). Although Caputo's final pronoun reference is appropriately ambiguous, it is the war and not the classical impulse that has been voided. Reconstituted rather than vanquished, it remains the bearer of a historical statement of rare honesty and continuing importance. Like Tim O'Brien, Philip Caputo holds up a new reflecting surface to a land of wild beasts and wild men.

3

HEARTS OF DARKNESS

"These are great days we are living, bros. We are jolly green giants, walking the earth with guns. The people we wasted today are the finest individuals we will ever know. When we rotate back to the World we're gonna miss having somebody around who's worth shooting. There ought to be a government for grunts. Grunts could fix the world up."

THE SHORT-TIMERS

"I am a civilian."

NO BUGLES, NO DRUMS

When Stanley Karnow described the plight of Ho Chi Minh and his forces confronting American might and technology as "a microbe facing a leviathan," he also offered unintentionally appropriate figures for a dominant reading of the American soldier's condition in Vietnam. Those writers who attempt to present the society of grunts as an authentic subculture whose language, rituals, and attitudes define that society as both a retributive envoy and a helpless prisoner of American myth, as both historical agent and victim, often produce protagonists whose first and last line of defense against the forces that placed them in Vietnam is the purest form of dark irony or gallows humor, the use of the comic voice to delineate national tragedy and personal victimization. Karnow's figures of the microbe and the leviathan are apt, for the Vietnam participant–resister in fiction and memoir is most often a historical voice whose only true weapons are language and attitude. As he carries out the directives of a powerful jailer, he is likely to use black humor as an applicable analytical tool for the exploration of his prison house. His employment of the darkly comic impulse is not a deflection of historical seriousness but a concerted movement toward it, a funneling of the energy of the absurd and the grotesque whose origins lie in aspects of entrapment, in the perception of small sensibility buffeted and shaped by huge, seemingly impervious economic and political forces. The joke that the gallows humorist tells is an inside one, a report from the very heart of the prison existing obliviously about him. The knowing grin of the Vietnam participant–resister is the signifier of the jungle-wise social critic and fledgling historian. Although he reaches an emotional and spiritual terminus in Vietnam, the American soldier as black humorist is a long-standing tradition, a figure who, like the natural warrior and the quester for classical knowledge, has a number of precursors in American war writing.

Melville's *Israel Potter* is an early example of class consciousness in the American war novel; Melville's running joke, of course, is the consistent ignoring of the sacrifice made by those who actually fight the battles. As an economic process to rid the nation of its indigent, Melville's Revolutionary War is a glimmer of Vietnam's caste system working itself out in a new historical frame, a prophetic and telling comic portrait of what was to become a repetitive American narrative. The darkly comic treatment of the new power of American technology in Twain's *Connecticut Yankee* foreshadows another Vietnam theme. If the participant–resister is the unwanted human surplus of an inequitable system, he is also the manipulator of a new Excalibur, the firepower of industry as historical and cultural bludgeon. Potter is an absurd victim of a military star system, but Hank Morgan is an example as well of a new American potential for mass destruction, the unreflective willingness to apply the deadliest engineering principles to the very roots of resistant cultures.

Both E. E. Cummings's *The Enormous Room* and Dalton Trumbo's *Johnny Got His Gun* employ accelerated notions of the absurd to point to new forces quickly moving out of control. Cummings's imprisonment in *La Ferte* is as much symbolic history as it is real prison chronicle. Suggesting that life in the twentieth century is now the story of the small against the large, that any individual or collective struggle against budding or realized totalitarian tendencies may discover as one of its more serious weapons the assertion of humanity through the comic mode, Cummings concludes that the deflation of unjustified hegemony might begin with the overloading of its pretensions through an absurd treatment, by a refusal to grant it the reverence of the imprisoned. Trumbo's dismembered, vegetable-like protagonist is the ultimate product of modern warfare, the most grotesque figure in all of World War I writing, who becomes the hub of the author's social and economic critique. As the human refuse who survives as the most telling symbol of who pays the bill for the unreflective application of national mythology, Trumbo's shattered soldier resides within the national memory as a permanent wound, the hero of a tract that discards subtlety for images sufficient in graphic power and rage to do justice to the omnivorous historical configurations of a violent century. Cummings's resort to the absurd at the moment historical shackles appear and Trumbo's hellish humor help to define an American sensibility in which the comic pratfall is transformed into the most visible, permanent cultural injury.

Aspects of the absurd and the grotesque find new levels of development and concern in a number of second-generation World War II novels, particularly Joseph Heller's *Catch-22*—the work cited most often by Vietnam writers—Kurt Vonnegut's *Slaughterhouse-Five*, and Thomas Pynchon's *Gravity's Rainbow*. Heller's Yossarian, Vonnegut's Billy Pilgrim, and Pynchon's Tyrone Slothrop are true beneficiaries of the twentieth century as fragmented, repetitive war chronicle, a narrative in which violence and death are no longer events but permanent afflictions without medicinal aids. All three protagonists receive the history lesson that they are inmates as much as warriors, that the forces that place them in clear and present danger are not only indifferent to their personal survival, but also unlikely to be toppled or even deterred. The power of the economic cartels and power blocs to amass men and materiel for crass aims and to produce a propaganda machine to write an acceptable historical gloss for those interests signifies a cultural condition in which notions of free will, collective action, and personal ethics are anachronistic. As the war machine becomes synonymous with the peace machine, imprisonment in the nose of a B-25, the fire storms of a Dresden crowded with refugees, and the fearsome parabola of the V-2 rocket suggest that the deepest fears of historian Henry Adams are now ongoing practice. Yossarian makes a flight for Sweden, but his rowboat seems an unjustified deus ex machina. More appropriately, Billy Pilgrim becomes unstuck in time in Vonnegut's violent century, and Slothrop actually disperses

within Pynchon's narrative, a small figure lost forever in the post–
World War II terrain known only as The Zone.[1]

But the horrific post–World War II visions of Heller, Vonnegut,
and Pynchon, despite the new historical data they incorporate, should
be read as the updating of an established tradition, the use of the
blackest comic voice to respond to real threats to indigenous idealism
and democratization. Black humor is a reply to a world seriously out
of joint. It is, in the hands of its most effective practitioners, not a
helpless, absurd waving of the arms before unswayable powers but a
signal for social, economic, or political revision that entails the keeping of an already jaundiced eye affixed to official versions of historical
truth and necessity. *Catch-22*, *Slaughterhouse-Five*, and *Gravity's
Rainbow* may seem from one perspective the most hopeless of historical responses, but they contain within the bellies of their respective beasts the germ of a new agenda, the irreducible stuff of moral
fiction—albeit a new and nerve-rattling variety.

Black humor, on more than one level, is an offensive weapon, the
inflation of a historical configuration already in perceived bad taste to
the bursting point in order to make its hidden assumptions recognizable. It is the tactical sortie of the threatened against the origin of
the threat, a comic device that reveals itself to be the most direct,
unflinching, and accessible form of high seriousness. Black humor is
the unlikely combination of the funeral shroud shaped as coxcomb,
but it demands that its wearer be no supercilious fool. It promulgates
the hopelessness of art only to enfold a guarded hopefulness toward
history, and if it announces itself as the grimmest possible report, it
includes as well implicit suggestions for what a humane historical
balance might entail.[2]

As the weapon of the entrapped, the threatened, and the disenfranchised in a world in disarray, black humor might be expected to
be more a mainstream mode of expression among Vietnam writers
than it actually is. Certainly, the war—the implantation of accumulated American myth into a foreign landscape that became increasingly surreal—was a historical event threatening constantly to become
its own worst parody. As an endless war of attrition waged in the
shadow of nuclear Armageddon, it was simultaneously a deflection
and a realization of the darkest aspects of its cultural origins. Any
part of it seemed to illustrate the deadly repetitiveness of the remainder. It was not the war it was feared might be fought, but the
only one that could be, a release of coiled American potential in a

controlled frame, a tragicomic inevitability in which history and myth were hopelessly intertwined in a danse macabre of lights and shadows. Vietnam was *Fort Apache* repeating itself in new technological variations, but it was also warfare according to Beckett and Ionesco, a true no-exit historical matrix for the soldiers who populated its asymmetrical topography and burrowed in its mythic terrain.

To expose the essential disparities between means and ends, theory and practice, announced objectives and revised readings, the Vietnam absurdist or black humorist did not need to apply a comic veneer to lived history, but only to tap the potential that already existed within the new data. Gallows humor was not so much a strategy as an archaeological discovery, the extraction and presentation of the darkest ironies inhabiting the gap between the words and the actions of the soldiers in the field and the war's managers and apologists. Even in the most rigorously controlled attempts at serious realistic treatments of the war—Halberstam's and Del Vecchio's, for example—there is a drift toward dark comedy in which one discerns the subversive influences of the absurd and the surreal. Black humor and the absurd in Vietnam War writing are not modes distinct from the projects in traditional and experimental realism or the exploration of the classical impulse, but become the hub of a grouping of novels and memoirs as matters of emphasis and rearrangement. If *A Rumor of War* and *If I Die in a Combat Zone* contain junctures of Helleresque logic, so the most absurdist or darkly ironic works bear the stuff of lived tragedy and serious historical analysis. The technique of black humor, however, demands a deft textual hand. Its negative energy and capacity for historical caricature are likely to grant to a partial success the appearance of unqualified failure.

Asa Baber's *The Land of a Million Elephants* is an attempt to forge an absurdist parable that broadens to the widest ideological applications. Essentially the story of a mythical land called Chanda subjected to economic and political coercion and tampering by the world's superpowers, Baber's work offers its Southeast Asian domino as a historical text in which Cold War mythologies are tested and reconstituted within a traditional culture that proves ungiving to either Soviet or American machinations and overreaching. Unfortunately, Baber breaks the historical allegory by inventing an eclectic, self-appointed defense contingent called "The Crew," which expels foreign interests by relying on an undefined mystical source known as "phi." Baber's fable falls prey to the most dangerous literary strategy, the enhancement of absurdist and fantastic elements until the break from recognizable history is complete. The book eventually recedes into memory as its own form of historical wish fulfillment, a daydream that breaks on the realities of lived history.

A work owing heavy debts to both Heller and Melville is Robert Littell's *Sweet Reason*, one of the few naval accounts of Vietnam, which presents the American destroyer *Eugene F. Ebersole* as an up-dated version of Melville's man-of-war as social microcosm. Littell's vessel is a floating concentration of American social, economic, and political interests, a symbolic ship of state that includes blind ambi-tion, antiwar activism, racial inequities, and the essential discrepancy between the real practices of the war and the historical versions of it proffered by politicians, high-ranking officers, and journalists. Littell frames Vietnam more as career opportunity and public-relations cam-paign than as military or political necessity, themes central to sec-ond-generation World War II writing, but *Sweet Reason*, although achieving a certain effectiveness in its caricature of the cultural types operating within the historical configurations of Vietnam, is more descriptive than interpretive. When the *Ebersole* is rammed and sunk by an American carrier at the conclusion of the novel, Littell's deline-ation of the war's secret history goes down with it; the opportunity for rigorous analysis of the assembled data is relegated to Davy Jones's locker. Littell's unfocused protest is defused by its submerging be-neath lived history.

Len Giovannitti's *The Man Who Won the Medal of Honor* is an example of Vietnam black humor whose rage is restricted to a narrow channel of historical data and interpretation. Treating the war as an exclusively American atrocity, Giovannitti takes the "good Viet-namese–bad American" thesis to new extremes of absurdity, offering a protagonist named David Glass, who receives his nation's highest military award for valor against the enemy, when in reality he has executed a number of racist, atrocity-purveying American soldiers in Vietnam. Summoned to the White House to receive his medal, Glass meets the president, telling him, "I'm not one of your heroes, Mr. President. I think your war is an obscenity" (197). Giovannitti's dark joke is that Glass ends the narrative falsely accused of having tried to kill the president, although his real murders, his and his coun-try's secret history, remain buried under layers of cultural rationaliza-tion and obfuscation. Within the strictures of his interpretation, Giovannitti uses gallows humor adroitly, but the shadow in the text of the history he ignores precludes the novel's right to be read as a complex response to Vietnam. Like the war and the culture it purports to criticize, the novel itself is sorely out of balance, a limited reading of an experience demanding a fuller and more considerate vision.

One of the few attempts at a genuine Vietnam War metafiction is James Park Sloan's *War Games*, an entropic account of a nameless protagonist's decision to write the definitive war novel. Most of the narrative is devoted to the hero's efforts to get himself into a combat role to garner the necessary background for his novel. In Sloan's inversion of the familiar narrative pattern of the American separate peace, the hero fires a salvo of verbal pot shots at the military while struggling to get to the war rather than to escape it, but Sloan's attempts at absurdity spin centrifugally away from their historical referents, making *War Games* seem the most self-reflexive but dehistoricized tract of the war, a book that uses rather than interprets a significant American experience. Although in complexity, craft, and style it operates on a much higher level than the many Vietnam potboilers that offer the war as a setting for the telling of exciting adventures, *War Games* appropriates history in the same way. Without a considered response to the complex configurations in which it resides, without a moral burden growing out of a recognition of historical imbalance, the joke falls flat.

Those Vietnam practitioners of black humor and the absurd who succeed do so because their interpretations originate and remain within the central experience of the soldiers in the field, the society of grunts whose response to the collectively perceived tasteless joke of the American presence was to offer a stronger and more pointed one. If their nation could talk of destroying villages in order to save them, then some of the soldiers, directly and immediately threatened by the new logic, would need to move beyond *Catch-22* to couch appropriate historical replies. Gustav Hasford's *The Short-Timers* and Charles Durden's *No Bugles, No Drums* portray the grunt as a member of a violent class characterized most strongly by the blackest of shared historical jokes, the persistent grin on a grotesque visage. In these works, the new American reading of the Vietnam participant–resister achieves its darkest overtones, its grisliest lessons.

The application of the aesthetic shock treatment of black humor to a historical subject bears within it an unspoken conclusion: that more subtle, politic, or genteel prose strategies will fail to move the reader to the level of textual awareness that begins in turmoil but moves toward artistic equilibrium and historical understanding. Black humor, in its essential exchange of delicacy for maximum energy, is a calculated aesthetic risk that even with the most expert handling may foster a reader response characterized more by aesthetic trauma or disaffection than by critical cultural reappraisal. The danger inherent in the mode of writing is that of any extreme strategy: that the aspects of authorial control and moral sympathy necessary for its success may remain unnoticed behind the immediate, fearsome surface. The reaction to traveling through a literary house of horrors may keep one from discerning an intricate design and a larger purpose.

The crafted, self-conscious employment of black humor for the purpose of rendering a meaningful historical statement on Vietnam has suffered critically from a confusion of means for ends, from an attention to graphic surface rather than larger strategic purposes. Gustav Hasford's The Short-Timers is the most unrelenting of Vietnam War dark jokes, a work that deliberately sacrifices character for caricature and aesthetic diplomacy for textual frontal assault, but Hasford's stripped, terminally vicious field of action is neither a deflection of historical complexity nor a retreat into a position of nihilism. Delineating his society of field Marines as a distinctly American rogues' gallery, a concentration and culmination of cultural influences, he represents the Vietnam War as the most tragic but inevitable historical realization of a nation's most dangerous hidden assumptions. A first-person narrative told entirely in the present tense, the novel is a moment-to-moment study in cultural overload, a spare but minutely rendered poetics of evil.[3]

Hasford's choice to employ the novel as shock therapy for collective historical amnesia is a strategy that has been met with more than a modicum of critical resistance. Roger Sale has called The Short-Timers "a shapeless and chaotic novel" (19), a work whose graphic humor is finally its own reason for being. Assessing Hasford's approach to the war as the worst form of historical obfuscation, Sale describes the darkly comic surface of the work as an ineffective shield rather than a weighty historical cutting edge: "It is as though Hasford and his buddies during the war relied so much on the protection of arch jokes that he had only Creative Writing 201 prose to offer when the protection was removed" (19). James Wilson is even harsher in his estimation of Hasford's aesthetic choices. Mistaking the surface effect for the historical message, he asserts that the novel should be read only as "an overdose of surreal fantasies of carnage and machismo that become absolutely pointless" (50–51). Failing to discern the cultural lessons offered within the controlling band of the book's negative energy, Wilson dismisses *The Short-Timers* and other "dope and dementia" works with a sweeping and problematic critical charge: "Because of what they omit, these books display their dexterity in a moral and political void" (52). Within Wilson's assessment and the many others like it, the narrative method and tactical madness of black humor are necessarily antipathetic conditions.

Other critical responses to *The Short-Timers*, however, provide needed counterstatements to the accusations of nihilism, moral bankruptcy, and historical evasion. Philip Beidler has characterized both Hasford's work and Charles Durden's *No Bugles, No Drums* as books whose hub is the voice of a true subculture, a "brotherhood of death" (165)—his near oxymoron is appropriate—that insists that its dark history lesson be heard. Arguing for both conscious design and moral sympathy in the work, Walter Clemons has said of *The Short-Timers* that it is "narrated with a fastidious nonchalance that only a careless reader will mistake for lack of feeling" (60). Beidler's and Clemons's insights should be read as linked responses, for Hasford's presentation of his Marines as a form of violent American class consciousness is the organic historical development from which the tone and style naturally spring. The novel succeeds because the form and content of Vietnam as both reality and imaginative association are melded into a synchronous expression of the grotesque. By portraying the war as a heartless cartoon in which the characters fail to rise after their individual pratfalls, Hasford presents a merciless polemic against the mythic influence that produces real catastrophe. He argues by example that the most violent caricature not only may reveal secret history, but also may be a pathway to a revised statement of humanity amid the debris.

Hasford's grunts reside at one end of the spectrum of presentations of the Vietnam participant–resister, an absolute limit of violent possibility in terms of both attitude and action. Hasford's narrator, Corporal Joker, and his buddies are the tools of new American practice, but they are recipients and emblems of all that is darkest within a tradition. Hasford makes clear that the mythology of the Marine

Corps and of Hollywood is so deeply entrenched within the recesses of American belief that its application to new historical configurations is not even questioned. Vietnam may be a fresh American tragi-comedy, but the figures who become its principal characters are trapped within the most unreflective command performance, one whose run is as indefinite as it is murderous.

The first section of the novel, "The Spirit of the Bayonet," is the familiar basic-training sequence common to mainstream American war fiction from World War I onward. But Hasford's presentation of the Marine boot camp at Parris Island, South Carolina, is basic with a difference, an early indication that his Vietnam history lesson will be something other than the infantry company as a smoothly operating organism under fire. Hasford's combat community is rife with tensions that are struck continually throughout the novel by the mallet of military and popular myth. Hasford assembles the familiar hazing techniques of Marine indoctrination, but his narrator asserts that the physical punishment of Parris Island is "not that I'm-only-rough-on-'em-because-I-love-'em crap civilians have seen in Jack Webb's Holly-wood movie *The D.I.* or in Mr. John Wayne's *The Sands of Iwo Jima*" (7).

The narrative fulcrum of "The Spirit of the Bayonet" is a struggle between the drill instructor Gerheim and a slow recruit named Leonard Pratt, a figure who is given the unfortunate nickname "Gomer Pyle." Gerheim is the black humorist's rendition of the drill instructor as shaper of men and dispenser of tradition. He reminds his charges that "at Belleau Wood the Marines were so vicious that the German infantrymen called them *Teufel-Hunden*—'devil dogs' " (13), a reference that Joker updates as "werewolves" when he and his cohorts enter the gothic horror movie of Hasford's Vietnam. But Gerheim is capable of grislier, more contemporary folklore. To en-courage proficiency among his young men on the rifle range, he "brags about the marksmanship of ex-Marines Charles Whitman and Lee Harvey Oswald" (17), a citation less shining myth than its historical Other.

Gerheim conducts "the siege of Leonard Pratt," a recognizable variation of the war-movie convention of the dedicated professional transforming the most incompetent recruit into a battle-ready war-rior. But Hasford puts the convention to new uses. Under Gerheim's steady pressure, Pratt develops a relationship with his rifle, a new love object he calls Charlene. Transformed not into a functioning cog within the machine or a young soldier who realizes his potential for bravery and sacrifice in combat but into a deadly, silent psychotic, Pratt underscores the company's graduation ceremony by murdering Gerheim and then himself with his lovingly anthropomorphized weapon. Hasford indicates that Pratt is not to be understood as an aberrant product of the mythic machinery, but merely as a more advanced student. As Joker and his peers, the newly galvanized tools of American historical practice, ready themselves for their tours in Vietnam, the narrator offers this complication of Pratt's apparent psychosis:

> I hold my weapon at port arms, as though she were a holy relic, a magic wand wrought with interlocking pieces of silver and iron, with a teakwood stock, golden bullets, a crystal bolt, jewels to sight with. My weapon obeys me. I'll hold Vanessa, my rifle. I'll hold her. I'll hold her for a little while. I will hide in this dark dream for as long as I can. (32)

With this lyrical admission by Joker, Pratt becomes in death the true standard bearer of Hasford's "newly minted Marines" (32), who go to Vietnam as captives of what is most irreducible in their nation's dark reverie.

"Body Count," the long middle portion of The Short-Timers, is an unusual narrative strategy among Vietnam novels. Discarding the customary scenes of young soldiers being gradually shaped, informed, and disillusioned by new American history in Vietnam, Hasford presents Joker and his peers as fully formed black humorists, men whose historical response and accompanying linguistic strategies are developed and bitterly locked into place. Concentrating on the key historical pressure point of the 1968 Tet offensive, the true chronological fault line of the American involvement, Hasford conjures a Vietnam that is the stuff of surreal nightmare, a demonic realization of Melville's suggestion in The Confidence-Man that the reader is to be offered a strange world but one to which he feels a connection. Hasford retains a faithfulness to facts on one level—the destruction of Hue and the siege of Khe Sanh are his prime story elements—but he rends the expectation of documentary realism and substitutes a fictional terrain that has the geometric feel of Caligari's cabinet, the unwanted announcement that the deepest forebodings of historical fancy are more than imaginative projections. Imploding the melting-pot naturalism of Mailer's The Naked and the Dead, Hasford offers a battlefield society populated by two-dimensional cartoon characters, an assemblage of nicknamed dark functionaries who are presented deliberately as tools of cultural dementia rather than as sympathetic personal histories. In place of the John Andrewses, Frederic Henrys, and Lieutenant Hearns of mainstream American war fiction, Hasford offers Crazy Earl, who uses a Red Ryder BB gun against the enemy; Alice, a huge black who collects the feet of dead Vietcong in a blue shopping bag; and a character known to his fellow grunts as T. H. E. Rock, a walking emblem of the entropic power of Vietnam to drain traditional notions of the human and the humane.

The inherent danger, of course, in this sort of violent caricature is that Vietnam as a recognizable but alternative universe may seem disconnected finally from lived experience, but Hasford succeeds not only in retaining his historical referent, but also in rigorously interpreting it. In "Body Count," Joker is a combat correspondent, a conduit of the war's official, censored history, but he is also Hasford's tour guide for that history's horrible antithesis. Aware that the confident grin of high command is the mere assertion of optimism in a historical near void, he knows as well that he is one of the managers' most necessary tools. His attempts to capture the truth of his war in words are "shit-canned" at higher levels, and his sanitized press releases are "paper bullets fired into the fat black heart of Communism" (59). Castigated by his peers for his status as halfway grunt, Joker is capable of identifying his complicity in the writing of the careful mixture of myth and reality that becomes acceptable public fabulation:

> You know I do my job. I write that Nam is an Asian Eldorado populated by a cute, primitive but determined people. War is a noisy breakfast food. War is fun to eat. War can give you better checkups. War cures cancer—permanently. I don't kill. I write. Grunts kill; I only watch. (60)

Beyond his writing of two Vietnam War histories—the public revisionist one of half-truths and ignored facts and the private compensatory monologue the reader overhears—Joker is the teacher and protector in "Body Count" of a young combat photographer called Rafter Man, a would-be grunt who is Hasford's device for a grotesque rendering of the traditional American war *Bildungsroman*. When Joker's charge experiences his first action, he invents his own spontaneous bonding ritual with his new brothers. Picking up a small portion of a mortared American soldier, "Rafter Man puts the flesh into his mouth, onto his tongue, and we think he's going to vomit. Instead, he grits his teeth. Then, closing his eyes, he swallows" (74). Rafter Man's ticket of admission to the society of grunts is not only the acquisition of the black humorist's tone, but also the willingness to put that attitude into historical practice, to indulge in rites that in the most graphic way define that community as a true historical terminus, a cold instrument of secret history that offers its members only the most unstable bonds of friendship and cooperation.

Beneath Hasford's savage imagery, his choreography of a historical danse macabre unprecedented in American war fiction, is a substratum of moral sympathy and humanism that battles continuously with the novel's drift toward pure horror. Without that level of concern and sensibility, *The Short-Timers* would be a tract unrivaled for its devaluation of the real tragedy and human sacrifice, a book that not only misrepresents but also insults the memory of the living and the dead. But unlike those writers who appropriate Vietnam for dehistoricized assertions of the absurd and the demonic, Hasford reveals gradually but clearly that his dark humor is merely a surface beneath which his real historical message resides. The key to understanding Hasford's reading of the war is the recognition that for him and his narrator, the "arch jokes" of grunt society are a protective device for the historically trapped, a buttressed historical pose that by novel's end crumbles before the power of human feeling and vulnerability. Tucked under the crust of the gallows-humor defense mechanism, *The Short-Timers* is one of the war's most poignant documents, a careful if graphic argument that the devil dogs of myth are only scared young men trying to live long enough to get home.

Harry Brown's World War II novel *A Walk in the Sun* is a representative work of that war in that in tone and substance it portrays the rifle platoon as a necessary, well-operating society. Brown's soldiers perform competently; individual complaints are deferred; and there is a tired matter-of-factness, a sophistication toward the intrusion of violent history. The job is to be done as cleanly as possible and then left behind, an unwelcome but accepted imperative for collective action. Although personal vainglory and overt patriotism are missing from Brown's work, there remains the sense, admitted grudgingly, that Hitler has to be stopped, that history has provided a horrible but incomplete narrative. Even in a second-generation work such as *Catch-22*, Yossarian, the prime captive of violent history in all of

World War II literature, does not assert that he is fighting on the wrong side; his complaints stem from having been forced to fly into the flak too often, and his disengagement is more personal than ideological.

The Short-Timers offers a new relationship among the individual, the group, and history. Like Del Vecchio's think-tank specialists, Hasford's Marines are practiced analysts of their historical configuration, but in the surreal terrain of Hue and Khe Sanh during Tet, their complaints, attitudes, and conclusions are less tempered and equivocal. They share the thesis that history has indeed betrayed them, that they have been stripped of just cause or even decent explanation for their function, and that their entrapment by the mythic machine is complete and irrevocable. As Joker suggests, "What you do, you become" (133), a historical aphorism that isolates the tragic juncture where national hubris and individual victimization meet. Hasford's grunts wisecrack, swagger, and wear a grisly visage, but unlike Brown's soldiers, who are able to walk away from a dirty, necessary job, or Yossarian, who opts for Sweden, they find no escape or release from the forces that condone their most extreme practices without providing a validating explanation for them.

For Joker and his cohorts, Vietnam becomes not a disquieting interruption of their lives but a permanent state of mind, recurrent nightmare as sole reality. Responding to Alice's description of the war as a historical madhouse, Joker retorts, "No, back in the World is the crazy part. This, all this world of shit, this is real" (123). The grunts comport themselves like the werewolves of legend, promulgating and extending the dark joke in which they reside, but they are also aware of the individual and collective price for living too long and too obsessively in a historical event that presents itself not as cultural necessity, but as self-justifying violent fact. When national purpose drops from history like a husk, the individual soldier is forced to provide his own explanations, to create a personal center where larger ones implode. As spokesman for all of Hasford's grunts, Joker offers the terrible lesson behind the joke telling. Recalling at one point his first confirmed kill, the needless shooting of an old farmer, he says,

> I was defining myself in bullets; blood had blemished my Yankee Doodle dream that everything would have a happy ending, and that I, when the war was over, would return to hometown America in a white silk uniform, a rainbow of campaign ribbons across my chest, brave beyond belief, the military Jesus. (133)

No less than Tim O'Brien in a different mode of expression, Hasford works with determination through the black joke to explore the lasting ramifications of exposed, shattered myth, indicating again that the strategies and techniques of the writers of Vietnam War literature, although originating in different philosophical and aesthetic commitments and beliefs, more often than not offer variations of the same cultural report.

The critique of history among Hasford's grunts is as much attitude as detailed analysis, and the shared sense of imprisonment dictates that any career military person is by definition excluded from their society. "Lifers are a breed," says Joker. "A lifer is anybody who abuses authority he doesn't deserve to have" (63), a charge that Vietnam is more a study in class warfare than an American collective effort, more a steady antagonism between jailers and inmates than an equitable cultural enterprise. Even in basic training, Joker learns enough of his true position to assert that "Marines are not allowed to die without permission; we are government property" (13), but as the Tet offensive is breaking as both real and symbolic news, a character called Chili Vendor intensifies the collective apprehension. Reducing large, anarchic history to a smaller, accessible one, he summarizes, "We're prisoners here. We're prisoners of the war. They've taken away our freedom and they've given it to the gooks, but the gooks don't want it. They'd rather be alive than free" (67). The potential for this sort of instant abstract is a collective one, a shared need to reduce historical chaos to the magnitude of personal and group understanding. Despite the continual danger of reductive reasoning, the black humorists as a reflective, resentful class launch their historical salvos as natural retaliatory gestures.

The grunt as a prisoner of violent history does not hesitate to offer sociological and political readings concerning the plight of soldiers in adjacent prisons. A prime theme in all of Vietnam War writing is the unstable, often explosive relationship between American and South Vietnamese forces, one in which the ARVN soldier most often is devalued and denigrated for his lack of commitment and his desire to allow the American combatant to bear the brunt of the fighting. Hasford's grunts consider themselves a separate society from lifers, but they are not without the capacity for peer identification with other contingents of the victimized. During the battle for Hue, Joker and Rafter Man spot a group of South Vietnamese soldiers looting a mansion, an image that elicits from Joker the common American reading: "Remember this, Rafter Man, any time you can see an Arvin you are safe from Victor Charlie. The Arvins run like rabbits at the first sign of violence. An Arvin infantry platoon is about as lethal as a garden club of old ladies throwing marshmallows" (82). Joker's comments are standard fare; resentment of the South Vietnamese military can be discerned in a hundred variations throughout the novels and memoirs. But Joker as spokesman for the entrapped also offers another assessment of the ARVN soldiers. Despite concluding that the ARVN are useless, he offers a rare example of solidarity with the South Vietnamese soldier, one that originates in the cultivated self-reflexivity of grunt society: "Don't believe all that scuttlebutt about Arvins being cowards. They just hate the Green Machine more than we do. They were drafted by the Saigon government, which was drafted by the lifers who drafted us, who were drafted by the lifers who think they can buy the war" (82). Joker is aware that the South Vietnamese are putting into historical practice their disaffection in a way the grunts are not. Despite their cogent readings and grisly demeanor, they remain short-timers, men striving for only one goal as they count off the days of their sentences. As the platoon leader called Cowboy asserts, "My job is to get my people back to the World in one piece" (9–10).

Joker and company find the greatest illumination of their true status, however, in their relationship with the enemy. A character called Mr. Payback verbalizes a core emotion among the entrapped toward those who would terminate them: "When Luke the gook zaps you in the back and Phantoms bury him in napalm cannisters, that's payback. When you shit on people it comes back to you, sooner or later, only worse" (64). But the revenge factor that promulgates the deadly effectiveness in Hasford's Marines is only one response toward their historical other; a deeper identification than that with the South Vietnamese, one based on the perception of efficacy and tenacity, is another. At one juncture during the Hue sequence, Crazy Earl attempts to encapsulate the strange bond between rival professionals: "The gooks are grunts, like us. They fight, like us. They got lifer poges running their country and we got lifer poges running ours. . . . We kill each other, no doubt about it, but we're tight. . . . I love the little commie bastards, man, I really do. Grunts understand grunts" (93).

The destruction of Hue is one epitome for Hasford of the true effect of American mythic machinery in Vietnam. Covering the battle as a combat correspondent, Joker offers a piece of narration that frames the essential relationship of grunt society to Vietnam War history. As fighting rages about the Citadel, the most treasured and symbolic architecture of old Vietnam, he submits the sort of news dispatch to the reader that no official censor would fail to bury:

> We are big white American boys in steel helmets and heavy flak jackets, armed with magic weapons, laying siege to a castle in modern times. One-Five has changed a lot since the days when it was the first battalion to hit the beach at Guadalcanal.

> Metal birds flash in and shit steel eggs all over the place. F-4 Phantom jet fighters are dropping napalm, high explosives, and Willy Peter—white phosphorus. With bombs we are expressing ourselves; we are writing our history in shattered blocks of stone. (97)

After Joker and the grunts leave Hue, Hasford offers two incidents that powerfully illustrate the unusual bonds between enemies and friends. Observing a group of enemy soldiers on an island in the River of Perfumes attacked by Cobra gun ships—a small tableau of American technology versus indigenous, overmatched tenacity—Joker and the grunts spontaneously become a cheering section for the one "ant" who succeeds in swimming to the river bank. There he conducts an absurd one-man stand against the pursuing helicopters, destroying one and holding his ground until two more expend their ammunition, prompting one of the American cheerleaders to assert, "That guy was a grunt" (126). Responding to the ultimate victory of the underdog, Joker summarizes the mood of all the historically imprisoned:

> While we wait for the gunboats to come and take us across the River of Perfumes we talk about how the NVA grunt was one hell of a hard individual and about how it would be okay if he came to America and married all our sisters and about how we all hope that he will live to be a hundred years old because the world will be diminished when he's gone. (126)

The battle of the ants is followed quickly by the death of Rafter Man, Hasford's battlefield initiate, who dies stupidly and senselessly under the treads of an oblivious American tank that bears the telling inscription BLACK FLAG—We Exterminate Household Pests. Early in "Body Count," the same symbol of uncontrolled power runs over a young Vietnamese girl, prompting the overzealous driver to query,

"Don't these zipperheads know that tanks got the right-of-way?" (79). The grotesque demise of Joker's understudy is another emblem of the failure of the unreflective practitioners of power to discriminate between prisoners of war. Joker's response to the loss of a peer points to the disjunction between internal and external response in Vietnam. Standing over the crushed remains of a failed pupil, he can only admit, "I want so much to cry, but I can't—I'm too tough" (129).

"Body Count" ends with a confrontation between Joker and a mad career officer that combines the inverted logic of Joseph Heller with the iconography of Bela Lugosi and Lon Chaney. Reprimanded for the peace symbol on his helmet and offering the incorrect historical response to the query "Do you believe that the United States should allow the Vietnamese to invade Viet Nam just because they live here?" (137), he fends off with a wooden bayonet the officer who "bares vampire fangs" (139) and reports Joker's insubordinate attitude and appearance to higher authority. Stripped of his function as combat correspondent, Joker is made a full werewolf in his nation's longest continuing grade-B horror movie, a transformation that elicits the response, "I tell them I'm glad to be a grunt because now I won't have to write captions for atrocity photographs they just file away" (140). Ordered to Khe Sanh, he becomes an additional projection of the history that he and his fellows have already terminally judged.

Hasford begins the concentrated final section, called "Grunts," with an evocation of Khe Sanh, the historical outcropping on which are concentrated the deepest American hopes and fears. Joker reminds the reader that forebodings of another Dien Bien Phu have resulted in the application to the hills around the American compound of "the greatest volume of explosives in the history of war" (146). But he also asserts that immediate history has already become "a faded daguerrotype" (146), an enjambment of memory and new experience. Now both victim and enactment of national fears, he can assert, "In the darkness I am one with Khe Sanh—a living cell of this place—this erupted pimple of sandbags and barbed wire on a bleak plateau surrounded by the end of the world" (146). The black absolute center of anarchic history, Khe Sanh is also the setting for the black humorist's deadliest jokes and the humanity they would enfold and protect. Leaving the compound on the novel's final mission, Joker and his squad acknowledge a familiar figure, Hasford's updating of the dark prophet of Melville or Coleridge:

This time we do not salute Sorry Charlie. Sorry Charlie is a skull, charred black. Our gunner, Animal Mother, mounted the skull on a stake in the kill zone. We think it's the skull of an enemy grunt who got napalmed outside our wire. Sorry Charlie is still wearing my old black felt Mouseketeer ears, which are getting a little moldy. I wired the ears onto Sorry Charlie as a joke. As we hump by, I stare into the hollow eye sockets. I wait for the white spider to emerge. The dark, clean face of death smiles at us with his charred teeth, his inflexible ivory grin. Sorry Charlie always smiles at us as though he knows a funny secret. For sure, he knows more than we do. (147–48)

In the bush, Hasford's society defines itself most purely and completely. "We hump, werewolves in the jungle," says Joker. "God has made this jungle for Marines. . . . To show our appreciation for so much omnipotent attention we keep Heaven packed with fresh souls" (150). But the hard surface of grunt society is only the protective sheath for more than one layer of vulnerability. Hasford's Marines are aware of their failure to do more than count their days. When one soldier begins to offer the anti-lifer speech, Joker suggests that "we all brown-nose the lifers" (160), an observation that elicits agreement from Alice, the foot collector: "That's an amen. . . . We talk the talk, but we don't walk the walk" (160). Conscious of both their complicity and their imprisonment in an American nightmare, they acknowledge the bonds of feeling among them only grudgingly and in the most extreme circumstances; the tone of feigned indifference or hostility is more typical. As a member of Joker's squad tells a new arrival, "Don't follow me too close, New Guy. If you step on a mine I don't want to get fucked up" (164).

The final sequence of the novel is the ambush of Joker's squad by a sniper, a small horror within the larger one that forces the black humorist to discard at long last his costume and to reveal himself as another form of Vietnam eiron. When Alice, the point man, is shot, Joker asserts internally, "I'm glad it's him and not me" (167), but he and the rest of the squad will not abandon Alice. A medic named Doc Jay shows Hasford's understanding of the other face of Vietnam. A figure who "wants to save all the wounded, even those killed in action and buried months ago" (155), Doc Jay is killed trying to administer aid to the fallen point man. The final dark joke of *The Short-Timers* originates in sacrifice, not cynicism; it is the sniper's knowledge that the grunts will die one by one trying to save one another. The ramifications of the joke are everywhere, the final irony being the failure of the young werewolves to live up to their mythic billing as callous killers. As Joker notes, "Sooner or later the squad will surrender to the black design of the jungle. We live by the law of the jungle, which is why more Marines go in than come out. There it is. Nobody asks why we're smiling because nobody wants to know" (175). When Cowboy, the squad leader, is wounded as well, Joker ends the procession of death and sacrifice by committing a mercy killing as he puts a bullet through "three pounds of gray butter-soft high protein meat where cells arranged like jewels in a clock hold every thought and memory and dream of one adult male *Homo sapiens*" (178).

Joker realizes that Comboy's murder has altered permanently his relationship with his men, asserting that "they'll never see me again; I'll be invisible" (178). But he understands also the necessity of reestablishing immediately the protective device of the black humorist, observing of his fallen leader that he "looks like a bag of leftovers from a V. F. W. barbecue. Of course, I've got nothing against dead people. Why, some of my best friends are dead" (179). The book ends with Joker assuming command, he and the grunts trapped in a frozen historical moment, but his final line of dialogue captures the essence of *The Short-Timers*, an explosive combination of tasteless humor, calculated rage, and heartfelt regret. As a novelist, Hasford means to offend, but as a serious historian of his nation's power of blackness, he also offends to mean.

When Leslie Fiedler, in *Love and Death in the American Novel*, characterizes our national literature as a case of arrested development and suggests that our great novels seem to belong most properly on an adolescent's book shelf, he is also identifying a particularly American relationship with history, both in fiction and outside it. The persistent concern with innocence in American fiction and within American culture does not originate in the failure to read history; rather, it is the violent refusal to accept the cultural demands of duplicity, inequity, and moral compromise that full membership in that history presents. If post–World War II war fiction has offered characters who would escape or refuse the more absurd demands of a newly powerful but immature culture—James Jones's Robert E. Lee Prewitt and Heller's Yossarian are prime examples—that form of heroism is mainstream in all of the most lasting writing of the period. Bellow's Augie March, Updike's Rabbit Angstrom, and Salinger's Holden Caulfield are all intuitive students of history—that is, of the American cultural landscape of almost unlimited power, voracious competition, and moral bankruptcy.

The postmodern protagonist or the new American antihero, however, is only a heightened, more deeply threatened variant of a figure who has dominated our national literature from its beginnings. The new industrial state that emerged from World War II has enlarged and intensified the central American argument with history, but it has not fundamentally changed it. Natty Bumppo, Hester Prynne, Ishmael, Nick Carraway, and many others are examples of protagonists who assert natural innocence in the face of unacceptable historical demands. The threat of personal compromise or complete corruption is part of the American Faustian pact, prompting more often than not the cultural Peter Pan syndrome that Fiedler addresses. The alternative to entry into corrupting history is the spiritual or psychological trek to unspoiled terrain or the refusal to be moved from occupied territory, a process in which the hero self-consciously defines himself or herself as the cultural outrider, the endangered but unrelenting innocent who forgoes full citizenship in absurd history for the preservation of private virtue. The hero involved in such an unsustainable personal confrontation is also the emblem of the key American mythic paradox, the belief that both material progress and collective goodness are possible, that the American can avoid the deadly exchange of spiritual well-being for worldly success. The recurrent hero in American fiction knows that the attainment of both worlds is unlikely, that the move to one garden entails the loss of the other. Twain's Huck Finn is our prime example of that recognition, the hero who is convinced on his floating reading room that to become historicized is to relinquish too much to powerful currents, that lighting out for the territory is the one alternative to the loss of both heart and soul.

Recent American history, however, forces the recognition that, beyond the disappearance of the geographical frontier, the diminishment of psychic and spiritual terrain for the innocent outrider is acute, if not absolute. As a new frontier for the playing out of the American mythic paradox—the belief in the happy reciprocity of idealism and historical progress—Vietnam proved to be a tragedy of unprecedented dimensions, a national narrative drift from confident assertions of justice and goodness to the bleakest sort of euphemistic pragmatism. John Kennedy could cast the use of Special Forces teams as American knight-errantry and be believed, but by the time Richard Nixon was speaking of "Peace with Honor," the paradox had revealed its true colors and its explosive composition. For those soldiers who would resist the narrative drift and assert private innocence and virtue within the walls of absurd history, their task was a great deal more hazardous than Huck's, for the discovery of spiritual elbow room was almost nil, the likelihood of the darkest complicity practically guaranteed. If the voice and spirit of Twain's Mississippi sojourner permeates any work of the Vietnam War, it is Charles Durden's No Bugles, No Drums, a novel that is a true yardstick of how much the American historical outrider has changed and where, if anywhere, his new spiritual territory may exist.

"Right off I knew things were gonna be fucked up as a picnic in a free-fire zone. Had to be. Number one in the Jamie Hawkins Index of Worthless Activities is: everything that starts before noon" (1), begins Durden's narrator, a lower-middle-class white soldier from Georgia who squares off with his historical moment no less fervently than Huck. But Hawkins finds the official "stretchers" of history he is offered better developed, more intractable, and more immediately threatening; assigned to fight on the last American frontier, he faces dangers more tangible than imminent moral compromise. A prisoner of war no less than Hasford's grunts, Hawkins offers a reading of the war that begins in the assertion of pure innocence and ends in the admission of total complicity. In comparison with Hasford's efficient, entrapped werewolves, Hawkins and his peers share their shackles but radiate none of their grisly preparedness. Describing the departure of his unit for Vietnam, Hawkins presents Kilo Company not as *Teufel-Hunden* but as "life-sized GI Joe dolls, toys taken to the ultimate— real rifles, packs, duffel bags, steel helmets, 'n' weak stomachs. The last word in disposable goods. Soldiers, I mean. Throwaway people" (3). As James C. Wilson rightly suggests, No Bugles, No Drums presents "a war fought not for ideology, but for economics" (74), but Hawkins, unlike Heller's Yossarian, enters his war with his polemical stance well formed. Whereas *Catch-22* offer a heroic movement of initial cooperation, gradual disaffection, and optimistic escape, No Bugles, No Drums reshapes the absurd war fiction into a pattern of initial disaffection, gradual complicity, and disengagement marked not by hopefulness, but only by rage and alienation. Yossarian's history is escapable, and he wins his personal battle with the military; Hawkins knows that his odds are too high and that his defeat is inevitable. Sucked into an American vortex with no real or imagined Swedens to which to run, he admits,

> "The goddamn Army picked me. They're winnin'. They put us here like this, all bunched up, nothin' to do but wait to get killed. They give us guns, cannons, airplanes, bombs, every fuckin' kinda shit they can ship in here. Then they wait. Sooner or later, man, you're gonna kill somebody." (105)

The essential difference between the absurdist fictions of Heller and of Durden is that the former can discover or at least assert a territory that affords individual withdrawal from the unacceptable aspects of new history; for all its careful delineation of the power of economic imperatives—Milo Minderbender and M&M Enterprises as the ultimate international cartel—Catch-22 retreats from its own inverted logic and offers Yossarian's success as individual wish fulfillment. Heller demonstrates that Eisenhower's warning of the military-industrial complex has become an irresistible reality, but he reintroduces Huck's raft as Yossarian's handy inflatable lifeboat. Hawkins's Vietnam is closer to Cummings's La Ferte than it is to Huck's raft. A closed system without windows, it offers only constricted possibilities for individual moral choice and liberation. Like Huck, Hawkins deflates with piercing rustic humor the pretensions and duplicities of his American society, but his grand refusal is a much more qualified one, and he conducts his historical struggle at a far greater distance than does Yossarian. Twain's and Heller's heroes may at least entertain the notion of being successful outriders; Hawkins is allowed only the retention of an "unshakeable bad attitude" (287) within his defeat by history. Vietnam indicated that assertions of national innocence have become insupportable but that reassessments of collective moral purpose are desperately needed. By closing off Hawkins's escape routes, Durden becomes an absurdist who suggests new historical readings and makes serious cultural demands.

The typical Vietnam soldier in fiction and memoir is one whose sole value becomes individual and group survival within chaos, but Hawkins confronts history with an additional pressure. Mired in a moral test of wills with the army, he is determined not to kill anyone, a difficult position when the survival of each soldier depends on the

resolve and cooperation of the rest. If Hawkins and the rest of Kilo
Company are acutely aware of their historical entrapment, that feeling
is exacerbated by their shared intuitions of their essential unpreparedness. They have neither the individual commitments to war that add
up to group resolve nor the necessary knowledge and orientation that
afford the protective shield of effective cooperation in the field. They
are not the pop-culture icons that have permeated their adolescent
lives. Says Hawkins on arriving in Da Nang, "Like it 'r not, we'd all
been raised on late-night TV movies that glamourized Americans
wadin' ashore under an umbrella of palm fronds 'n' 40mm cannon fire
from the fleet. And the only guys who got killed were the extras" (3).
Vietnam has been called the living-room war because of its impact
through television on the American psyche, but the war was just as
much a receiver of cinematic images as it was a producer of them.
When preexisting myth faced new historical reality in Vietnam, the
interchange was often the immediate betrayal of unconscious trusts.
When Hawkins admits that "none of us looked like John Wayne, or
even Steve McQueen" (3), one great supporting lie falls like a cheap
historical stage front.

    As Kilo Company travels by truck convoy to its area of operations,
it is ambushed by a small force of Vietcong, an attack that produces
panic and paralysis in the untested, bewildered initiates. The Americans huddle in trenches and behind burning trucks, failing to return
fire against the numerically inferior assailants, but as Hawkins observes, "What happens in an ambush depends mostly on whether
you're the ambusher or the ambushee. And how green you are. God
knows we were green" (14). Kilo's leadership is no more prepared to
transfer Hollywood iconography to lived history than are Hawkins
and his peers. Kilo's commander, a black captain named Jefferson
who is known to his men as the Chocolate Soldier, becomes immo-
bilized by fear during the one-sided battle, and an inept lieutenant
named Whipple, who is fresh from the Boston National Guard, orders a senseless counterattack against the enemy, even though he has
himself failed to fire a shot. The ambush is kept from becoming an
even larger debacle when a veteran NCO named Ubanski faces down
Whipple and shakes the comatose company out of its collective paralysis, but as the dead and wounded of Kilo are being evacuated,
Hawkins and company realize that the cinematic light show of the
invincible American warrior has already been edited into a ludicrous
short subject. When Hawkins's platoon discovers that a tape recorder

has been left running during the ambush, the men listen to the première of their own lived history and partake of something quite different from *The Sands of Iwo Jima*: "Tha's us on there," narrates a black soldier named Jinx. "Tha's us. Cryin' like women. You believe that shit?" (25). Hawkins searches for something in his tradition to dignify and to justify Kilo's first battle, but he finds the classical tone of an O'Brien or a Caputo inapplicable; instead, the disposable banality of something more contemporary seems suitable. Imagining one illusion speaking to another, he conducts his war's version of the naming of parts:

> Seventeen dead, just like that. Welcome to Vietnam. Sure's hell somebody's said somethin' noble about those that die in defense of their country. I'd even bet Bartlett's got it written down somewhere. I couldn't think of anything. Not a fuckin' thing. The first verse of "Flanders Field" came to mind. And that Pepsi ad . . . *You've got a lot to live, and Pepsi's got a lot to give.* Maybe that's the thing, the epitaph, I guess it's called, for this war. . . . Over 'n' over it went through my mind. Try to remember your mother's birthday. Or your social security number. No way. But a fuckin' commercial you can't get rid of. You've got a lot to live. Horseshit. Their days were done. And I had a feelin' ours were numbered. (23–24)

Like Hasford's werewolves, Durden's bawling initiates are a society that shapes its language, attitudes, and rituals according to the absurd history in which it is mired. Kilo Company defends not Bastogne, Wake Island, or the Chosin Reservoir but the Song My Swine Project, an experimental pig farm that is Durden's concentration of the war's competing histories and Kilo's updated experience of Cummings's *La Ferte*, a prison in which the true logic of the controlling economic and political forces may be discerned and analyzed. The project is a study in the discrepancy between official theory and real practice: "We came only to guard their pigs. To win their hearts 'n' minds" (36), says Hawkins, but he soon learns the real effects of the American presence:

> . . . as soon as it was safe for Saigon tax collectors to show up— tax on pig farmin' went up. Five or six to the tax man for the government, a couple more to the same tax man as a bribe to stay in his good graces . . . and the same two 'r three to the VC. They didn't stop comin', just changed their hours of collection or

had the hogs brought to 'em. So much for winnin' hearts 'n' minds. (37)

Violent rifts in traditional Vietnamese society extend beyond the immediate economic upheaval. Amid the bamboo huts of the village of Song My, the hamlet chief lives in a new teak domicile and has "a refrigerator, lights, a radio, and a Honda. He smiled a lot when we wandered by" (29). American engineering operates in Song My with the same absurd logic that energizes Heller's M&M Enterprises. Milo, Heller's entrepreneur, tells Yossarian that he must eat chocolate-covered Egyptian cotton for the sake of the cartel; when Luke Davis, a slow-talking southern soldier with rural common sense, suggests that the Vietnamese do not like the "miracle rice" raised in the rice paddies surrounding the farm, Whipple informs him that "the VIETNAMESE haven't as yet acquired a taste for it but it makes excellent food for . . . the swine" (38). When the overall configura- of the American experiment with traditional Vietnamese agriculture is explained to him, Davis can offer only an incredulous summary: "they raise the rice to feed the hogs 'n' sell the hogs to buy rice . . . ? Is that hit?" (38). Told his role in Vietnam is not to question official policy, Davis, another spokesman for all the Americans Hawkins de- scribes as "doin' convict labor in the rain" (28), offers a considered response to Whipple that laps over the immediate absurdity into larger historical assessment: "Ah s'pose not, Looten't. . . . But Ah b'lieve if Ah'd reasoned hit out ah'da come up with a better idea" (39).

Hawkins's historical project at Song My has little to do with mir- acle rice or village urban renewal. He wants only to remain an un- initiate among the unprepared, an outrider between innocence and experience on his own internal frontier. His predicament is compli- cated, however, by his becoming bound to his fellow inmates by in- stinctive loyalties he would prefer not to recognize. Once inside the walls of absurd history, he cannot resist the vestiges of humanity that present themselves. Ubanski is one of the few professionals in Kilo, a "lifer with eighteen years, two Silver Stars, three Purple Hearts and a hard-on for anyone who wasn't wed to the Army" (8). He is one of Durden's reality principles for Hawkins and the rest of the innocent, the new American guide and frontiersman who tries to keep the ini- tiates alive until they can learn the rules, boundaries, and hazards of the history they are writing. Hawkins recognizes Ubanski's value to his platoon but isolates as well the reason for his probable failure:

"We had him, and we shoulda had the best platoon in Kilo. Prob'ly the whole battalion. Except we were mostly fuckoffs" (8). Ubanski's assessment of Kilo complements Hawkins's, but the history lesson he administers merely illustrates the platoon's ignorance rather than diminishes it. Told by Ubanski that he has seen units like Kilo in a previous war, Hawkins asks, "What happened to the companies in Korea?" (40), an inquiry that receives the most abbreviated historical analysis: "Dead" (40). Hawkins demands of Ubanski a reasonable explanation of Kilo's imprisonment and asks, "How come they grabbed us from nowhere, guys who'd never even seen each other before—lots of 'em—just threw us altogether, bang-bang, here we are? Why?" (41), but when Ubanski offers a cryptic reference to the Tet offensive, Hawkins ends the guide's lesson with another question: "Tet? Wha'th'fuck's Tet got to do with it?" (41). The members of Kilo look the part of GI Joe in their combat scenario, but they have been given only partial historical scripts and no motivation for their performances. Considered easily replaced tools rather than reasoning men by the powers that placed them in Vietnam, they can only nod collectively to Hawkins's desperate leitmotif: "I definitely didn't feel ready" (42).

Durden's Kilo Company is the melting-pot naturalism of traditional American war writing rendered with a surrealist's brush, the antithesis of Ubanski's and the army's hope of a smoothly operating machine that will perform adequately with a minimum of friction and complaints. Hawkins explains that he is the latest in a long line of reluctant warriors. His great-grandfather had declared a one-man truce at Gettysburg, telling all on his trek south that the Civil War was over. A study in regional and ethnic tensions, Kilo is Shiloh or Vicksburg revisited. Hawkins and Davis find in Bobby Lee Poe, a right-wing senator's son from Virginia whom Hawkins accuses of "slummin'," another member of a Confederacy rife with class tensions. The "Yankees" include two silent urban blacks named Black and Decker but known, of course, as the Drill Team, who eventually desert for Sweden, and Angelo Bruno Cocuzza, "Crazy Dago," who operates a numbers game on the daily ARVN casualty figures. Durden complicates his sociologist's nightmare by offering a character such as Garcia, a Mexican soldier who becomes a victim of culturally induced machismo when he claims to be a matador and is gored by a Vietnamese water buffalo. The society of throwaway people is a distinct class defined by its violent historical pressurization, but it is also the American dream of opportunity for all showing its most absurd cultural underpinnings. Durden's Vietnam is no American aberration; rather, it is the accumulated tensions of a culture based on contradiction springing from a Pandora's box of its own careful construction—in short, a historical inevitability with traceable antecedents, visible roots.

Hawkins's bond of friendship with Jinx becomes Durden's updating of Huck Finn's central moral dilemma. Jinx is one of "McNamara's 100,000," a program aimed principally at blacks and other ethnic groups to raise their literacy skills to the level of the army's entrance exam, an opportunity that Hawkins refers to as "retrainin' the retards" (43), the most obvious and reprehensible example of the new American soldier as a disposable commodity. Jinx may arrive in Vietnam from "the compost heap of America's hopeless" (43), but when he puts into practice the new black Vietnam aphorism "Ain't no VC ever called me nigger" and becomes an adviser to the Vietcong, Hawkins is confronted not only with the necessity of killing, but also with the imperative of terminating a close friend who threatens the survival of Kilo. Huck's No in Thunder, his refusal to surrender Jim to absurd cultural dictums, is a preservation of personal principles; Hawkins's elimination of Jinx is a debilitating personal defeat. Hawkins becomes fully historicized by making a moral decision, but it is one forced diabolically by the violent circumstances in which he is snared. He understands that his killing for the greatest good for the greatest number is only a necessary evil, a nonchoice from an abbreviated list of historical options. Huck's stand toward history ends in the adamant preservation of an individual moral impulse; Hawkins's moral choice as a prisoner of war is the culmination of the shattering of his principles by his historical jailers. One hero can mature or refuse to mature in a still open frontier; his descendant can choose only bad or worse in a sealed universe.

Hawkins conducts a double-edged quest throughout *No Bugles, No Drums*. His assertion of nonviolence within violent history is coupled with the demand that the circumstances of his war speak to him in logical terms. Luke Davis's approach to history is similar to Ubanski's; once condemned to operate within a violent field of action, he knows that moral and philosophical debate ceases, that individual and group survival is the only issue. Davis clarifies Hawkins's dilemma, describing him as "a nine-year-ol' kid who still thinks there orta be some sense t' things" (95) but demanding of him the needed quotient of cooperation, including the consent to kill: "Well, what you goan do? If we git lit up 'n' need you, you goan be there?" (72). Hawkins's philosophical stand, his class consciousness, his economic reading of the war, and his demand for logical explanations make him the ultimate example of the participant–resister within Vietnam War writing. Like O'Brien's quest for classical wisdom in *If I Die in a Combat Zone*, Hawkins's attempt to salvage personal scruples and larger national imperatives from a historical machine that radiates only its own capacity for destruction is doomed.

As the features of the smiling, unspeaking face of absurd history become increasingly readable, so do the immediate pressures of his war. The price demanded for his inclusion in an advanced seminar in cultural surrealism is as basic as it is irresistible. Hawkins shields himself against the essential demand—smoking dope at every opportunity, deflating the absurdity with irreverence and black humor, hiding behind the small proficiency that exists in Kilo—but his personal defense perimeter is infiltrated easily by the same dark secret that Hasford's Joker hears laughing in his jungle primeval: " 'Course, reality has a way of snatchin' right back. You don't fuck reality around too much" (127), admits Hawkins. Humor, drugs, and personal resolve are inadequate to protect him, and the warnings of Davis and Ubanski speak with high seriousness, oblivious to his convictions and unpreparedness: "The whole thing of killin' people might be okay for movies. And seein' some other dudes dingin' people on Huntley-Brinkley is fine 'cause I can change channels. But the bare-ass brutal truth of it all is it ain't just dinks that die" (72).

When Ubanski leads a patrol outside the farm, Hawkins and his squad stumble across their deepest fears at a river bank: "nine of Uncle Ho's finest—playin' frisby. You think I'm kiddin? I couldn't believe my eyes. They gotta be South Vietnamese I figured. They can't be North Vietnamese 'cause nobody that stupid could be winnin' a war" (52). The ensuing action is less a battle than a slaughter—"Like dynamitin' for fish" (52)—but Hawkins returns to the farm from the ultimate Mad Minute a redefined outsider: "Walkin' back to Kilo everybody had a souvenir. Mine was nausea and bile puddled in the back of my throat" (52). Hawkins does not fire a shot during the massacre, but the images he absorbs force his historical analysis of this war to a more personal level of magnitude, emphasizing the unbreakable tension of the participant–resister between internal conviction and practical necessity. In moments of relative safety that afford the possibility of broad historical reading, Hawkins can maintain his nonviolent stance:

> So I go off to answer my country's call, to defend it against aggression, to help maintain peace in the world, and next thing I know I'm in this silly-ass place to shoot people who ain't no more a threat to my country than the Beatles are to Beethoven. Any country that's been around long as this one and still uses two sticks to pick up one grain of rice and one stick to pick up two buckets of shit ain't likely to keep me awake nights wonderin' when they're gonna invade California. (95)

But the events at the river illustrate in the most graphic way the disjunction between expansive analysis and immediate imprisonment; the nine shattered enemy bodies are the true adversaries of reason and personal refusal, and Hawkins records and correlates the smaller lesson within the large:

> Here I'd spent a fair amount of time tryin' to live down Life's clichés, or at least those I thought were a lotta shit. So Life says okay, wiseass, here's your first fuckin' meaningful choice: kill or be killed. I felt pretty much underwhelmed by both of 'em. As choices, I mean. And beyond the point of academic choosin' I couldn't say I was ready for either one. (55)

When Second Lieutenant Stephen Eric Levine joins Kilo, Hawkins finds his greatest friend and his most demanding reality principle. Neither rigidly and retrospectively gung-ho like Ubanski nor clearly incompetent and myth-laden like Whipple, the Boy Ranger, as he is dubbed by Hawkins, is Durden's updated example of another figure in American war writing: the trapped professional officer who is soured on his war but who redefines decorum and proper action to realize the primary goals of survival and order. When he first confronts Levine, Hawkins asserts class distinctions—"ain't it against the law for officers to talk to grunts" (77)—and smiles at Levine's restatement of Ubanski's doctrine: "I want a tight platoon. I don't want anybody to die because they were off on their trip. Everybody does his job, works together, keeps his head straight . . . we'll all make it" (78). But Levine ascertains immediately his charge's historical dilemma, for it is a variation of his own. As committed to saving the military within absurd history as Hawkins is to escaping it, he offers an analysis of Vietnam as absolute as his pupil's. Beyond the problem of avoiding unnecessary casualties, he admits a larger goal: "Trying to save the US Army. It's falling apart. If it were just Vietnam, I'd say screw it. But this isn't the only war we're going to have to fight. Not so long as people are what they are. The Army's got to survive and this goddamn war is destroying it" (267).

Hawkins rejects Levine's historical imperative but responds to him as an example of logic within absurdity. When Garcia is gored by the water buffalo, Dago concocts a scheme in which he disposes of Garcia's body and substitutes a small fortune in drugs in the casket for transport to the United States. Hawkins is included in the funeral detail by Levine and accompanies the casket to America, where Dago explains to Garcia's family that he is still alive on a secret mission, thereby maximizing his and their profits and granting the fallen matador "another year of life." When Dago explains that he has voided the stupidity of Garcia's death by making him a hero, Hawkins finds in the entrepreneur's reasoning the same dark duplicity of his historical jailers but admits, "There was a certain logic in what he was sayin'. It was against everything we been taught about right 'n' wrong, truth, whatever. But he was right" (153). Hawkins goes on a Las Vegas holiday with his drug profits, falls in love with a kind-hearted prostitute named Linda, and seems about to exercise Levine's unspoken historical escape clause, but, like Dago and the American high command, he finds he has developed his own situational ethics. Still defining himself and Kilo as "the ultimate luxury in a throwaway society" (166), he decides to return to Vietnam, telling Linda, "I got a friend in Nam. Coupla friends, I guess. I s'pose we're sorta in this together" (167). Admitting that irrational bonds have overridden cultural analysis, he discovers the limits of personal as well as historical logic. Having become another small absurdity within a cosmos of them, he departs again for Song My to void the pardon that Levine has extended to him.

When he returns to Kilo and Levine, Hawkins learns that history has altered its countenance and intensified its threats. The enemy has increased its pressure on the Swine Project, and Jinx, facing a court-martial for a racial incident he did not provoke, has become a weapons expert for the Vietcong. Despite the admission of real bonds with his friends, Hawkins attempts to reassume his stance of nonviolence, to restate his refusal to become a full member of the brotherhood:

There's gotta be a hundred million Americans who say it's right and a hundred million Americans can't be wrong. Fuck the French, it's Americans who gave us Fords, frozen food 'n' free-fire zones. Mass production, goopy strawberries 'n' legal murder. I'm weird. I like Italian cars, fresh fruit and I'm goddamned if I'm gonna go round lightin' up people without a better reason than I've gotten from anyone yet. (178)

But the war has escalated to the point where Hawkins's fears of the kill-or-be-killed proposition are realized. He resists his own awareness that Jinx's decision has altered the rules, that one moral decision has fallen like a domino and will force his own. When the farm is attacked and Poe and other men are killed, Hawkins numbs himself with drugs and attempts to declare a separate peace. Stretched to the breaking point between the twin realities of violence and loyalty, he seeks a netherworld of his own design, one that is more than a veiled reference to the literal flight of Twain's young sojourner:

I say I smoked the whole thing, but I'm guessin'. After three hits I couldn't hardly find my mouth. The last thing I remember is tryin' to whistle "Waitin' on the *Robert E. Lee*" while I was changin' clothes. Dago said he found me packin'. I was wearin' my Levis, a sweatshirt with a picture of W. C. Fields on the chest. . . . I said I was goin' home, fuck the war 'n' all the horses the warriors rode on. (212)

Like his great-grandfather at Gettysburg, he would declare the war finished, yet Hawkins has already voided his one ticket home. He asserts to Levine, "I am a civilian" (219), a cry that is only a half-truth, a denial of the irrational commitment that wars with his hope of disengagement.

Any aspirations that Hawkins retains to remaining on the sidelines of his war are expunged when he and Davis walk into an ambush in a supposedly friendly village. Hawkins's entrance into the rites of blood comes when he kills a booby-trapped little girl whom Davis has come to know and to befriend. Hawkins saves the wounded Davis by dispatching a number of the enemy cadres, and even Ubanski regards him as having achieved a level of maturation. While recuperating from his own wounds, Hawkins refutes internally his new designation as hero. Davis gives him his Greener, the shotgun with which Hawkins has saved both their lives; although Hawkins accepts the physical symbol, he rejects the philosophical implications of friendship under fire: "I nodded. My eyes were fillin' with tears. Not from gratitude. From pain. From the realization that, in his eyes, and probably in Ubanski's, Jefferson's, maybe even Eric's, I had grown up. I'd slaughtered people and symbolically earned my manhood" (235). Despite his apparent admission to the combat brotherhood, Hawkins remains resentful and tension-ridden, Durden's example of the additional pressures that the felt absence of just cause produced within the society of grunts in Vietnam. In a single meditation, Hawkins can admit, "I started feelin' lonely. Maybe it was thinkin' about the ones that were gone" (247), but he can also display how one prime component of American war mythology was altered by the Vietnam War:

> There's this bullshit fairy tale about the Army as a great melting pot, and Army buddies. . . . I think the thing is that once you've had the shit scared outa you while you were sharin' a hole with someone you're s'posed to forever cling to that moment. That's the myth. But the fact of it is, generally, once you've shared that moment the last thing you want is to remember it. . . . Maybe I'm wrong. Maybe it wasn't like that before, maybe it's only *this* goddamn stupid war. Or maybe it's just me 'n' my bad attitude. (247–48)

The completion of Hawkins's historical initiation is also the moral decision that, like the war itself, is more a product of attrition and exhaustion than of conviction. When Kilo Company undertakes a search-and-destroy mission, Hawkins spots Jinx operating with a body of Vietcong cadres but hesitates before telling Levine, his final and fatal moment of divided loyalties. Kilo is mortared by the formation Jinx is advising, and Levine is killed, decapitated by a piece of shrapnel. Hawkins gathers up the headless body, refusing to leave his historical guide behind. In his description of the return voyage to Song My, Durden makes his most overt connection between Hawkins and Huck, one that suggests how far the American myth of innocence has been extended. Having earlier killed an old peasant for his river raft, Hawkins and the squad board it again, this time with the lifeless body of their leader:

> We floated, drifted, ran aground, floated . . . I didn't have any idea of where we were goin'. I hadn't bothered with the map. I thought Eric would be with me, no matter what. He was, but not

quite in the way I'd seen it. The River Styx . . . it ran through
my head like a goddamn jingle . . . You've got a lot to live, and
Pepsi's got a lot to give . . . the Pepsi Generation. Throwaway
people . . . over 'n' over 'n' over, until I heard the chopper, up
high 'n' movin' fast. (274)

Durden adds the additional irony of having the raft's occupants mis-
taken for the enemy by the helicopter crew. The raft is destroyed—a
prime symbol of new frontiers forever vanquished—and Hawkins saves
the floating survivors only by disrobing partially and offering an unmistakable American gesture: "Not even that gun-happy nearsighted
sonofabitch could mistake my fleshy white ass for a Cong" (275).
When Hawkins returns to base, he presents the remains of Levine to
the lieutenant's father, a high-ranking officer who has helped plan the
mission, and the bedraggled, bitter initiate and his cargo become the
most obvious, unwelcome symbols to command of the true nature
of new American history:

> To them I musta looked like the end of their world, the ultimate
> insult—a bare-assed buck private holdin' a headless body without
> even a free arm to salute. So this is it, this is what our army has
> come to, from Valley Forge to Vietnam, two hundred years of
> tradition to produce a madman. I don't know. Maybe they were
> just pissed that I hadn't had the decency to get myself killed. (276)

Later, Hawkins takes Davis's Greener and, ambivalence replaced
by tired resolve and a new sense of historical justice, garners safe passage to the Vietcong village where Jinx resides. Having been there
before in a failed attempt to re-form broken loyalties—Jinx's and his
own—Hawkins kills his black friend and four other enemy soldiers,
adding a new coda to Huck's moral decision on racism. What Huck
learns, Hawkins assumes; but the killing of one piece of disposable
goods by another is Durden's final assessment of historical lessons
learned. Hawkins remembers nothing of his actions after leaving the
enemy village and has to read the official report on "Subject Hawkins"
to learn that he "returned to his company and killed a large number
of pigs, threatened several officers and noncoms, went absent without
leave and refused to return to his post, in violation of a direct order"
(287). Hawkins is given a psychiatric discharge and achieves finally
the separate peace he had already claimed was declared. But, not to

be denied a final opportunity to correct the official record, he offers the reader his final moment of secret history the army's account omits:

> Later, I walked back to Kilo, collected some personal stuff 'n' started for Atlanta. I was still carryin' the Greener. I told everybody the war was over, that I was goin' home. Nobody started arguin' with me until I got to Danang. The farther I got from the fightin', the harder it was to make people believe the war was finished. (285)

Like Hasford, Durden argues that the American historical terrain of both Huck and Yossarian—the untainted assertion of both innocence and victimization—is closed off by Vietnam. They also demonstrate that one proper aesthetic response to a world out of joint is not cynical acquiesence to absurdity, but the powerful enhancement of that world to reveal the humanity that still lives within. Jamie Hawkins assesses his inclusion in a dark chapter of American history with an insightful contradiction: "It isn't funny, but it is" (67). The finest practitioners of a new brand of historical humor in the Vietnam novel know that both propositions are not only possible but true.

4

THE WRITER AS ALCHEMIST

Straight history, auto-revised history, history without handles, for all the books and articles and white papers, all the talk and the miles of film, something wasn't answered, it wasn't even asked. We were backgrounded, deep, but when the background started sliding forward not a single life was saved by the information. The thing had transmitted too much energy, it heated up too hot, hiding low under the fact-figure crossfire there was a secret history, and not a lot of people felt like running in there to bring it out.

DISPATCHES

". . . just as happiness is more than the absence of sadness, so is peace infinitely more than the absence of war. Even the refugee must do more than flee. He must arrive."

GOING AFTER CACCIATO

If there is a crucial historical lesson offered by the American involvement in Vietnam, it might be that no culture—no matter how confident and powerful its machinery of official explanation—can wage a war successfully if its people cannot identify a just cause or a moral center within the enterprise. The American managers discovered that they could fight an undeclared war in Vietnam and muster the necessary human and technological resources, thereby skirting real issues of legality and purpose, but they could not prevent the erosion of national support when it became apparent to an increasingly disgruntled populace that the configurations of myth and belief that cloaked not only the war but also larger cultural imperatives were endangered by new history. When collective vision adjusted to the distortions of the ideological fun-house mirrors erected in Vietnam, the reflection was of a national face most Americans found disquieting and unwelcome. The tendency—what Philip Caputo calls collective amnesia—was to look away, to search for images that would not subvert the national belief system. The Vietnamese village is known as xa, the place where the spirits are worshipped, but Americans, operating in a culture whose hallmarks are fluidity, invention, and progress, center themselves not in a geographical grid but within a mythic one, an elastic network that incorporates the seemingly contradictory aspects of constancy and change. As an American ideograph, the Vietnam War illustrated that the network has limits. When placed under the unprecedented pressures the war produced, unexamined precepts of goodness and innocence became unstable propositions. The Vietnam War was never a military defeat for the United States, but it did indicate that a nation might become a spiritual refugee from its own professed ideals, that when the linguistic strategies buttressing national myth fractured, there might be nothing left but a desperate attempt to pull the pieces back together.

To determine how much of official history was believed by its writers and how much was merely strategically asserted may be an impossible task, for the war always radiated the capacity for what James Thomson calls "collective self-deception" (18), the failure at the decision-making level to read available texts, to explore the long and twisted cultural roots of the conflict. American blind ambition in Southeast Asia lacked neither idealism nor the will to act out those ideals. What it did lack was an examined historical frame of reference to make those actions seem self-validating both to the people who fought the war and to those who merely recorded the daily casualty figures at home. From Truman through Nixon, the story changed so frequently and unpredictably that the collective historical revisions seemed to approximate a serpentine movement, the track of a mythical creature that led everywhere and nowhere. The consolidation of Vietminh power in the North after World War II was considered validation of the deepest American fears, but 2,000 years of Vietnamese-Chinese antagonisms was a cultural fact unrecorded or disregarded within new history. No one suggested after 1954 that recognition of two sovereign Vietnamese states was to operate with a cultural blindness that was almost complete; too late did critics remark that to invent almost daily new strategies for pacification and democratization was to ignore a huge bank of readily available data. The willful combination of cultural-engineering principles and the evangelical impulse produced what Thomson calls "America's sentimental imperialism" (17), an enterprise that required the most elaborate and self-sustaining network of linguistic and imagistic invention at the managerial level.

The writers who have produced what are likely to be the most lasting documents of the war are those who have assessed and incorporated into their works the battle of words and images that transformed the war into something as much symbolic as real. To do battle in compensatory history with the managers' capacity for illusion and euphemism, the writer is required to first retrieve and then re-create the feelings, rhythms, and specific images that remained largely sequestered behind conveniently reconciled history and to place those components in opposition to the dominant text: in effect, both to reconstruct and to invent a historical debate. The failure of the managers to supply validation for human sacrifice is the true American defeat in Vietnam, one that placed the responsibility for the retrieval of meaning firmly on the shoulders of each soldier, citizen, journalist, and artist. It became obvious to the most perceptive observers that official history not only failed to seal off threats to its own mythic influence, but also was becoming increasingly haunted by its capacity for contradiction. In short, the pure energy of the managers' narrative had become at some date—1968 and Tet serves for many critics—a study in diminishing returns; historical momentum had become transmuted into spiritual inertia. Responding to the trend of official history to become handcuffed in its own cat's cradle, Frances FitzGerald has observed in "How Does America Avoid Future Vietnams?" that "Gen. (William) Westmoreland has, I think, a linguistic lesson to teach us. He used language in a very extraordinary fashion many times during the war. But the lesson that comes to mind is this: if there is a verb 'to attrit,' it is almost certainly reflexive" (303).

The power of official history to furnish neologism and euphemism for its activities produced finally a surface of language that functioned much like a one-way mirror. One could view the furious workings of myth from outside, but once seduced by the official illusions, an observer would find only the invented story reflected back, access to the historical referent precluded by sealed narrative. The responsibility of each writer on Vietnam is to recover as much of the lost referent as possible, to speak to those aspects of human experience—individual and national—that could only be jettisoned when the mythic imprint began to set and to harden in Vietnam. If history is not what is real or possible but only what can be harmonized with established cultural patterns, the task is to work antagonistically against the false limitation of available space in the larger text. If the best Vietnam writers seem textual rowdies crashing the proceedings of a genteel historical society, it is only because the initial invitations were bestowed according to privilege, not merit. The writers know as well that amnesia is not a right but an affliction and that the symmetry and solidity of a number of retrospective visions are suspect. And many argue that the way to a more complete history is not the further publicizing of the war but the necessary personalizing of it, the inventing of new aesthetic equipment through which the overlooked historical data may be sifted and understood. Ward Just, a fine novelist and memorialist himself, has traced the historical chore clearly and succinctly: "The Vietnam War must be scaled down to life rather than up to myth" (Swiers 198).

Del Vecchio with revised, complicating realism, Caputo with self-conscious classical memoir, and Hasford with antagonistic black humor succeed in producing forms of compensatory Vietnam War history, but their works do not fill the entire spectrum of textual possibilities. The realists, the classical memorialists, and the absurdists, although they must be granted their achievements in refurbishing and extending traditional modes, fall short of finding new forms to serve up all that was unique about Vietnam. *The 13th Valley, A Rumor of War,* and *The Short-Timers* are enlightened examples of the aesthetic choices they incorporate, but within those works are discernible still the speaking voices of Mailer, Hemingway, and Heller. Not overtly imitative, they explore new cultural terrain, but they do so by keeping one foot in a more familiar modernist sensibility.

At the managerial level, a war that was at its core postmodern both in form and in historical message was offered to the American people as the most recent chapter in a coherent tradition: the selfless, idealistic bestowing of the vision of the new City on the Hill to a culture that was surely needful of it. The collision of cultures in Vietnam, however, produced a narrative that resisted aesthetic incorporation into traditional modes. Fragmented, surreal, episodic, ungiving to singular readings, and resistant to convenient closure, the war seemed not the extension of an established tradition but something more akin to a collective nervous breakdown, an overload of the mythic circuitry that the managers sought to thread through the paddies and villages of an unreceptive culture. To the managers themselves, the war seemed more and more a grand cabal to thwart dedicated Cold Warriors, to subvert an incipient Great Society, to desecrate Peace with Honor. A supreme work of the American imagination, the Vietnam War became a historical narrative detested by its own authors, a mythic enterprise gone wrong for which no one wanted to assume responsibility. To the soldiers and journalists in the field, who saw first hand the effects of the new narrative in Vietnam, it was apparent that the attempted insertion of an entire body of American myths into a historical field incapable of receiving it was producing the most dire results, that the psychological and spiritual distance between private and public history was filled by a widening ocean of official confidences and sealed press releases.

When it became obvious that official history had broken irrevocably with the new facts of war, the press corps was placed in a new professional and ethical position. The idea of a collective war effort, one shouldered by combatants, citizens, reporters, and managers, became the grand illusion by the time of Tet, and a new antagonistic journalism emerged through mainstream news conduits. When *Time* and the *New York Times* became overtly critical of the official story, the problem of reliable history was not alleviated by the newly petulant voices but complicated by them. An already unstable narrative now displayed fresh, conflicting reports. The effect at home was to intensify confusion, impatience, and alienation, for the negative reports were coming not only from peripheral, disenfranchised voices, but also from the desks of CBS News and the *Washington Post*; the furrowed brow of Walter Cronkite produced reactions that a battalion of editors of free presses could only hope to foster. Once they broke from the managerial version, the news media soon assumed an unaccustomed function that often resulted in increased fragmentation of the master narrative but did not replace it with a credible one. Assessing the new role of the press in Vietnam, Peter Arnett, a Pulitzer Prize–winning correspondent, has said, "Our generation of reporters opened a Pandora's box in Vietnam. We chose to write about what we saw with our own eyes and heard with our own ears, rather than practice the selective reportage that enthusiastically enhanced national objectives in previous wars" (132). A large number of journalists had strong intuitions that the war had gone wrong, that its managers were telling a story that demonstrated imaginative power but lost the historical referent about which they draped their confident narrative. Morley Safer, perhaps remembered best for his television news story that included the haunting image of GIs setting huts ablaze with Zippo lighters,[1] has said of the press corps that "most of the reporters smelled something terribly rotten about this war from day one of their tours—that it lacked a moral or intellectual or strategic core" (162). Misgivings, however, usually did not encourage television to do more than offer cryptic anecdotes and scattered images, a pattern of reporting that may have imitated the war formally but that succeeded in first jarring and then alienating the American public. Television did not provide an interpretive alternative to the master narrative, which it had rejected and now uncertainly opposed.

When the war's managers declared Tet a decisive American and South Vietnamese military victory, the press corps offered pictures and stories of the destruction of Hue and of the battle around the American embassy in Saigon, but the disturbing images remained uncorrelated and suggestive, intimations that a darker narrative might reside beneath the bright one that came from the halls of Washington and Saigon. The press was limited by its faith in traditional reportage to cope with new historical developments.[2] No longer believing the official press releases but asserting their duty to transmit them, the journalists encountered their own form of historical entrapment. As Michael Arlen has argued, "television dutifully passed on the body counts—a distant, alienating kind of announcement—but almost never showed us death, which might have been more meaningful" (102).

Between official truth and a suspicious press lay the persistent reality of the war—not the sanitized, unreal deaths of the new quantifying principle, but individual, unvalidated ones. There were during the war many attempts to codify the new history in terms of military tactics and political policies, but for more than a few recorders, the truths of the Vietnam War—its most obvious, irreducible lessons— were being overlooked or deliberately ignored. For some of the writers, the way to the missing history was not through a heightened attention to the heterogeneous groupings of facts and images but through the shaping and transmuting of the many puzzle parts with the power of individual imagination. To salvage history from the grip of the official master narrative, something more than anecdotal reportage and imagistic documentary realism was required. What buried history demanded were reportorial strategies that would restore the referent but admit the imagination to synthesize, to connect, and to create where it must.

A new war of discontinuous, competing narratives could not be brought into high relief with old sources of illumination, and the two most inventive works of the war—Michael Herr's *Dispatches* and Tim O'Brien's *Going After Cacciato*—assume not only the primacy of the imagination, but also the necessity of inventing new aesthetic strategies for the rendering of new history. In the presence of intractable official truth and ill-equipped traditional reportage, both writers have explored varieties of self-conscious Vietnam War romanticism. They assert that the only history worth recording entails the stripping away of abstractions and preestablished categories and the working outward from the individual creating imagination's encounter with new cultural data. Both writers incorporate in their aesthetic structures the official master narrative of the war in order to subject it to a process of textual alchemy in which it is pressurized, tested, and, finally, transmuted within the laboratory of personal sensibility. As distinctly new for the Vietnam War as *In Our Time* and *The Enormous Room* were for World War I, *Dispatches* and *Going After Cacciato* demand that the reader accept some apparent contradictions: to record facts, one must transform them; to remember the war, one must reinvent it; and, finally, to establish a credible public memory, one must first explore and chart every imaginative recess of the private one. Herr and O'Brien present the most demanding literary documents of the war, texts that assume maximum reader activity as they display their authorial ingenuity. Although they announce themselves as evocative displays of textual virtuosity, they are also much more. As radical aesthetic restructurings of cultural upheaval, both works restate the romantic argument while laying claim to historical validity.

Images of the immense power of America's "sentimental imperialism" were everywhere in Vietnam. Evangelism, technology, and spontaneous engineering produced a new topography in the war zone that rivaled the work of Hieronymus Bosch in its eclectic intensity, its combinations of the familiar and the strange. Cam Ranh Bay became the ultimate shopping center: any imaginable item of American disposable goods could be discovered there; grunts in the field could call down artillery or air strikes like express-delivery packages from an omnipotent deity; and technological marvels like Starlight scopes, electronic people sniffers, and ultrasensitive listening devices enhanced the sensory powers of the army of occupation to superhuman levels. It seemed only logical early in the war that indigenous guerrillas who lived on rice balls and who improvised booby traps from the overflow of American materiel could not hope to withstand the awesome goods and services that made the American soldier the most mobile, best equipped, and best supported combatant in the history of warfare. The helicopter—the dominant metaphor of ubiquitous American ingenuity—hovered above the refashioned landscape like a technological avenging angel, the most pervasive image of war as symbolic action and cultural will-to-power.

But the powerful tide of goods and services—the ideological–economic mix that was thought at the managerial level to be America's trump card—did not prove to be the decisive factor in Vietnam. The most perceptive observers knew that the real battle was being waged not in the new geographical landscape of men and machines, but within the terrain of collective imagination, an area where the surface images of the war became a mere light show that dissolved in the stronger illumination of persistent cultural realities. The power of invention that engendered the deadly images also enfolded the germ of its own destruction, for its confident spontaneity produced cultural and ideological seeds that would not take root in Vietnamese soil. If bases that looked like cities could be built and supplied, if an army designed for set-piece battles in Europe could adapt to guerrilla warfare, then it was logical that American improvisation also could create in its own image a South Vietnamese government out of nothing, uproot and reshape a traditional village structure, and fertilize the very cultural ground of Vietnam so that equivalents of American social and political patterns would spring organically from the alien soil.

To provide a new map of the cultural enterprise in Vietnam is Michael Herr's self-imposed task in *Dispatches*, a project that both removes official diagrams and discovers through the power of memory and imagination the emotional and spiritual terrain of the war. As map maker, Herr does not draw the borders of violent history with traditional tools of measurement; he is not the fact gatherer of discoverable, preexisting truths but assumes, as Philip Beidler suggests in *American Literature and the Experience of Vietnam*, "the role of public artificer" (142), the historian who follows to its textual limits the proposition that the faithful recording of the war is synonymous with the imaginative creating of it in a language sufficiently elastic, poetic, and associative to overcome the reconciled history already receding into public memory. More than any other chronicler of the war, Herr attempts to discover within the materials of individual consciousness a historical lexicon and syntax with enough originality and power to do battle with those of the master narrative. As Vietnam alchemist, he would filter a war whose message resides largely in its form through personal imagination and render a textual analogue of its deepest rhythms and structures. Herr attempts a dangerous aesthetic feat in *Dispatches*, for his choice to present his own evolving historical consciousness as an adequate encoding of Vietnam invites charges of arbitrary subjectivity and factual obfuscation. As he offers the reader the co-pilot's seat in the "collective meta-chopper" (7) in which he traverses the promontories and chasms of a Vietnam of the creating imagination, he accepts willingly the risk that his textual method will reveal him finally to be both Daedalus and Icarus, mythic artificer and ludicrous, prideful victim of an ill-advised flight of historical fancy.

The first section of the memoir, a remarkable meeting of minute observation and poetic suggestiveness called "Breathing In," is both an essay on the writing of history and a complete history of this war. The title itself lends shape to Herr's method. The Vietnam War is not a finished event that may be passively photographed, recorded with a neutral language, or studied and understood with classical categories of objectivity. It is not a destination but a point of departure, the catalyst of individual consciousness that enfolds it and shapes it; the revised facts of war—the organic flow of images, feelings, and associations—are not observed as much as they are figuratively inhaled and transmuted by personal consciousness. Herr is faithful to facts in a classical sense—he dutifully accumulates image, statement, and event in episodic documentary style—but he complicates his history by subjecting those facts to the unfiltered light of the creating consciousness, by deliberately seeking the point where imagination is most energized by the catalytic historical referent.

The historian as self-reflexive active agent within his data has precedents within American writing. The exploration of history as partnership between event and the creating imagination is a prominent theme in such journalism as Truman Capote's *In Cold Blood*, Mailer's *The Armies of the Night*, and Tom Wolfe's *The Electric Kool-Aid Acid Test*, works as much about their own aesthetic revisions and inventions as about the events and personalities they describe. Herr does not single-handedly invent a method of reporting, but extends and refines a methodological belief system that awaited an event as mythically resonant as Vietnam to be truly tested. As Peter Davis, one of the producers of the controversial Vietnam documentary *Hearts and Minds*, has observed, "The self-designated 'new journalism' was born before the war, but Vietnam was a perfect place for it to grow" (99).

Herr's new journalism, however, for all its original power and inventiveness, should also be understood as American romanticism restated and reexamined. *Dispatches* is the poetic theory of Emerson's "Nature" and "Circles" applied in language of new elasticity and power, the practice of Thoreau's *Walden* transferred to a dark and violent historical configuration. The romantic and the new journalist may differ on the origin and nature of Spirit in regard to categories of transcendence and immanence, but the fact remains that the aesthetic ground and practice of both groups of writers look remarkably the same. Herr would agree with Emerson that his generation has become retrospective, and like his forerunner, he strips his moment of constricting categories to free the organic power of the image and of the word. Revised romantic that he is, Herr reads his book of nature only to rewrite it as an individual spirit of history, as both complicating and completing artificer.

Appropriately, the first image of "Breathing In" is a map on the wall of Herr's Saigon apartment that offers a Vietnam marked by the old French divisions of Tonkin, Annam, and Cochin China, a topography that "was a marvel, especially now that it wasn't real anymore" (1). Herr knows as well that a reliable high-relief rendering of the American presence is unavailable and that his task as personal historian is to fill that void, to correlate the many voices speaking within the spiritual, emotional, and psychological data he both observes and contains:

> It was late '67 now, even the most detailed maps didn't reveal much anymore; reading them was like trying to read the faces of the Vietnamese, and that was like trying to read the wind. We knew that the uses of most information were flexible, different pieces of ground told different stories to different people. We also knew that for years there had been no country here but the war. (1)

What Herr seeks in *Dispatches* is a voice that allows the historian both to approximate in language the internal rhythms of the war and to demonstrate how those rhythms were lost under the increasing volume of the official mythic voices attempting to assert their re-sounding American epic by sheer force of will.

Herr's retrieval of secret history begins with the observation that the historical event he confronts is incomplete, that it suggests possi-bilities rather than imposes obvious interpretive strategies. Early in "Breathing In," he recounts meeting a soldier who tells him the em-blematic war story, one that brings home the insight that traditional recording devices are obsolete and in need of replacement:

> "Patrol went up the mountain. One man came back. He died be-fore he could tell us what happened."
>
> I waited for the rest, but it seemed not to be that kind of story; when I asked him what had happened he just looked like he felt sorry for me, fucked if he'd waste his time telling stories to anyone dumb as I was. (4–5)

Like this single sphinxian riddle, Vietnam overall presents itself to Herr as a series of discontinuous, discrete images that demand indi-vidual completion, portents and promontories of historical significance that reveal their possible relationships only through a process of per-sonal absorption, connection, and invention. The powerful current of images can be overwhelming, the exhaustion of sorting through them a substitute for interpretation—"I came to cover the war and the war covered me" (20), he confesses—but the beginnings of per-sonal differentiation and integration lie not in passive, objective re-ceiving but in the reciprocal exchange between the historian and the history that challenges the imagination to place it into a readable configuration. Phillip Knightley has argued of Vietnam that "no one correspondent could hope to get a broad, general experience of it; all that most correspondents succeeded in doing was obtaining a limited, spotty experience" (108). Finding a historical configuration not of incipient congruity but of broken puzzle pieces, Knightley contends that no equipment existed for the writing of the necessary comprehen-sive statement: "Vietnam was such a complex tragedy that the re-porters, like everyone else, were overwhelmed by it" (109).

But Knightley does not include in his assessment the restatement of the romantic's bargain that Herr attempts. If existing language structures are insufficient to speak to history as it evolves, then the aesthetic equipment of the historian must demonstrate a corresponding violent evolution; the formal structures of the journalist must be reshaped to allow the entrance of the new data that resist traditional fact gathering. What is required is the discarding of old tools and the discovery of new ones. When unchallenged, shared notions of objective reporting produce only the undifferentiated quilt of statement and image that Knightley describes, greater reliance on subjectivity and invention is required. In short, the journalist becomes not a medium but a component of history, a builder rather than a retriever of public memory. Confronting the new data of Vietnam, Herr confesses that

> the war made a place for you that was all yours. Finding it was like listening to esoteric music, you didn't hear it in any essential way through all the repetitions until your own breath had entered it and became another instrument, and by then it wasn't just music anymore, it was experience. (67)

As alchemist, Herr defines himself as a new figure in American war writing, what Gordon Taylor describes as "the protagonist more as witness than as hero" (300), the recorder who willingly enters the historical bargain of enduring and re-creating for the reader "self-encounters enforced, in landscapes of the mind, by the environments of war" (300). Herr proves successfully in *Dispatches* that more than one kind of chimerical movement is possible, that an encounter of individual imagination with history can begin to sketch the features of a credible collective record.

Fredric Jameson has assessed Herr's achievement in *Dispatches* as the successful charting of "the space of postmodern warfare" ("Postmodernism" 84), a historical and aesthetic project that assumes the obsolescence of standard methods of recording and evoking. A war that manifests its historical configuration as one resistant to modernist notions of narrative requires inventive textual strategies rather than unreflective applications of well-traveled modes. Assessing Vietnam's cultural demands, Jameson states,

> This first terrible postmodernist war cannot be told in any of the traditional paradigms of the war novel or movie—indeed that breakdown of all previous narrative paradigms . . . along with the breakdown of any shared language through which a veteran might convey such experience . . . may be said to open up the place of a whole new reflexivity. (84)

Herr abandons chronological narrative—and, with it, the familiar contours of the classical memoir—in favor of an exploration of space:

psychic space, mythic space, ideological space. In "Breathing In," Herr guides his meta-chopper through not only the sensory jolts and psychic disorientations that individual consciousness received in Vietnam, but also the struggles for mythic control and possession of public memory. High command could reside in the ethereal categories of winning hearts and minds—imaginative projections that spoke only to their own abstract seductiveness—but Herr can remember in passing the cryptic announcement of a black paratrooper of the 101st Airborne Division: "I been *scaled* man, I'm *smooth* now" (28) is the kind of cool, spontaneous metaphor that subverts the official story so completely that it seems almost beyond antagonism, a true signifier of the breach between public and private visions.

Most often, Herr's Vietnam describes a historical configuration that seems the product of the combined imaginative resources of Lewis Carroll, Samuel Coleridge, and the most fearsome, uncontrolled acid dream. Vietnam is such a powerful cultural stimulant, such a tangible alteration of aesthetic consciousness, that artificial mind-expanding agents are superfluous: "Going out at night the medics gave you pills, Dexedrine breath like dead snakes kept too long in a jar. I never saw the need for them myself, a little contact or even anything that sounded like contact would give me more speed than I could bear" (3). Ideological imperatives, cultural-engineering principles, and categories of practical military necessity have produced not a variant of American order and control in Vietnam, but a collective falling through an improvised looking glass into a disorienting jungle of mythic undergrowth, a passage that places the chore of historical reading on grunt, reporter, and manager alike. A volunteer among the many levels of the historically imprisoned, Herr seeks high aesthetic ground within the American antithesis of the pleasure dome, a vantage point from which to gauge its composition and its workings:

> You'd stand nailed there in your tracks sometimes, no bearings and none in sight, thinking, *Where the fuck am I?*, fallen into some unnatural East-West interface, a California corridor cut and bought and burned deep into Asia, and once we'd done it we couldn't remember what for. . . . There was such a dense concentration of American energy there, American and essentially adolescent, if that energy could have been channeled into anything more than noise, waste and pain it would have lighted up Indochina for a thousand years. (44–45)

James Wilson finds in *Dispatches* the most fully realized example of the "dope and dementia" grouping of Vietnam histories, a work that expends its aesthetic resources "denying the possibility of structure" (45), but Herr's discernible fracturing of traditional narrative is not an announcement that the textual analogue for the Vietnam War must be hopeless discontinuity. Certainly, Herr operates in Vietnam in what Gordon Taylor calls "a black hole in moral space" (305), but he also fashions an aesthetic apparatus from the materials of personal sensibility that allows him to overcome the almost terminal gravitational pull of new history. For Wilson, Herr's imaginative flight is a historical fool's errand, one that "does not replace the wornout map with a new one" (46); however, he fails to consider fully the capabilities of Herr's linguistic chopper. The connections among image, statement, and discrete event in *Dispatches* are fluid, organic, demanding imaginative completion and extension by author and reader. Meaning resides not in single, unviolable correspondences, but between and among the plenitude of possible relationships. Herr refuses to place limits on the the associative power of his method, to ring in interpretive possibilities, and invites the reader to extend the narrative how he can in a textual partnership that is finally a moral enterprise as much as an aesthetic opportunity.

Herr's Vietnam is not the shaped configuration of official policies and tactics, but the place in the imagination where "all the mythic tracks intersected" (19). Realizing that "you couldn't use standard methods to date the doom" (51), he needs the full range of imaginative vision. He can suggest that the war's true managers may be "the proto-Gringos who found the New England woods too raw and empty for their peace and filled them up with their own imported devils" (51), but he also finds the new end product of indigenous tendencies a victim of its own mythic overload, incapable of speaking coherently or consistently of its origins and true motivations. Beneath assertions of order and purpose—the collective vision of a tidy war fought with a clear moral imperative—the enterprise offers itself to Herr more as "a big intertwined ball of baby milk snakes" (41), a collision of cultures that has transformed buried national neurosis into the most debilitating form of compulsive historical behavior.

Herr's style in *Dispatches* is an attempt to render historical substance through restructured aesthetic form. His prose reaches the reader through a redesigned personal transmitter, a manic teletype within the creative imagination that is always in danger of being short-circuited by the plenitude of words and images being fed through it. The small dispatches function as historical poetic conceits, concentrations of symbolic energy emitting bands of suggestiveness that intersect with others to form a corruscating network of correspondences. One of the crowning statements of high-modernist prose style was Virginia Woolf's assessment of life not as a series of gig lamps but as a luminous halo, a new appreciation of the relationship between the lived world and individual consciousness demanding appropriate aesthetic equipment for its presentation. Herr's postmodern war complicates Woolf's notion, for history presents itself to the subject not as a bright continuum but as a puzzling network of interlocking and overlapping sources of illumination, a shifting play of light and shadow that presents a new configuration with each changing vantage point. Herr finds the antithesis of his new historiography in the struggle by the war's spokesmen to limit the possible readings of the war, to shape a mercurial cultural event into a fixed form, to shatter the expanding rings of unwelcome data:

> That fall, all that the Mission talked about was control: arms control, information control, resources control, psycho-political control, population control, control of the almost supernatural inflation, control of terrain through the Strategy of the Periphery. But when the talk had passed, the only thing left standing up that looked true was your sense of how out of control things really were. Year after year, season after season, wet and dry, using up options faster than rounds on a machine-gun belt, we called it right and righteous, viable and even almost won, and still it only went on the way it went on. When all the projections of intent and strategy twist and turn back on you, tracking team blood, "sorry" just won't cover it. There's nothing so embarrassing as when things go wrong in a war. (50)

In his shuttling in helicopters between periods of hazy reflection in Saigon and total immersion in the dark imagery of the fire bases and the bush, Herr begins to trace a more expansive variety of historical continuity. The early days of the American involvement, the covert operations and improvised, unannounced tactics of "the romance of spooking" (53), have planted in Vietnam a historicized version of Wallace Stevens's jar. Taking mythic dominion everywhere, it is also beyond the control of its makers: "Their adventure became

our war, then a war bogged down in time, so much time so badly ac-
counted for that it finally became entrenched as an institution because
there had never been room made for it to go anywhere else" (53).
The dangerous outcroppings and residual effects of blind ambition
are everywhere, signifiers of a history that has been concentrated and
catalyzed by a powerful but visionless instrumentality. Herr is intrigued with American technology as a virulent, delusory form of symbolic action, and his own meta-chopper is a concentration of the conflicting, seductive aspects of the American presence. An integration
of recorded image and imaginative extension, it is the ultimate Vietnam conceit:

> . . . in my mind it was the sexiest thing going; saver-destroyer,
> provider-waster, right hand-left hand, nimble, fluent, canny and
> human; hot steel, grease, jungle-saturated canvas webbing, sweat
> cooling and warming up again, cassette rock and roll in one ear and
> door-gun fire in the other, fuel, heat, vitality and death, death
> itself, hardly an intruder. (7)

As historian, Herr confronts the unimaginable, a war of almost pure
style whose capacity for eye-fooling illusion becomes its most common
message, but the symbology of American omnipotence is only a self-
deception. The realities that reside beneath the sleight of hand of the
new machine have deep roots and the potential to strike back with
vehemence. "Just a projection," admits Herr, "that was the thing
about the chopper, you had to come down sometime" (39). He discovers the need for personal resources beyond a resistance to historical
air sickness and the ability to identify American hubris. Beneath the
spinning rotors of technological magic lies another historical vision,
one with simpler definitions of tenacity and purpose:

> The ground was always in play, always being swept. Under the
> ground was his, above it was ours. We had the air, we could get up
> in it but not disappear in to it, we could run but we couldn't hide,
> and he could do each so well that sometimes it looked like he was
> doing them both at once, while our finder just went limp. (13)

On the ground, in Saigon and in the field, Herr discovers the most
resonant images of mythic cause and effect running beyond official
control. Saigon is the "only place left with a continuity," but spending time there is also "like sitting inside the folded petals of a poison-

ous flower" (44), a lived analogue to Baudelairean imaginative space where the information is too concentrated and undifferentiated. Official confidences center their energy in the southern capital, but so do the darker projections that have been engendered by the cultural exchange. Herr listens to an officer explain a war out of control in nutritional terms, a small reading that indicates how much many others have become powered by their own invented sources: "We were a nation of high-protein, meat-eating hunters, while the other guy ate rice and a few grungy fish heads. We were going to club him to death with our meat; what could you say except, 'Colonel, you're insane'?" (63). For others, the failure of attrition sparks intimations of escalation, the application of the ultimate American technological trump card: "Once I met a colonel who had a plan to shorten the war by dropping piranha into the paddies of the North. He was talking fish but his dreamy eyes were full of mega-death" (63). Saigon is the nexus of energy "fed back into town on a karmic wire" (43), but it is the receiver and mixer of historical transmissions, not the originator of them. Like Greene's Fowler, Herr knows that the access to secret history is not in the air-conditioned hotels and bars of the information centers; there he can record the after shocks and residual effects of the story he seeks, but his new historiography requires complete personal immersion rather than detached observation and conjecture:

> It seemed the least of the war's contradictions that to lose your worst sense of American shame you had to leave the Dial Soapers in Saigon and a hundred headquarters who spoke goodworks and killed nobody themselves, and go out to the grungy men in the jungle who talked bloody murder and killed people all the time. (43)

With his lessons learned in the jungle, Herr attempts to fashion a transmitting device that will not condemn his data to the file of sanitized reports and incomplete stories already locked in place. The style of Dispatches is not the outgrowth of sequestered aesthetic theory, but the organic form rising from Herr's sympathetic union with his data. If, as John Hellman contends, the memoir is "the journey of the author through his own consciousness" (142), it is also something less hermetically subjective. The record of the reciprocal exchange between a creating consciousness and the most powerful kind of historical data, Dispatches is an effective argument—as an example of historical romanticism in fully realized form—that the light refracted by the prism and the prism itself cannot be discussed independently without losing all ability to discriminate within the bands. Herr offers what seems to be a new journalistic egocentricity, but his strategy is the alchemy of romantic sensibility announcing its claim to historical terrain; what seems on the surface tangential confession is most often a short discourse on method:

> After a year I felt so plugged in to all the stories and the images and the fear that even the dead started telling me stories, you'd hear them out of a remote accessible space where there were no ideas, no emotions, no facts, no proper language, only clean information. (31)

To retrieve and to transmit the "clean information" with which individual consciousness has joined, Herr discovers that his imaginative resources must be stretched continually to a limit that is near absolute, that the threats to personal sensibility inherent in the passage into the war's dark center have duration and depth. To break free of the master narrative is also to work psychologically and aesthetically without a net: "Going crazy was built into the tour," claims Herr, "the best you could hope for was that it didn't happen around you, the kind of crazy that made men empty clips into strangers or fix grenades on latrine doors" (61). He discovers that much of grunt society has broken so completely with the master narrative that variants of primitive superstitions and practices are doing battle with the influence of American technology. Energies flowing within the historical configuration other than the sanctioned ones prompt men to arrange themselves around a "charmed grunt," a soldier who has lived long enough or who has escaped death miraculously enough to be considered endowed with magical properties. "Flip religion," as Herr dubs it, offers spontaneous social groupings and practices—strange signifiers of the battle for control of collective memory—found neither in the army handbook nor in the clean journalism of Time and Newsweek. Far away from the influence of the managerial narrative, "you couldn't blame anybody for believing anything," argues Herr. "Guys dressed up in Batman fetishes, I saw a whole squad like that, it gave them a kind of dumb esprit. Guys stuck the ace of spades in their helmet bands, they picked relics off of an enemy they'd killed, a little transfer of power" (59).

Assuming the role of romantic as historian, Herr attempts at all times to be both sensitive seismic device for the energy of his configuration and creative medium through which the multiple associations of new history may be allowed to catalyze the imagination of his readership. The challenge, however, of composing a narrative faithful to facts even in Herr's expanded sense is prohibitive. He occupies imaginative terrain that seems like "some black looneytune where the Duck had all the lines" (63), attempting to test the master narrative against field stories such as the one "about the man in the Highlands who was 'building his own gook'" (35) and against an enemy sensibility sufficiently attuned to postmodern irony to place on the body of a dead American soldier the small textual message, "Your X-rays have just come back from the lab and we think we know what your problem is" (36). Herr tests the waters of a referent as simultaneously real and symbolic as Thoreau's Walden Pond, but his pool of data presents more immediate dangers to the romantic imagination diving into its murky depths:

> It was bottomless and alive with Lurps, seals, recondos, Green-Beret bushmasters, redundant mutilators, heavy rapers, eye-shooters, widow-makers, nametakers, classical essential American types; point men, *isolatos* and outriders like they were programmed in their genes to do it, the first taste made them crazy for it, just like they knew it would. You thought you were separate and protected, you could travel the war for a hundred years, a swim in that pool could still be worth a piece of your balance. (35)

Herr views close up the dominant attitudes and practices of the violent, pressurized society of grunts as he reads the historical text that America's "best killers" write daily in the jungle. One of the many hallmarks of *Dispatches* is Herr's willingness to chart the shifting ratio of sympathy and revulsion he feels in Vietnam. The decision to give voice to feelings that other writers leave sequestered behind liberal rage or shopworn apology is Herr's act of aesthetic courage; his personal confession within the full range of historical response makes the memoir the most necessary addition to the public record:

> Disgust doesn't begin to describe what they made me feel, they threw people out of helicopters, tied people up and put the dogs on them. Brutality was just a word in my mouth before that. But disgust was only one color in the whole mandala, gentleness and pity were other colors, there wasn't a color left out. I think that those people who used to say that they only wept for the Vietnamese never really wept for anyone at all if they couldn't squeeze out

at least one for these men and boys when they died or had their
lives cracked open for them. (70)

If Saigon is the pressurized center of postmodern space in Vietnam, the windowless arrangement of conflicting reports, the Tet offensive is for Herr the chronological nexus that gathers together the
war's past and future history into synchronous readability. In the sections entitled "Hell Sucks" and "Khe Sanh," Herr evokes within the
particulars of the destruction of Hue and the siege of the Marine
compound the intricate relationships between American theory and
practice, word and deed, reality and symbology. Tet is the event
within events that makes the buried assumptions of the American
presence most available to the romantic sensibility, that forces the
interconnected planes of language and action to become accessible to
the imaginative extension of the new historian. The "romance of
spooking" and the fall of Saigon congeal within present time in the
Citadel and behind the wire at Khe Sanh; the diachronic is transmuted into the synchronic within individual consciousness as Herr
says of Tet,

> We took a huge collective nervous breakdown, it was the compres-
> sion and heat of heavy contact generated out until every American
> in Vietnam got a taste. Vietnam was a dark room full of deadly
> objects, the VC were everywhere all at once like spider cancer, and
> instead of losing the war in little pieces over years we lost it fast
> in under a week. After that, we were like the character in pop grunt
> mythology, dead but too dumb to lie down. (74)

Herr notes the American machine's capacity for the reflexive repara-
tion of its most visible components: "We took space back quickly,
expensively, with total panic and close to maximum brutality. Our
machine was devastating. And versatile. It could do everything but
stop" (74). For Herr, "losing the war" is not a matter of body count
but the collective apprehension that the master narrative has im-
ploded in public view, that the deepest historical premonitions of
even the war's staunchest apologists have become real. At Hue in
"Hell Sucks," Herr evokes the former beauty of the ancient city, only
to underscore its methodical shattering with the horrible understate-
ment of new history operating without respect for or contemplation
of its own origins and effects:

One Marine next to me was saying that it was just a damned
shame, all them poor people, all them nice looking houses, they
even had a Shell station there. He was looking at the black napalm
blasts and the wreckage along the wall. "Looks like the Imperial
City's had the schnitz," he said. (79)

Although the city is retaken, Herr chooses his symbolic details in
order to underscore the failure of the master narrative to remain intact. A single, well-chosen image, suggests Herr, offers more information of the attack's ramifications than a hundred official synopses.
When a GVN flag, signifying the return of southern control, is
raised in one part of the battered city, "the rope snapped, and the
crowd, thinking the VC had shot it down, broke up in panic" (88).
In the Imperial Palace itself, Herr creates a small tableau of the true
condition of a traditional culture subjected to too many violent historical visions:

> The large bronze urns were dented beyond restoring, and the rain
> poured through a hole in the roof of the throne room, soaking the
> two small thrones where the old Annamese royalty had sat. In the
> great hall (great once you scaled it to the Vietnamese) the red
> lacquer work on the upper walls was badly chipped, and a heavy
> dust covered everything. The crown of the main gate had collapsed
> and in the garden the broken branches of the old cay-dai trees lay
> like the forms of giant insects seared in a fire, wispy, delicate, dead.
> (88–89)

In the "Khe Sanh" section, Herr concentrates his imaginative
powers on the significance of the defense of the Marine compound,
which becomes "a passion, the false love object in the heart of the
Command" (113), demonstrating both why Khe Sanh became the
locus of official hopes and fears and how, once again, most journalistic
accounts missed the most obvious truths. Framing his exploration of
the obsession with an evocation of the Highlands of Vietnam, the
terrain referred to officially only as "I Corps," Herr argues that the
managerial lexicon was only "a cosmetic" but that because "most of
the journalism from the war was framed in that language . . . it
would be as impossible to know what Vietnam looked like from reading most newspaper stories as it would to know how it smelled" (98).
Herr supplies the missing context of sensory and psychological knowledge, the anti-image of the "unbearably spooky" terrain around Khe
Sanh in which the most readable example of American symbolic ac-

tion takes place. The war refuses consistently to conform to American imaginative projections, and much of the cause for that denial is discoverable in the Highlands, an area that offers both unique mysteries and an eerie sense of mythic repetition. Describing the topography enfolding the most visible promontory of the new City on the Hill, Herr suggests,

> The Puritan belief that Satan dwelt in Nature could have been born here, where even on the coldest, freshest mountaintops you could smell jungle and that tension between rot and genesis that all jungles give off. It is ghost-story country, and for Americans it had been the scene of some of the war's vilest surprises. (100)

American hopes and fears, suggests Herr, extend back far beyond the immediate official nightmare that Khe Sanh may become Dien Bien Phu revisited or the bright dream that the enemy here may finally be coaxed into "a set-piece battle where he could be killed by the numbers, killed wholesale, and if we killed enough of him, maybe he would go away" (114). Khe Sanh symbolically returns America to its historical beginnings, concentrating space and time into an objective more imagined than real. It is little wonder, offers Herr, that the unofficial theme song of the Marines and reporters at Khe Sanh becomes the Beatles's "Magical Mystery Tour."

Of the Marines, Herr observes that "they were killers. Of course they were; what would anyone expect them to be? It absorbed them, inhabited them, made them strong in the way that victims are strong" (109–10), but his portrayal of the defenders moves beyond the immediate presentation of violent function and strikes larger responses of sympathy and understanding. Herr's achievement in the "Khe Sanh" section, and in the memoir as a whole, is the careful juxtaposition of intuitive response and imaginative extension with the most glaring omissions of the official narrative; as he probes the lived history at Khe Sanh, Herr attempts to penetrate the superficial aspects of grunt sensibility and to probe the deeper effects on individual sensibility of the high command's obsession. As the hills ringing Khe Sanh are razed by American firepower, so the defenders experience the most telling internal transformations. Herr presents the familiar statistics— "we delivered more than 110,000 tons of bombs to those hills during the eleven-week containment of Khe Sanh" (162). But he extends obvious cause and effect into more far-reaching and unexpected correspondences:

. . . the bigger hills were left with scars and craters of such proportions that an observer from some remote culture might see in them the obsessiveness and ritual regularity of religious symbols, the blackness at the deep center pouring out rays of bright, overturned earth all the way to the circumference; forms like Aztec sun figures, suggesting that their makers had been men who held Nature in an awesome reverence. (162–63)

The powerful imagery of new history is the catalyst for personal reorientations, slides into historical readings so terminal and unspoken that no familiar recording devices can bring them to light. Reading the book of nature at Khe Sanh suggests that Vietnam is the concentrated mythic space where Frederick Jackson Turner might meet Milton or Dante, the place in the imagination where primal forces and cultural imperatives meet. Night vision at Khe Sanh can offer spontaneous iconography to the imagination that official history cannot hold:

Then it is night again, and the sky beyond the western perimeter is burning with slowly dropping magnesium flares. Heaps of equipment are on fire, terrifying in their jagged black massiveness, burning prehistoric shapes like the tail of a C-130 sticking straight up in the air, dead metal showing through the gray-black smoke. God, if it can do that to metal, what will it do to me? (117)

The concentration of American energy—technological and imaginative—at Khe Sanh produces smaller personal obsessions within the public one. For management and media alike, the Marine compound seems to order the chaos: "Khe Sanh said 'siege,' it said 'encircled Marines' and 'heroic defenders.' It could be understood by newspaper readers quickly, it breathed Glory and War and Honored Dead. It seemed to make sense" (111). But as a concentrated metaphor of the strange mix of fact and fiction in Vietnam, it is for the inhabitants of its dark center the most persistent illogic. Within pressurized postmodern space, time takes on new significance. It is on a personal level not the stolid regularity that governs tactical calendars and supply schedules, but an internal presence influenced directly by the perceived configuration of the newly created landscape. Herr's description of a black soldier from Detroit known to his fellow grunts as Day Tripper illustrates the new psychology of the purest of short-timer's syndromes:

No metaphysician ever studied Time the way he did, its components and implications, its per-second per seconds, its shading and
movement. The Space-Time continuum, Time-as-Matter, Augus-
tinian Time: all that would have been a piece of cake to Day
Tripper, whose brain cells were arranged like jewels in the finest
chronometer. (126)

When Operation Pegasus is conducted to relieve Khe Sanh, Herr
notes that "it soon came to look more like a spectacle than a military
operation, a non-operation devised to non-relieve the non-siege of
Khe Sanh" (166). He observes as well how quickly the imaginative
incursion of the American obsession into ghost country can dissipate
its energy. The hills around Khe Sanh, which "had held such fearful
mystery," Herr describes as being "transformed as greatly as if a
flood had swept over them" (173), and the many voices asking how
Khe Sanh could be so suddenly diminished in strategic importance
are informed politely that "the situation had changed" (173). Herr
completes the section with an image of organic compensation as he
describes the jungle about the abandoned compound growing "with
a violence of energy now in the Highland summer, as though there
was an impatience somewhere to conceal all traces of what had been
left by the winter" (173-74). If for General Westmoreland, Khe
Sanh is a great victory, "a Dien Bien Phu in reverse," it is for Herr
the most readable mix of natural and newly invented images, a discursive part of the whole text that speaks of the origins, nature, and
direction of American historical drift.[3]

Herr assumes a connection among the images and statements in
the grid he assembles, but it is one that reveals itself in a most associative, indeterminate way. Meaning can never be isolated in any one
area of the grid, nor can the possible correspondences be made absolute; as he dispenses with the false textual security of the univocal
narrative, he offers as its replacement spots of light that bring the
grid into relief from a number of angles. In "Illumination Rounds,"
Herr fires at the reader in quick succession telling vignettes that
bring momentarily darkened history into view. As the fading suggestion of each image hangs in the textual air, he launches a new one
to bring the reader closer to the historian's problem of focusing on
and correlating within individual imagination the plenitude of suggestions, of dealing aesthetically with the nonstop accumulation of
quick glimpses and possible correspondences. Herr's metaphor suggests a diachronic gathering and re-creation of image, but the final

effect is of synchronic arrangement of response and association, the simultaneity of suggestions. Philip Beidler has said of *Dispatches* that "any single observation or datum will eventually be seen to have pointed at once backward and forward to any number of others bearing it some complex relation" (*American Literature* 146–47), a fair assessment of how Herr fashions postmodern textual topography to stand as a linguistic analogue for the imaginative space of lived experience.

In "Illumination Rounds," Herr recounts listening to another reporter's small interchange with a young soldier, a nonconversation more suggestive of the overall effect of the American presence than a hundred polemical novels:

> There was a standard question you could use to open a conversation with troops, and Fouhy tried it. "How long you been incountry?" he asked.
>
> The kid lifted his head; that question could *not* be serious. The weight was really on him, and the words came slowly.
>
> "All fuckin' day," he said. (189)

The relation of personal knowledge to public memory is most accessible not in elaborate treatises and situation reports, but in quicksilver glimpses into the recesses of other historians' internal perceptions. Herr describes meeting a young career officer overcome by the discrepancy between theory and practice whose reception of one more confident intelligence report prompts the offering of a small vision:

> "I've been having this dream," the major said. "I've had it two times now. I'm in a big examination room back in Quantico. They're handing out questionnaires for an aptitude test. I take one and look at it, and the first question says, 'How many kinds of animals can you kill with your hands?' " (197)

In "Colleagues," Herr recounts his own journalistic exploits and those of fellow romantics such as Tim Page, Sean Flynn, and Dana Stone in the context of the overall performance of the media in Vietnam, but the section is much more than the familiar anecdotal version of the hard-bitten war correspondent sharing the dangers of combat with camera and pad in hand. Herr relates that the reporters, if they were to cover the story with new methodology and adjusted

vision, had to overcome as best they could the massive mythic influence being played out daily in Vietnam. "Colleagues" extends and
complicates Herr's discourse on method, and, again, the section is an
example of theory being transmuted spontaneously into effective
practice. He admits that the "glamour" of his role is inscribed in the
historical narrative with a mythic quill, that a heightened self-consciousness is more likely to feed residual Hollywood fantasies than
to expunge them. "I never knew a member of the Vietnam press
corps," says Herr, "who was insensible to what happened when the
words 'war' and 'correspondent' got joined" (199). Like Philip
Caputo casting himself in a blood-and-guts crusade scenario, Herr
confesses an envy for those writers who had a mythically pure war in
which to act out the deepest cultural wish fulfillment, but he is sensitive enough to the new developments within the interface of life
and art in Vietnam to realize the personal and professional dangers
in applied fantasy:

> In any other war, they would have made movies about us too,
> *Dateline: Hell!*, *Dispatch from Dong Ha*, maybe even *A Scrambler
> at the Front*, about Tim Page, Sean Flynn and Rick Merron, three
> young photographers who used to ride in and out of combat on
> Hondas. But Vietnam is awkward, everybody knows how awkward,
> and if people don't even want to hear about it, you know they're
> not going to pay money to sit there in the dark and have it brought
> up. (*The Green Berets* doesn't count. That wasn't really about
> Vietnam, it was about Santa Monica.) So we have all been com-
> pelled to make our own movies, as many movies as there are cor-
> respondents, and this one is mine. (200)

Herr's "movie" in "Colleagues" is not a dispersion of established
mythic influence through aesthetic self-consciousness, but an enfolding and complicating of it. Attuned to the message that the war is
an energized, increasingly uncontrolled performance within redefined
mythic space, he chooses to demonstrate how art and history continually merge in Vietnam and how any attempt to separate them is
doomed. He redefines journalistic honesty not by retreating from the
mythic aspects of war but by emphasizing them, by illustrating that
no pure exchange between referent and romantic sensibility is possible. There is, however, the recognition that the imaginative extension of lived history within the memoir has for its aesthetic foundation the reciprocal bond between preexisting mythic influence and

the engendering power of newly created history; in short, Herr knows that myth creates his war, but he charts as well how the war shapes new myth. When he contends that for the journalists "all styles grew out of the same haunted, haunting romance" and reflexively dubs his coterie of romantic historians, "Those Crazy Guys Who Cover The War," he is deliberately overloading mythic influence to see what aesthetic excess will produce.

Herr sees at every juncture the power of the cultural influences already locked in place. "You don't know what a media freak is," he says, "until you've seen the way a few of those grunts would run around during a fight when they knew there was a television crew nearby," but he knows that the performance aspect of the war is not cast in Vietnam: "They were insane, but the war hadn't done that to them" (223). For grunts and journalists alike, mythic influence is omnipresent: "That feedback stalked you all over Vietnam" (224). But Herr knows that powerful influence cannot shield the sensitive recorder from truths even more deeply entrenched:

> It was the same familiar violence, only moved to another medium; some kind of jungle play with giant helicopters and fantastic special effects, actors lying out there in canvas body bags waiting for the scene to end so they could get up again and walk it off. But that was some scene (you found out), there was no cutting it. (223)

Beneath the new choreography of old mythic patterns lies secret history, the main narrative few are reporting, "a story that was as simple as it had always been, men hunting men, a hideous war and all kinds of victims" (228). Herr contends that, like grunt society, the correspondents who burrow beneath the ready-made myth of Hollywood and the spontaneous one of management compose an "authentic subculture" (252), one whose willingness to pursue the story entails complete immersion in the data the grunts already know intimately. The class structure within the press corps is described not by rank or privilege but by proximity to the essential facts, and Herr and his peers chart from the inside the repercussions of traditional reporting. Too many correspondents, he contends, dutifully transmit the master narrative without undertaking the necessary task of personal immersion in the experience of this war: "It was inevitable that once the media took the diversions seriously enough to report them, they also legitimized them" (229). Herr and his fellow romantics are not James Wilson's "dope and dementia" practitioners, but self-conscious political reporters cut from a new cloth: political in the sense of disputing the dominance of the master narrative by supplying counterstatements to it and its mainstream reportorial versions.

Herr's aesthetic strategy, his exploration of the war through a careful charting of minute alterations within his own recording consciousness, is finally what Gordon Taylor calls "a 'witness act' for the voiceless dead" (304), an enterprise whose moral and philosophical imperatives are discoverable in furious aesthetic invention, ingenuity made necessary by what traditional records are regrettably reinforcing. Of conventional journalism, Herr contends that "all it could do was take the most profound event of the American decade and turn it into a communications pudding" (232). His reply, and that of Page, Flynn, and the other new historians, is to travel to the war's dark center and to transmit their narratives from as many vantage points within the historical configuration as possible.

At the center of new history, the relationship between the correspondents and the grunts is volatile and ambivalent. "They *had* to be here, they knew that," says Herr. "We did *not* have to be here, and they were sure enough of that too" (202). Recognition of difference and the accompanying suspicions, however, are overcome often by other readings, the realization among many soldiers that the correspondents attempting to retrieve the buried story are the only historical conduits for what most reports miss or pretend does not exist; in a passage that captures both the ambivalence and the desperation of the grunt–reporter connection, Herr summarizes the tenuous bond:

> And always they would ask you with an emotion whose intensity would shock you to please tell it, because they really did have the feeling that it wasn't being told for them, that they were going through all this and that somehow no one back in the World knew about it. They may have been a bunch of dumb, brutal killer kids (a lot of correspondents privately felt that), but they were smart enough to know that much. (220)

The outlandish personal style of Herr's journalistic subculture can be disorienting or intimidating for the soldiers, but the reporters' willingness to accept the same risks as those threatening the grunts—the immediate dangers of personal immersion—is often the key to finding at least a temporary solidarity. Sean Flynn, the "Son of Captain Blood," is the most immediately romantic figure, an experience for the grunts "like looking up to see that you've been sharing a slit trench with John Wayne or William Bendix" (207). But underneath Flynn's status as a walking emblem of popular myth, Herr contends that his "playing was done only on the most earnest levels" and that his personal immersion affords him "a vision of Vietnam that was profound, black and definitive, a knowledge of its wildness that very few of his detractors would have understood" (209). The correspondents' commitment can inspire acceptance and, at times, admiration, but it can also receive the most serious demands from those unable to exit the war zone when they choose: "Okay, man, you go on, you go on out of here you cocksucker, but I mean it, you tell it. You tell it man. If you don't tell it . . ." (221). And there is always hatred, admits Herr, deep resentment of figures who are perceived by many to be parasites rather than committed historians. Understanding that his method of retrieving secret history will confront its own heartfelt counterstatements, he recounts overhearing the frozen comment of a soldier watching a jeepload of correspondents recede from the war's dark center: " 'Those fucking guys,' he'd said. 'I hope they die' " (222).

The concluding section, called "Breathing Out," is both a personal release from the war and a recognition that the merging of the historian's consciousness with the war experience has forged a most permanent connection. On one level, there is necessary individual closure: "The war ended," says Herr, "and then it really ended, the cities 'fell,' I watched the choppers I loved dropping into the South China Sea as their Vietnamese pilots jumped clear, and one last chopper revved it up, lifted off and flew out of my chest" (277). But Herr finds the transition to former realities as difficult as that of the combat veteran. He discovers the new historical dimensions wrought within the imagination by the war and confesses, "It wasn't just that I was growing older, I was leaking time, like I'd taken a frag from one of those anti-personnel weapons we had that were so small they could kill a man and never show up on X-rays" (277). He is brought finally to the recognition that what he has seen and felt are merely heightened examples of long-standing cultural knowledge. In a remarkable passage, Herr combines a postbellum personal diagnosis with a final contention that Vietnam is not an American historical aberration:

Home: twenty-eight years old, feeling like Rip Van Winkle, with a heart like one of those little paper pills they make in China, you drop them into water and they open to form a tiger or a flower or a pagoda. Mine opened out into war and loss. There'd been nothing happening there that hadn't already existed here, coiled up and waiting, back in the World. I hadn't been anywhere, I'd performed half an act; the war only had one way of coming to take your pain away quickly. (268)

The final act of the romantic sensibility as historian is one of both private and public alchemy. As a new register for what resides beneath official history, Herr reintegrates the self as he presents it as a document for collective examination, observing that there are "no moves left for me at all but to write down some last few words and make the dispersion, Vietnam Vietnam Vietnam, we've all been there" (278). As a model of how the successful union of form and function may transmute private vision into public understanding, *Dispatches* remains the war's most distinctive and eloquent voice, its most abundant and demanding compensatory history.

The persistence of memory is as much a forward- as a rearward-looking condition; the potential for the new historical application of revised myth resides always beneath the illusory stasis of harmonious retrospection. Herr's furious personal invention and extension of the Vietnam War might be only so much textual virtuosity if his historical data were inert rather than active mythic material. All attempts to forge a credible, comprehensive record might be construed as academic exercises for the interested specialist if Vietnam were a finished experience, one that could be allowed to recede peacefully into the collective archive, but such is not the case. If the revised configuration of national myth is applied to a Nicaragua or to some yet untargeted geopolitical complex, Vietnam will quickly shed its image as an event frozen in time and sensibility and reveal its active historical potential. Small examples of that exchange have in fact already occurred, for a medical student on Grenada remarking that the approach of American helicopters reminds him of *Apocalypse Now* is a tiny signifier of the mythic potential that awaits only a historical referent of sufficient depth and duration for its power to be fully unleashed.

The persistence of memory encourages calculated revision and convenient forgetfulness, and the master narrative of the Vietnam War continues to be edited and rewritten in a number of ways. To gain congressional funding and public support for the imperatives of new American foreign policy, Ronald Reagan can retread the prime metaphor of Del Vecchio's GreenMan and characterize the Vietnam War retrospectively as a football game that was well played. The current crop of popular films centering on American avengers rescuing MIAs in Vietnam indicates not only that the public imagination is ready only ten years after the fall of Saigon to accept two-dimensional stereotypes of the Oriental as venal and inhumane, but also that a collective desire exists not to reappraise the darker passages within the public record but to delete them. The mythic apparatus, however, cannot reshape so easily its new contours; although the power of the new revisions is undeniable, the disparities between memory and artifice forced by them can prove to be anxiety-producing only through time. Like morphine administered for a broken limb, convenient editing of the narrative is a temporary assuaging of pain from a wound that requires deeper cures. The experience of the war was too traumatic, too disruptive of what Americans hold most dear of themselves, to allow easy revisions or quick rewritings to stand as acceptable peace making.[4] In an interview with Eric James Schroeder, Robert Stone indicated why both individual and collective imagination must trace more honest, painful paths from Vietnam if they are to find enduring methods of reconciling reality and desire, powerful new data and mythic imperatives:

> Vietnam was a terribly important thing for this country. It's like a wound covered with scar tissue or like a foreign body, a piece of shrapnel, that the organism has built up a protective wall around, but it is embedded in our history. We will never get it out of there. (154)

To come to terms with the new information offered by Vietnam, Herr demonstrates, individual sensibility must become intimate with the facts, remain respectful of them, but not be controlled by them; the power of private imagination to complicate and to correlate new experience is the task at hand, a job requiring the powers of the recorder and the artificer—the combinative ability to foster a meaningful cultural exchange between memory and imagination. The irony not only of Vietnam War writing but also of any historical narrative, Herr suggests, is that to make sense of facts, one must break free of their obvious authority so that they may be reinscribed in a new way. *Dispatches* takes the reader on an imaginative flight through personal consciousness that ends with extensive burrowing in revised notions of facticity, and that accomplishment is a narrative that seems to bear only a tenuous resemblance to a more traditional memoir, such as Tim O'Brien's *If I Die in a Combat Zone*. The novel, however, would appear to be the more likely imaginative terrain for a true test of how far individual imagination may range from established categories of factual reportage and still be considered a valid historical document. Somewhere between the opaque report of pure documentary realism and the unhinged fantasy of the cinematic American avenger lay the exploration of how faithfulness to experience could be retained and personal vision extended so that neither essential component would have its historical testimony diminished.

Beyond Herr's identification in *Dispatches* of the essential irony inhabiting the shared terrain of fact and fiction, the corpus of Vietnam works offers at least one other. Proving himself no less an alchemist than his fellow memorialist, Tim O'Brien transmutes the moral center of *If I Die in a Combat Zone*, the war's most classical personal history, into the most experimental fiction any writer on Vietnam has produced. In *Going After Cacciato*, he replaces the meta-chopper with the more familiar locomotive principle of left foot after right, but his trek, like Herr's, is a voyage through inner space where facts confront imagination.

Going After Cacciato raises the same difficult questions as *If I Die in a Combat Zone*: how to act properly within a configuration that affords the entrapped soldier little historical understanding or moral justification as he experiences the most jarring imagery of waste and death. During one night's watch in his observation tower by the South China Sea, Spec. Four Paul Berlin attempts to meld the data of memory and imagination into an interpretive strategy that is both a departure and a pursuit, a quest whose narrative is bracketed by the tracking down and retrieving of the one soldier who has declined further participation in the violent facts of the war. Cacciato, "Dumb as a bullet. . . . Dumb as a month-old oyster fart" (14), has set his sights on Paris and has walked out of the war toward freedom, a self-designated beacon to Berlin's 3rd Squad of what imagination and determination might accomplish. He is the quarry, the test of individual duty and group cooperation, but he is also the guide, the encouragement to extrapolate freely from the essential facts of repetitive, violent death. In his tower, Berlin reiterates the essential inquiry of *If I Die in a Combat Zone*, to which experience and imagination make their separate cases and file their differing historical reports. Charting step by step in his imagination Cacciato's 8,600 mile flight to Paris and integrating with it the real horrors of his war as he remains mired within Vietnam, Berlin isolates the problem that is both the impetus for the flight and the argument for why it must be halted:

> The issue, of course, was courage. How to behave. Whether to flee or fight or seek an accommodation. The issue was not fearlessness. The issue was how to act wisely in spite of fear. Spiting the deep-running biles: that was true courage. He believed this. And he believed the obvious corollary: the greater a man's fear, the greater his potential courage. (100)

Identification of the novel's moral center has often been a secondary concern to critical assessments of O'Brien's intricate weave of fact and fantasy in *Cacciato*. In his review of the work, Bruce M. Firestone praises O'Brien's basic conception but observes that "it's difficult to tell what's past and what's present, what's real and what's fantasy" (2513), a complaint that betrays a failure to recognize the moral center about which aspects of the real and the imagined arrange themselves. Pearl K. Bell argues that *Cacciato* "stands the war on its head and turns it into a picaresque fantasy" (76), but such a perception confuses a part as the whole and sidesteps the very real ground on which O'Brien's debate occurs. In the confrontation between memory and imagination, Berlin joins what he has seen, felt, and done with what might be possible—indeed, necessary—in response to that experience. He confesses, "Pretending was his best trick to forget the war" (24), but his imaginative extension of Cacciato and the squad's trek is no mere evasion of violent contingency but a true test of what proper action might entail. Bell ignores the reciprocal exchange between experience and imagination within Berlin's creating consciousness, arguing of the narrative that "the alternating faces of the story—the one a cinematic daydream, the other a walking nightmare—do not fuse in a dramatically realized whole" (76). But O'Brien insists that traditional distinctions between dream and reality are not admissible in Berlin's moonlit tower by the sea where the most serious form of expostulation and reply is conducted. Berlin breaks from the facts to order them, and he leaves Vietnam to explain it within himself. His night reverie is neither pure memory nor historically disenfranchised fantasy, but the necessary interpenetration of the two, a joint activity that is also the most concerted personal debate of multiple testimonies. No fantasy, Berlin and the 3rd Squad's pursuit of Cacciato through Mandalay, Delhi, Tehran, Athens, Zagreb, and Bonn into the cafés and sidestreets of Paris is an imaginative activity deeply rooted in the lived experience of Vietnam, not a denial of reality but a deeper exploration of it. No less than Herr's narrative voice in *Dispatches*, Berlin understands the irony of having to leave Vietnam in order to arrive and acts on the knowledge of having to create in order to record:

> Paul Berlin, whose only goal was to live long enough to establish goals worth living for still longer, stood high in the tower by the sea, the night soft all around him, and wondered, not for the first time, about the immense powers of his own imagination. A truly awesome notion. Not a dream, an idea. An idea to develop, to tinker with and build and sustain, to draw out as an artist draws out his visions.

> It was not a dream. Nothing mystical or crazy, just an idea. Just a possibility. Feet turning hard like stone, legs stiffening, six and seven and eight thousand miles through unfolding country toward Paris. A truly splendid idea. (43–44)

Richard Freedman has said of O'Brien that he "counterpoints the gritty realism of combat against a dreamlike state" (21), but such a bifurcation of the novel into opposed sections of memory and fantasy makes *Cacciato* appear to be a clearly demarcated textual lawn game in which the ball is always in one court or the other. Berlin's moral debate is more intricate than that; experience and imagination face each other, but they also compose a continuum, a different kind of frame tale of which the architecture, like the eye-fooling geometry of an Escher print, seems to defy natural laws of space and proportion. Reality tests the limits of imagination in *Cacciato* as imagination enters and informs the nature and quality of memory. By extending rather than abandoning the reality of the Vietnam War, O'Brien simultaneously speaks more fully of it as he enfolds that experience with larger issues. Freedman makes the inevitable connection when he says of O'Brien's narrative, "Clearly we are dealing here with what the South American novelists would call 'magical realism'" (21). Magical occurrences present themselves in *Cacciato*, as they do in Gabriel García Márquez's *One Hundred Years of Solitude*, but neither author would be delighted to hear that his novel is the mere appropriation of historical elements for a virtuoso display of technique. James Park Sloan's *War Games* is the most disappointing kind of Vietnam metafiction because of its failure to respond to the moral and ideological issues that dwell within the configuration it fabulates. O'Brien never breaks with his facts; the pursuit of Cacciato is one in which "each step was an event of the imagination" (48). In a crucial passage, Berlin is forced to admit, "Even in imagination we must be true to our obligations, for, even in imagination, obligation cannot be outrun. Imagination, like reality, has its limits" (378). O'Brien uses the latter statement to establish Berlin's personal position on duty and desertion, but he also is making an assessment of the writer's responsibility to his historical data.

Any reader will admit that O'Brien's use of the fantastic is the most eye-catching quality of *Cacciato*. Beneath the sparkling surface of the narrative, however, are the moral ruminations of a Hector or an Achilles. John Updike has noted the effect on the reader of O'Brien's extension of the facts, the feeling that anything may occur, that time and space have become infinitely elastic and that logic is now invitingly malleable. But he, too, misses the deeper relationship of fact and fantasy in the walk to Paris. Noting that the emplotment in the tower produces "the slightly insulating lacquer of self-conscious art" (130), he construes Berlin's activity as dream rather than idea, desertion rather than extension, and argues that "the effect, when the narrative returns to Vietnam, is that a little Ian Fleming unreality has rubbed off on the real action, and the reader slogs through the paddies waiting for the next bravura display of adventure writing. Violence that did occur, historically and unentertainingly, has been demeaned, lightened" (130). O'Brien's narrative cannot return to Vietnam, for it never leaves. His textual alchemy, like Herr's, is the most puzzling but successful kind, for as he spins the gold of his fantastic elements, he retains the quality and feel of the base metal from which they attain their glittering surface of transformed reality.

In the chapter called "A Hole in the Road to Paris," Vietnam seems to descend into a Lewis Carroll wonderland as Berlin and the 3rd Squad plummet into the ultimate enemy tunnel complex when the road magically becomes an entrapping chasm. Yet O'Brien's miraculous event is followed by "Fire in the Hole," Berlin's remembrance of the real destruction of the village of Hoi An, an incident so devastating and complete that the men "watched the village become smoke" (100). Indicating how the union of memory and imagination functions in the tower, Berlin recalls in minute detail the sensory impact of the attack: "The tracers could be seen through the smoke, bright red streamers, and the Willie Peter and HE kept falling, and the men fired until they were exhausted. The village was a hole" (100). Memory informs imagination, supplies it with horrible data for its alchemy, but the transformed internal landscape impinges on experience as well. O'Brien follows "Fire in the Hole" with "Falling Through a Hole in the Road to Paris," an intricate ideological encounter below ground between Cacciato's seekers and a Vietcong major, who informs the 3rd Squad that "the soldier is but the representative of the land. The land is your enemy" (107), a statement that is both philosophically far-reaching and immediately astute. "Upon Almost Winning the Silver Star," the next chapter, in which Berlin recalls the real deaths of Bernie Lynn and Frenchie Tucker as they search an enemy tunnel, is not the demeaning or lightening of real violence, as Updike suggests, but the centering and intensifying of it in the imagination as the power of fantasy and the persistence of memory complicate the historical record being etched in the tower. What seems mere counterpoint between distinct, inviolable realms is actually the transformation of both by their deep encounter. As Berlin attempts to move from war toward peace—"to imagine a proper ending" (38) rather than merely a happy one—he listens to the Vietcong major tell him he is "a prisoner of the war, caught by the land" (121), but he also remembers how his "fear biles" assert themselves when he fails to help Bernie Lynn in the real tunnel and watches Frenchie burrow to his death.

Berlin's fantastic moonlit pursuit of Cacciato is filled with the same immediate hazards, personal fears, and moral quandaries offered by the reality experienced in unfiltered Vietnam daylight. As Berlin investigates his "possibilities," he discovers that any imagined flight to Paris must take stock of the essential facts: Bernie and Frenchie dying in the tunnel; Pederson shot by an American helicopter crew; Lieutenant Sidney Martin fragged by his own men of the 3rd Squad; and "the ultimate war story," Billy Boy Watkins dying of fright on the field of battle, an incident so fearful for Berlin that by itself it could power him halfway to the French border. O'Brien's interchange between memory and imagination in *Cacciato* is the most elaborate test of the Hemingway dictum that a good novel is truer than anything factual can be, and in an interview with Eric James Schroeder, he explained why he found the need to embellish the experience of Vietnam in the novel: "Truth doesn't reside in the surface of events. Truth resides in those deeper moments of punctuation, when things explode. So you compress the boredom down, hinting at it but always going for drama—because the essence of the experience was dramatic. You tell lies to get at the truth" (141). It may be a fruitless question to ask how the author of *In Our Time* would have assessed the blend of fact and fiction in *Cacciato*, but one might guess that O'Brien's expanded understanding of historical accuracy and fictional imperatives would not be dismissed as bad reporting. "It wasn't dreaming and it wasn't pretending. It wasn't crazy" (46), contends Paul Berlin of the wild chase to Paris, claims that O'Brien illustrates, explains, and, finally, justifies.

The unpreparedness of the individual soldier to interpret his experience is a theme shared by many Vietnam works, but Berlin's narrative in the tower is the most complete study of the inability to connect immediate violent reality with larger historical and ideological components. In the chapter called "Pickup Games," O'Brien begins by describing the debilitating repetitions of Vietnam that provide the small sense of order offered Berlin and his peers:

> They cordoned the villages and searched them and sometimes burned them down. They never saw the living enemy. On the odd-numbered afternoons they took sniper fire. On the even-numbered nights they were mortared. There was a rhythm in it. They knew when to be alert. They knew when it was safe to rest, when to send out patrols and when not to. There was certainty and regularity to the war, and this alone was something to hold on to. (125)

When a lull in the established pattern ensues, the immediate ordering principles of new history are replaced by collective anxiety, "A milky film clouding the hot days. Lapping motions at night. Artificiality, a sense of imposed peace. A wrongness" (127). Trapped in a war that now emits neither small rhythms nor larger messages, Berlin and the squad fill their days playing basketball games in the quiet villages, an activity that provides transitory clarity and purpose, a sense of collective achievement between base lines that is the antithesis of their off-court predicament. Berlin admits that he "liked reciting the final scores: 50 to 46; 68 to 40; once in My Khe 2, a lopsided 110 to 38. He liked the clarity of it. He liked knowing who won, and by how much, and he liked being a winner" (128).

But basketball is too small an ordering principle to bridge the gap between the reality of death in Vietnam and the absence of historical understanding. "We're getting short-changed on conceptual supplies" (131–32), argues Doc Peret, the medic-philosopher who makes the diagnosis of Berlin's fear biles and encourages his activity in the tower by the sea. As the lull continues and the men grow more anxious and surly, Doc offers an analysis that speaks to the larger historical problem and explains the necessity for Berlin's imaginative project:

> "What we have here," Doc said at the start of the fourth week of peace, "is your basic vacuum. Follow me? A vacuum. For order you got to have substance, materiel. So here we are . . . nothing to order, no substance. Aimless, that's what it is: a bunch of kids trying to pin the tail on the Asian donkey. But no fuckin tail. No fuckin donkey." (131)

The one reliable fact of the war reasserts itself at the conclusion of "Pickup Games"—"When Rudy Chassler hit the mine, the noise was muffled, almost fragile, but it was a relief for all of them" (137)—but manifestations of larger purpose and individual understanding within the configuration remain elusive as the 3rd Squad walks through silent villages and explores potentially deadly tunnels.

Berlin's recollections of how he was oriented to fight his war clarify why the process of fabulation in the tower is more than the idle daydreaming of a frightened soldier. In "How They Were Organized," O'Brien describes how the soldiers arrange themselves about aspects of superstition, luck, trust, and pride, but he illustrates the discrepancy between "formal" and "informal" standard operating procedures, the former indicating tunnels are to be searched, the latter demanding they be sealed with explosives to bury their deadly potential. The informal principles are functional ones. The situational practices they produce occur in the absence of more expansive historical understanding. Berlin's training for existence within his violent grid is as portentous as it is ludicrous, a series of omens that imagination will have to supply what facts fail to provide. In the tower, he remembers his first lessons at the Chu Lai Combat Center.

He recalls sitting before a silent instructor who gazes at the sea for a full hour and then announces to the initiates, "That completes your first lecture on how to survive this shit. I hope you paid attention" (56). He attends a class on enemy booby traps and crawls through a make-believe minefield with no signs or objects to indicate where the fateful surprises may lie. Told he has just become a dead man, Berlin complains that there is nothing in the sand and is informed, "Course not, you dumb twerp, you just fucking *exploded* it" (57). The lack of useful knowledge is so complete that Berlin writes to his father and asks him to locate Chu Lai on a map, confessing, "Right now . . . I'm a little lost" (58). Herr's opening image in *Dispatches* is reinforced: reliable maps are difficult to locate when the only topography is the moment-to-moment apprehension of incipient catastrophe.

The data that Berlin collects from the experience of his war intensifies the real need to exercise his powers of imagination to find a way out of Vietnam that is also a pathway inward to a moral center. His initial orientation affords no meaningful frame of reference for action or inaction, but neither does daily contact with Vietnam's most horrible surprises. Where is the imperative, asks Berlin, for Lieutenant Sidney Martin's demanding them to search tunnels, and where is the moral justification for their terminating with a ritualized grenade his adherence to official policy and personal decorum? Is removing oneself from a situation in which a man may die of fright desertion or good sense? And, beyond the obvious practical problems, what might be the circumstances to support Cacciato's declination and the 3rd Squad's following their guide?

In a remarkable chapter called "The Things They Didn't Know," O'Brien indicates why the ground for morality and ideology remains unhinged from immediate practice. Berlin confesses that he allows himself to go to war "not because of strong convictions, but because he didn't know" (313). Personal pressures and larger cultural imperatives influence what is really a noncommitment, but so does Berlin's inability to articulate an effective historical counterstatement. He goes "because, not knowing, he saw no reason to distrust those with experience. Because he loved his country, and more than that, because he trusted it" (313). In Vietnam, he cannot explain to villagers that he is as entrapped as they because he does not know the language; he cannot make known within the daily death and destruction that his personal intentions are good, his need to understand intensely real. The gap between the official narrative and the horrible realities of Vietnam is too great. As the Paris peace talks flounder in trivial argumentation, Berlin and his peers continue to perform their stultifying tunnel and village searches, manifesting "no serious discussion. No beliefs. They fought the war, but took no sides" (320).

The necessity of individual and group survival despite an absence of historical understanding or sense of purpose is a central theme of the soldier's experience in Vietnam writing, but Berlin's personal narrative of Cacciato's trek is the most resonant exploration of how much pressure is placed on personal imagination to provide acceptable explanations. In a passage emblematic of how traditional American assertions of innocence were tested and complicated by Vietnam, O'Brien indicates why individual and collective understanding remained dangerously elusive:

> They did not know even the simple things: a sense of victory, or satisfaction, or necessary sacrifice. They did not know the feeling of taking a place and keeping it, securing a village and then raising the flag and calling it a victory. No sense of order or momentum. No front, no rear, no trenches laid out in neat parallels. No Patton rushing for the Rhine, no beachheads to storm and win and hold for the duration. They did not have targets. They did not have a cause. They did not know if it was a war of ideology or economics or hegemony or spite. . . . They did not know how to feel when they saw villages burning. Revenge? Loss? Peace of mind or anguish? They did not know. They knew the old myths about Quang Ngai—tales passed down from old-timer to newcomer—but they did not know which stories to believe. Magic, mystery, ghosts and incense, whispers in the dark, strange tongues and strange smells, uncertainties never articulated in war stories, emotion squandered on ignorance. They did not know good from evil. (320–21)

Berlin claims the status of the imprisoned innocent, but his complicity in the pact to frag Sidney Martin is an indelible stain on the moral fabric of his interpretive project, a symbolic as well as real act indicating that a separate peace, if possible at all, will not allow the escapee to emerge sinless from this war. Sidney Martin is not a bad officer. Adhering to the standard of "mission over men," he enforces the formal SOPs and makes his men search tunnels, believing that war exists "so that through repetition men might try to do better . . . so that men might not be robbed of their own deaths" (201). Martin dies not because his classical standards of endurance,

courage, and achievement are innately wrong, but because they are
not shared. His fatal flaw is not understanding that the human
material he assumes is malleable to his precepts is most often "dull of
mind, blunt of spirit, numb of history" (204). When Martin's replacement, the overaged, tired, and forgetful Lieutenant Corson,
adheres to the informal procedures and has the men seal tunnels
without exploring their depths, he becomes the ideal leader, a figure-
head of the new standard within this historical configuration that
men always precede mission and that the things they do not know
dictate new terms for peace.

Because of the way memory and imagination interact, Berlin's
fabulation in the observation post is filled with constant peril and
prodigious obstacles. Imagination can deal with the practical problems. Berlin asserts confidently, "Money could be earned. Or stolen
or begged or borrowed. Passports could be forged, lies could be told,
cops could be bribed. A million possibilities. Means could be found"
(153). Certainly, the series of linked vignettes that make up the
sections of remembered experience in the novel contain enough
catalytic energy for Cacciato's flight, but memory also dictates the
course and the particulars of individual disaffiliation. John Updike
has noted that "there are no villains in this book, only villainous
circumstances" (130). The images of unacceptable history imprinted
in Berlin's memory infest the desired purity of imagination, place
tethers on the fantastic journey, and fill it with issues and impediments that reshape its contours and determine finally its indeterminate closure. If Going After Cacciato is magical realism, the magic
is filtered discernibly through the real, Berlin's combinative observa-
tion-post narrative existing in its finished form as an assay of both
fact and imagination, a textual sample of reciprocal mental activities.
When Berlin asserts, "It could truly be done" (154), he is thinking
practically but also enfolding the practical solutions with the larger
question of whether it should be done. Many voices are allowed to
enter the debate as the 3rd Squad, O'Brien's fantastic variation of
Del Vecchio's jungle think tank, tries to decide whether going after
Cacciato is pursuit or flight, the discovery of proper action or the
denial of personal and collective responsibility.

Beneath the ingenious workings of its textual alchemy, Cacciato
seems an intensely classical work, a feeling instilled by O'Brien's
placing the problematic history of the war in an expansive moral and
philosophical context. Updike has suggested of O'Brien that "his

essential contrast is not between Vietnam and other wars but between war and peace" (133). The reciprocal illumination of large
moral questions and immediate historical quandaries is O'Brien's
true goal; he illustrates how as memory and imagination interact,
they have as the material for their shared project those larger categories of tradition and new experience that appear antipathetic but
that are always in dialogic relationship with each other in a complex
historical configuration such as Vietnam. The war is both subject
and catalyst in *Cacciato*, historical energy powering the imaginative
trek to Paris as it is framed and illuminated by it. In his discussion
with Schroeder, O'Brien has suggested how the novel differs from
more traditional American war writing:

> I think that as an outside reader, if I were to pick up my book and
> read it, my feeling would be that I wasn't reading a war novel; I
> would perhaps feel that a trick had been played on me. Here's a
> book passing as a war novel, but it's not really that: it's not like
> *The Naked and the Dead*, it's not like Quentin Reynolds, it's not
> like Hemingway's war stuff. It's quirky. It goes somewhere else; it
> goes away from the war. It starts there and goes to Paris. A
> *peace* novel, in a sense. (144)

The primary value of O'Brien's quirkiness is that, by expanding the
limits of how Vietnam may be recorded and explored, by freeing it
from its time-bound historical condition and restoring it as a subject
for the free play of the imagination, he has helped to reinscribe and
to stress its active mythic status and to plant necessary signposts along
the road to Paris toward a credible public memory, toward the acceptable peace that Berlin seeks.

The influence of memory on the narrative in the tower produces
periodic nightmare within the dream of flight. At one juncture in
Tehran, Berlin and the 3rd Squad watch what Doc Peret calls "one
of those true spectacles of civilization" (222), the public beheading
of an Iranian youth that is a grisly symbol of the true inertia on the
road to Paris. "You try, you run like hell, but you just can't get
away" (223), observes Doc, and as Berlin reflects in the tower on
the unexpected course of his own narrative, he asks,

> Why, out of all that might have happened, did it lead to a behead-
> ing in Tehran? Why not pretty things? Why not a smooth, orderly
> arc from war to peace? These were the questions and the answers

could come only from hard observation. Doc was right about that.
He was right, too, that observation requires inward-looking, a study
of the very machinery of observation—the mirrors and filters and
wiring and circuits of the observing instrument. (247–48)

He discovers that the facts of war—the discontinuous narrative of
the real deaths of his peers—infect the imaginative journey but do not
define it; they shape the terms but do not dictate the nature of a
possible peace. "The facts," thinks Berlin, "even when beaded on a
chain still did not have real order. Events did not flow" (248); like
the war, the imagined escape is a series of starts and stops, unpleasant surprises and deadly impediments. Berlin, like Herr, discovers that imagination must be an active force on undifferentiated
historical data, but he learns by doing the unexpected twists and
turns offered by an unavoidable faithfulness to facts.

The issues of desertion and personal fear are the hub of the
debate on the road to Paris, and although Berlin is a discrete character—one complicating voice—within his own fictive project, all the
characters on the journey are aspects of his moral questioning, voices
that must declare for personal flight or the formal SOPs. Cacciato
and the other real members of the 3rd Squad mix with personages of
pure invention: Sarkin Aung Wan, Berlin's Vietnamese refugee
paramour who, beyond Cacciato himself, becomes the greatest champion of the imagination; Fahyi Rhallon, an officer of Iranian internal
security who is the most demanding reality principle; the Vietcong
major who instigates ideological discussion in the *Alice in Wonderland* tunnel complex. The members of the squad retain their real
personalities as they describe distinct positions on the significance
and ultimate goal of the journey; they both help to extend Berlin's
flight and provide the drag of reality on its progress. Soon after the
3rd Squad crosses the border into Laos, the men take a vote to continue the pursuit, but Harold Murphy dissents: "Desertion. . . .
That's the word. Running off like this, it's plain desertion. I say we
get our butts back to the war before things get worse" (54). Murphy
walks out of Berlin's narrative and back to the war. Corson accedes
to Cacciato's example and tries to declare a separate peace in Delhi,
but he validates Murphy's reading as he does so, asserting, "The
war's not over. We *left* the bloody war—walked away, ran. Understand that? No more crap about duty and mission. It's over" (211).
The squad, arrested in Tehran and sentenced to death as deserters,

is saved only by a miraculous jail break engineered by Cacciato as a failure of imagination is reversed by force of will, and in Athens, the pursuers depart ship and walk safely through a phalanx of police, the power of Berlin's dream shielding them from detection. But after they reach Paris successfully and search half-heartedly for their quarry as they sample the fruits of rediscovered Western civilization, Oscar Johnson restates the facts of desertion and decrees the new strategy: "Catch the dude, hogtie him, and bring him in. March him right into the U.S. embassy, plop him down on the bargainin' table. Then we got ourselves a negotiating position" (346). Berlin and Sarkin rent an apartment that symbolizes the apparent victory of imagination, but the pull of fear, conscience, and obligation remains, not to be denied even in the parks and cafés of Paris.

The negotiating position of the imagination is a formidable one. In the chapter called "World's Greatest Lake Country," Berlin recalls how Cacciato deals with the pact to terminate Martin. Sitting before a rain-filled bomb crater with a line and a bobber, Cacciato fishes through the sheer power of imagination, telling Berlin that he is receiving "little nibbles, but the real thing. You can always tell" (284). The nibbles become "a real strong bite" as Berlin tries to get Cacciato to seal the pact by touching the grenade, but the fisherman offers a lesson of his own:

Cacciato's eyes never left the bobber in Lake Country. Releasing the boy's hand, Paul Berlin put the grenade away and watched as Cacciato played with the line as though feeling for weight, for life at the other end. He was smiling. His attention was entirely on the bobbing Secret in Lake Country. (286–87)

Suggesting that the peace of a big two-hearted river is possible even in the midst of a thousand bomb craters, Cacciato advises that through patience and concentration, the proper exercising of the imagination can be achieved. Within the real events of the war, Berlin finds a model for his own fishing expedition in the observation post: " 'Sucker took my bait.' Cacciato winked. 'But next time I'll nail him. Now that I got the technique' " (287).

Berlin's own developing technique powers Cacciato and the 3rd Squad to Paris, but in "The End of the Road to Paris," Berlin faces Sarkin Aung Wan, the new spokesperson for the untethered imagination, in his inward-looking version of the Paris peace talks. Encour-

aging Berlin to take the final step, Sarkin restates and extends Cacciato's position:

> "Having dreamed a marvelous dream, I urge you to step boldly
> into it, to join your own dream and to live it. Do not be deceived
> by false obligation. You are obliged, by all that is just and good,
> to pursue only the felicity that you yourself have imagined. Do not
> let fear stop you." (375)

Fear of censure, fear of reneging on obligations, and, beyond all, fear
of cowardice provide Berlin with his own necessary retorts, and as
reality makes its last appeal to dream, he asks,

> "Are these fears wrong? Are they stupid? Or are they healthy and
> right? I have been told to ignore my fear of censure and embar-
> rassment and loss of reputation. But would it not be better to
> accept those fears? To yield to them? If inner peace is the true ob-
> jective, would I win it in exile?" (377)

"Imagination, like reality, has its limits," concludes Berlin; the
necessary exploration of creative possibilities is insufficient to produce
the desired historical conclusion: "There is no true negotiation.
There is only the statement of positions" (378), he admits, but the
failure to write the final peace does not signify the uselessness of the
activity in the observation post. In his final meditation before daylight, Berlin prepares to return to the war with the knowledge gained
within the imaginative negotiations: "There was still a war and he
was still a soldier. He hadn't run. The issue was courage, and courage
was will power, and this was his failing" (379). He does not follow
Sarkin's beckoning, but his victory is the illumination and clarification fostered by the meeting of fact and fancy. The willed ingenuity
in the observation post produces finally a classical boon—self-knowl-
edge within travail, the partial ordering of chaos that even a statement
of positions can provide, the move toward, if not the attainment of,
a proper peace.

Going After Cacciato ends with a renewed challenge to both
memory and imagination. Berlin does not make up Cacciato's departure, but extrapolates from the facts in an imaginative feat of
revised historiography. For the rest of the 3rd Squad and for the
reader, the first chapter of an incomplete text is inscribed in experience, waiting for new war historians:

So the facts were simple: They went after Cacciato, they chased him into the mountains, they tried hard. They cornered him on a small grassy hill. They surrounded the hill. They waited through the night. And at dawn they shot the sky full of flares and then moved in. "Go," Paul Berlin said. He shouted it—"Go!"

That was the end of it. The last known fact.

What remained were possibilities. With courage it might have been done. (380)

In fear, Berlin fires his rifle, and Cacciato does escape, somewhere, even to Paris, if the imagination can sustain and find a moral center within such a venture. Corson concludes of the botched real pursuit that precedes Berlin's narrative, "I guess it's better this way. . . . And who knows? He might make it. He might do all right" (395). O'Brien's final implication is that several roads to Paris must wind through many more imaginations, each one necessary, each one an ordering principle for the unacceptable history of this war. As Cacciato and Berlin have already surmised, there are thousands of bomb craters in Lake Country, and a line and bobber for each one.

5

SHADES OF RETRIEVAL

This is not a settled life. A children's breakfast cereal, Crispy Critters, provokes nausea; there is a women's perfume named Charlie; and the radio sound of "We Gotta Get Out of This Place" (The Animals, 1965) fills me with a melancholy as petrifying as the metal poured into casts of galloping cavalry, squinting riflemen, proud generals, statues in the park, roosts for pigeons. My left knee throbs before each thunderstorm. The sunsets are no damn good here. There are ghosts on my television set.

MEDITATIONS IN GREEN

I told him my journey to the Zone was a necessity, and not a beginning but an end. A period to one sentence and after the period a long pause before beginning another. The Zone, I said, was the place where modern American history begins.

THE AMERICAN BLUES

The cultural trauma induced by World War I was captured best in American literature not in graphic portrayal of the new horrors of modern warfare but in a small study in noncommunication. Hemingway's short story "Soldier's Home" features a returned American veteran named Krebs, who appears outwardly the same young man who went off to fight at Belleau Wood and in the Argonne, but who has been inwardly transformed by the experience. Hemingway communicates the shattering effects of Krebs's war not so much by what is said but by what is not. The postwar experience is a silent naming of parts, the identification of the discrepancy between happy appearances and the psychological and emotional realities that language cannot be trusted to express. Distrust of received language is in tension with the private need to order the experience, however, to articulate it in such a way that its lessons are not falsified by a convenient closure.

When Krebs's mother tries to motivate her son to reintegrate himself into established social patterns, she resorts to an appeal that to Krebs, the bearer of new cultural knowledge, is unacceptable. Encouraging him to consider some normal employment that will halt his aimless drifting, she suggests, "God has some work for every one to do. . . . There can be no idle hands in His Kingdom," a throwback to prewar values that prompts in her son only resentment and embarrassment and the simple reply, "I'm not in His Kingdom" (151). Because Krebs cannot communicate successfully his new personal knowledge to those who have not seen the war, he continues to drift from his family at the story's end, contemplating a nonfuture in Kansas City, wanting only to live, as he puts it, "without consequences." He realizes that to tell comforting lies is to lose the "cool, valuable quality" of the few true lessons he has learned. Hemingway makes clear that, despite the nature of what his hero has witnessed, Krebs has something of value at his private core that language is likely only to diminish. The buried lesson is small but irreducible. In an important passage, Hemingway sketches Krebs's necessary comparison of private and public narratives, an emotional and intellectual process that is the true inscribing of his war's significance:

> He sat there on the porch reading a book on the war. It was a history and he was reading about all the engagements he had been in. It was the most interesting reading he had ever done. He wished there were more maps. He looked forward with a good feeling to reading all the really good histories when they would come out with good detail maps. Now he was learning about the war. He had been a good soldier. That made a difference. (148)

The irony of Krebs's "learning about the war" from reading history is unmistakable, but it is Hemingway's emphasis on what "made a difference" that recommends "Soldier's Home" as an important touchstone for appraising the Vietnam works that explore the condition of the returned veteran.

To conclude a war with written treaties is not to end it in a cultural sense; the commitment of a nation's human, economic, and technological resources to warfare creates a powerful historical momentum that produces aftershocks and makes demands within a national narrative long after the troops, victorious or defeated, have returned home. Hemingway's Krebs might be a new figure to himself—a transformed sensibility whose new knowledge makes familiar cultural patterns obsolete on a personal level—but as symbol of an unviolated national narrative, the returned World War I veteran presented little danger to the powerful myths that fostered modern warfare. The Hun was defeated, the warriors returned, the bands played, the speeches reverberated, and the celebrations were conducted within a continuing American historical fabulation. The lessons that prompted the modernist experiments of Hemingway, Cummings, and Dos Passos resulted in a new aesthetic stance toward history, one coexisting antagonistically with the reading of World War I as a successful crusade that had been concluded with the national components of virtue, idealism, and purpose intact. The many complaints against such a reading in postwar writing—demands that the darker aspects of culture that produced the carnage be considered—did not dislodge the popular narrative but persisted as counterstatements to it and as the stuff of compensatory history, the aesthetic project of the new antiwar novel.

For Hemingway and company, the shock of the new was synonymous with the decay of the old, but the Lost Generation sensibility was an aesthetically antagonistic minority voice contending with but not overthrowing collective memory.[1] The soldiers of World War II read and assimilated the warnings of the modernists, but they fought in Europe and in the Pacific without the profound sense of shock or protest of their predecessors. To perceive the clear and present historical danger of a Third Reich and a Japanese empire did not make the American soldier the idealistic crusader of World War I, but the perception did suggest that heroes and villains were still viable categories, that aspects of virtue and idealism remained applicable with more worldly sophistication and in less vainglorious tones than those of the earlier quest to save Western values. Despite the shadows cast in 1945 by the clouds over Hiroshima and Nagasaki, specific, private horrors were reconciled within the larger narrative of a shared, necessary struggle, and the returning American combatant was celebrated as the representative of a national commitment. The World War II protest fiction focusing on the endangered individual trapped within huge industrial forces—works such as *Catch-22*, *Slaughter-house-Five*, *The Thin Red Line*, and *Gravity's Rainbow*—appeared well after the myth of the well-conducted team effort had been permanently inscribed, and the late-blooming protesters had less effect in contending with the reconciled history of World War II than had the earlier contingent of the 1920s and 1930s—whose shock was deeper and whose aesthetic sorties were more concerted and prolonged—with the collective memory of World War I. After both wars, the shared sense of the desired American victory did much to defuse both the vociferous protests and the quieter reports of the returned veterans. Beyond his often real condition as a figure who was physically or psychologically debilitated by his admittance to a twentieth-century nightmare, the American veteran of either conflict could be incorporated successfully within comforting mythic patterns. He had fought and won, and his broken body or spirit could be repaired or, at the very least, explained.

The American veteran of the Vietnam War—the most immediately visible symbol of national will, virtue, and idealism in Indochina—often found on his return that Krebs's assertion of personal competence making a difference had become an unstable historical proposition. The country could not correlate the historical data of Vietnam with traditional mythic patterns and celebrate the hero's return as the final typological act in a continuing national drama. It chose instead to cancel the performance with what Caputo calls collective amnesia or to cast the veteran in a new role. Rather than the garlanded symbol of national goodness, the Vietnam veteran often became the despised and feared Other, the scapegoat for a variety of ills, the greatest of which was the failure to secure the familiar, unambiguous historical closure that is called victory. The veterans of World Wars I and II, despite their many individual refusals to celebrate the carnage of modern warfare, could not escape the happy inscription of their feats within the master narrative. The Vietnam veterans, feeling that they had performed as required, found dark new fabulations at home rather than gratitude or understanding.

The Vietnam veteran returned home to find he was still surrounded by enemies, and his new mythic status as scapegoat achieved quick prominence through the conduits of popular culture. George Swiers, a spokesman for the Vietnam Veterans of America and a decorated combatant himself, has described how the Vietnam veteran, surprised by and angered at the embarrassment and forgetfulness he induced, was metamorphosed into a new brand of cultural signifier, one that was asked to bear the weight of national historical neurosis:

> Hollywood, ever bizarre in its efforts to mirror life, discovered a marketable villain. *Kojack, Ironside,* and the friendly folks at *Hawaii Five-O* confronted crazed, heroin-addicted veterans with the regularity and enthusiasm Saturday morning heroes once dispensed with godless red savages. No grade-B melodrama was complete without its standard vet—a psychotic, ax-wielding rapist every bit as insulting as another one-time creature of Hollywood's imagination, the shiftless, lazy, and wide-eyed black. The demented-vet portrayal has become so casual, so commonplace, that one pictures the children of Vietnam veterans shivering beneath their blankets and wondering if Daddy will come in with a good-night kiss or a Black & Decker chain saw. (198)

To cast the veteran as a debilitated and dangerous domestic agent, to make of him an infestation that threatens national moral and social equilibrium, is to indulge in the most convenient historical metonymy. Separating the most readily available symbol of American will and idea from what produced it and forcing that figure to play the whipping boy for the whole is to attempt to heal collective wounds in a delusory way. As Swiers contends, "The myth of 2.5 million walking time bombs tells us that someone, somewhere, in some way, is paying the price for our national sin" (198).

To ask the veteran to play the villain is a way to quiet a loud memory, to rewrite a new national narrative so that it can be joined, without disturbance, to older ones. The human instruments of an aberrant American war must be aberrant themselves, or so the mythic syllogism would have it. But to sacrifice the Vietnam veteran on an altar of national humiliation or bad conscience or to exorcise him as a discomforting historical Doppelgänger is only to refuse the real lessons of Vietnam and to miss the opportunity to discover a national virtue that originates in experience rather than desire. Gloria Emerson has noted how notions of infirmity fostered a convenient failure of memory:

> I sometimes think there is a conspiracy to show the weaknesses and the grief, not the strengths, of Vietnam veterans. Because we see the Vietnam veteran as kind of a crazy, inadequate, second-rate, feeble, advanced neurasthenic, we never have to face Vietnam. Or

face what was required of him. We can keep our distance. ("Vietnam Veterans Speak" 183)

What the treatment of the veteran as either threat or damaged goods allows is the preservation of the American idea of Vietnam at the expense of its instrumentality. High motives can be reaffirmed by assuming a new form of American victimization. In short, if the conveniently denoted monsters now stalking our own shores are not of our own making, American innocence survives history.

The kind of portraiture Swiers and Emerson describe has been modified in recent times by renewed attempts to reinscribe the war as an American moral crusade. Films centering on the rescue of MIAs in present-day Vietnam, such as *Uncommon Valor* and *Rambo*, offer avenging veterans who still show signs of derangement, hostility, and residual shock but who now become the victims striking back not at the American mythic machinery that made them instruments of national will, but at updated Vietnamese stereotypes (and their inhuman Russian advisers). What seems most dangerous in such convenient extensions of conventional history is the disproportionate emphasis placed on the American avenger as victim and the denial of American failings through the doubling back of the veteran's rage against a venal enemy. The veteran as historical avenger becomes a different kind of scapegoat, one who ceases to be a social threat or embarrassment by serving as the refashioned tool with which mythic desire may write the desired conclusion, which was unavailable in the real jungles and villages of Vietnam. If the images of the final flight in 1975 from the American embassy in Saigon signified the most unacceptable closure imaginable, the avenging veteran becomes a corrective for the skewed narrative. As he saves his buddies from the prison camps of the enemy, he rights symbolically the wrongs of his nation. This evening of scores is an exploitation of a complex tragedy, however, a poaching on history. The veteran is done no more service by the new stereotype of the avenger than he is by those of ax-wielder or time bomb. Behind all the flickering images, ominous or comforting, the human dimension of the soldier's experience remains absent.

Beneath the layers of stereotypes of the Vietnam veteran resides the true legacy of the war: an inadequate GI Bill; health facilities illequipped or unwilling to deal with physical and psychological wounds; problems of readjustment, unemployment, and drug addiction; and postwar possibilities unique to this war—the threat to the mind of delayed-stress syndrome and to the body of the chemical mixture of 2, 4, 5-T and 2, 4-D known as Agent Orange. The dioxin used in the herbicide program is the most virulent symbol of the new variations of American cultural cause and effect in Vietnam. Residing in a dormant state in the body's fatty tissue, attacking suddenly other parts of the organism with no warning and with dire effect, it is the most horrible historical reminder of how synonymous the terms "agent" and "victim" were during the war. George Ewalt, Jr., a veteran who suffered a variety of physical problems after being in contact with herbicides, has described the carelessness, intentional or unintentional, of the users of the chemicals: "I believe that the army knew that the herbicides would not only punish the Vietnamese but also us, the survivors" (192). As one of the afflicted, however, Ewalt does not skirt the issue of complicity:

> During my tour in Vietnam, we were never informed of the herbicide program that has come to be known as Agent Orange. We drank the water from the streams and rivers and bathed in it. My tour was over on February 24, 1968, during the Tet offensive. We devastated the land, the trees, the rivers, and the people. The final result was that Vietnam was turned into an ashtray. We will always live with what we killed in Vietnam. (192)

Over 17 million gallons of herbicides—Agents Pink, Purple, Blue, and White as well as Orange—were used in Vietnam to deny the enemy the protection of vegetation, but what Herr calls the unannounced scorched-earth policy merely heightened the mixture of guilt and bitterness carried home by the Americans. In regard to both variables in the historical legacy, Ewalt attempts to speak for all the veterans when he says, "We are not asking for your pity, but only to be treated fairly" (195).

The Vietnam Veterans Memorial in Washington is perceived by many to be long-overdue recognition of the price paid by the American soldier, but the unstable, changing nature of national response to the veteran continues to make it an ambiguous artifact. The argument that the war was indeed a moral crusade misperceived by media and public and badly executed in the field is a historical proposition at the center of much current revisionist history. A block of stone may be a powerful text with many subtexts, or it may be an inert simplification of historical reality that assuages memory—it depends on the readership. In *Why We Were in Vietnam*, Norman Podhoretz attempts to catalyze the national healing process by reinscribing the mythic strands of the City on the Hill, but his argument, like a partial consideration of the black stone V, expunges admissions of wrongdoing as it underscores once again notions of indigenous virtue. Says Podhoretz,

> When Ronald Reagan, an unrepentant hawk, called the war "a noble cause" in the course of his ultimately successful campaign to replace Carter in the White House, he was accused of having made a "gaffe." Fully, painfully aware as I am that the American effort to save Vietnam from Communism was indeed beyond our intellectual and moral capabilities, I believe the story shows that Reagan's "gaffe" was closer to the truth of why we were in Vietnam and what we did there, at least until the very end, than Carter's denigration of an act of imprudent idealism whose moral soundness has been so overwhelmingly vindicated by the hideous consequences of our defeat. (210)

The testimony of the veterans comprises the necessary counterstatements to revisions such as Podhoretz's. Mixtures of rage and regret, guilt and expiation, their reports point steadfastly to the complexity and to the continuing influence of the historical configuration in which the American soldier was both brutal agent and endangered species. The need to articulate the experience is great, for, as George Swiers contends, "if we do not speak of it, others will surely rewrite the script. Each of the body bags, all of the mass graves will be reopened and their contents abracadabra-ed into a noble cause" (199).

The novelists who attempt to complicate the report by rendering in fiction the difficulties of the veteran's return offer necessary replies to comforting revisions and reconciled myth. As compensatory history, their fictions contain their own organic definitions of what a noble cause entails, knowledge originating in the dark data of a configuration already receded into private and public memory. Swiers summarizes the novelist's task when he speaks of the duty of each veteran: "A veteran who endures, and survives, the trauma of war has a moral obligation to articulate that experience to others. Not to do so is to totally abdicate one's responsibilities to the living, the once-living, and to generations yet unborn" (200). Hemingway's Krebs perceives that being a good soldier makes a difference, and he bears his lessons silently. The writers of Vietnam, attempting to fashion aesthetically an acceptable closure for their war, contend that what matters is not only the soldier's experience, but also the archival work that places the personal knowledge into public domain.

The great majority of Vietnam War novels and memoirs have as their substance the immediate experience of life at its dark center. They examine how the values of the participant—whether he is initially confident, ambivalent, or resistant to his immersion—are modified, transformed, or plowed under by the shattering effects and narrative inconsistencies of the new history he is helping to write. Of those works that end with the new American protagonist still in the jungle, the reader is left with the questions of what reassimilation into a suddenly alien American cultural grid will entail and whether physical return to "the World" can be accompanied by the necessary psychological, emotional, or spiritual adjustments that will allow the veteran to close the cover of the most threatening historical tract.

A reader can imagine only with difficulty Del Vecchio's Chelini sleeping peacefully without an M-16 close by, Hasford's Joker walking a country lane without studying the ground for booby traps, or O'Brien's Paul Berlin spending a week by the sea without the memory of beckoning tunnel complexes. The imaginative challenge inherent in the works that supply the narrative closure of the hero's return is not only assimilating, ordering, and interpreting the data they assemble, but also projecting the contours and particulars of the life that follows it. As Berlin and the 3rd Squad discover in *Going After Cacciato*, the fall into the entrapping history of this war is violent and unexpected, and clean escape from it seems improbable. Like the war, the peace that follows, if it is attained at all, will be a hazardous, intricate work of the imagination and the will, a retrospective ordering of chaos no less crucial than the improvised survival skills—the informal SOPs—needed by the soldier operating within the tangible threats of his war. What is likely, and what is asserted by the novelists and memorialists who treat at least partially the postwar experience, is that the war continues to be an active force long after its visible signs are gone. As recurring nightmare, as personal obsession, as historical enigma, the war returns with the veteran not as an inert cultural organism in a body bag but as the potential for renewed upheaval, for real catastrophe.

Those works that include the soldier's reentry into American society begin to sketch the continuing cultural repercussions of the fissures produced by Vietnam in the traditional American mythic pattern. Because the veteran cannot be celebrated as the crowning symbol of a successful national commitment, he is condemned to carry his new knowledge in silence. He is not perceived as the bearer of a great historical boon; instead, he is both participant in and witness to a national accident that few are interested in assessing or reliving after its apparent end. Rather than a conduit of insight, or even wisdom, he is the catalyst for embarrassment, anger, frustration, recrimination, and apology.

A prime theme in the works that deal even partially with the postwar experience is the radical difference in sensibility between those who have experienced the war and those who have not. The intensity of the experience—its horrible realities, its deep bonding of individuals within the most primal travail—produces a sense of anticlimax concerning everything that follows it. The deeply entrenched moral and ideological ambiguities of Vietnam exacerbate rather than diminish the primacy of new history as personal transformation. Because the war placed more individual pressures on the entrapped combatant to reconcile theory and practice than any previous American conflict, the returned veteran in fiction and memoir often experiences the strangest form of nostalgia for the war, a connection that makes the available social patterns and institutions at home seem pallid, delusory, somehow unreal. Of his feelings on return, Caputo states,

> In spite of everything, we felt a strange attachment to Vietnam and, even stranger, a longing to return. The war was still being fought, but this desire to return did not spring from any patriotic ideas about duty, honor, and sacrifice, the myths with which old men send young men off to get killed and maimed. It arose, rather, from a recognition of how deeply we had been changed, how different we were from everyone who had not shared with us the miseries of the monsoon, the exhausting patrols, the fear of a combat assault on a hot landing zone. We had very little in common with them. Though we were civilians again, the civilian world seemed alien. We did not belong to it as much as we did to that other world, where we had fought and our friends had died. (*Rumor of War* xvi)

The bitterness accompanied by nostalgia in Caputo is not always shared by other writers. In most, however, the personal significance of Vietnam heightens for the returned veteran the indifference, obfuscation, or willed forgetfulness he confronts within a newly alien domestic landscape. In *Born on the Fourth of July*, Ron Kovic rages against the uncaring attitudes he experiences and observes in veterans' hospitals, but his real adversary is the sequestering and rewriting of his experience within official narrative and public memory at the expense of its historical reality, the shattered men who ask only for fair treatment for their sacrifice. Like Kovic's memoir, Charles Coleman's novel *Sergeant Back Again* explores the veteran's battle with history in the context of physical and psychological rehabilitation in a veterans' hospital where the crippled warriors prompt more contempt and indifference than sympathy and understanding. Surrounding the immediate tasks of resurrecting body and mind from the effects of Vietnam is the equally pressing project of ordering memory, of writing a collective record that will not be lost within perceptions of the veteran as merely damaged or even disposable goods. Like Kovic, Coleman argues that the veteran requires more than rehabilitation. He needs to explain his experiences to himself and to those willing to listen. As Caputo suggests, however, the difficulty lies in explaining the aspects of personal transformation and new historical data in a culture of willed forgetfulness.

If disorientation and rage are concomitants of the Vietnam veteran's reentry, so is the issue of personal and collective guilt. The strong bonds and the intensity of the personal experience forged by the soldier's unusual historical position are complicated by deep feelings of complicity, wrongdoing, violent transgression. The returned warrior is not raised within collective myth as the familiar American victor; nor is he likely to reiterate on an individual level Krebs's identification of what makes a difference. James Webb's *Fields of Fire* offers an ambivalent soldier named Goodrich, whose inability to separate ideological resistance from necessary survival skills produces real human disaster in the field. Wounded in action, he returns home and is quickly exploited as a symbol of an unjust war by a campus antiwar group. But his uncertainty concerning political realities, moral imperatives, and personal ties to those dead or left behind continues. Trapped between his opposition to the war he has left behind and the deadly homilies of those who have not lived through its emotional and ideological dispersions, he is at novel's end the new historical isolate whose quotients of guilt and anger remain warring factions.

Larry Heinemann's *Close Quarters* concludes with the protagonist Philip Dosier's visit to the mother of his dead friend Quinn, a meeting in which the veteran's true report remains his secret as he merely explains that his comrade had been a good soldier willing to sacrifice himself for his peers. The reader, however, has been privy to the data that Dosier keeps secreted, the awareness of his and Quinn's capacities for cruelty, for killing without remorse, for moral callousness. The discrepancy between the sanitized Vietnam report that Dosier gives to Quinn's mother and the acquired knowledge of true historical evil is no less striking a closure than the conclusion of *Heart of Darkness*, but Heinemann, like Conrad, transmits to the reader what Dosier cannot: the knowledge of personal and collective transgression that is mixed inextricably with assertions of national sacrifice.

The conclusion of Jack Fuller's *Fragments* is a study of the guilt and expiation of a returned veteran in powerful symbolic terms. Having attempted to play savior to the people of a Vietnamese village, Fuller's hero, Neumann, must return to America with the knowledge that the mixture of idealism and engineering principles he applied within the village has resulted in the deaths of a number of Vietnamese, including a young girl he had come to love. The climax of Fuller's narrative is the meeting between Neumann and his best friend, Morgan, in which the former's sudden epiphany of the tragedy he has brought about almost results in new disaster. Morgan helps his friend begin the painful process of personal regeneration, but Neumann, mistaking dark memories for present realities, comes close to shooting his uncomprehending young daughter with the shotgun he carries as he relives the history he has kept only half-buried. Fuller shows through both his veterans not only the residual effects on personal sensibility of broken American myth—Morgan can sleep peacefully his first night home only by wrapping himself in his poncho liner on the cold concrete floor of the family garage—but also the unprecedented personal difficulties that arise when memory invariably produces a tension between guilt and victimization. Like Graham Greene's Alden Pyle, Neumann sees his attempts to inscribe in Vietnam the history he desires have tragic effect, but, unlike his foreshadower, he becomes his own judge and jury, a fully realized symbol of the enormous personal and national price paid for historical consciousness.

Of the works that deal centrally with the postwar experience, two recent novels are a striking stylistic contrast of how the Vietnam veteran's memory may be fictively explored. Stephen Wright's *Meditations in Green*, the fragmented, nervous, ominously malevolent account of a returned veteran, and Ward Just's *The American Blues*, the quietly meditative study of a journalist's obsession with the war, meet at the same historical nexus, the place within memory that contends that the war can end only when one recognizes that the war is not over. With divergent aesthetic strategies, Wright and Just argue that a credible public memory can be achieved not by burying or rewriting Vietnam's most persistent lessons, but by confronting them. Peace with honor, they assert, cannot simply be proclaimed. It must be personally and culturally earned.

When Converse, the heroin-smuggling correspondent of Robert Stone's *Dog Soldiers*, is preparing to return to the United States from Vietnam, Hicks, the American samurai who is transporting the drugs and who will eventually refight the war in the hills of California, tells him, "You'd better be careful. . . . It's gone funny in the states," an assertion that elicits from the would-be dope dealer the rejoinder, "It can't be funnier than here" (57). Converse's throwaway moment of comparative sociology, in which the data of Vietnam are connected to new developments, identifies another central theme in Vietnam War writing dealing with the postwar experience, that Vietnam is only the most visible promontory of a transformed American cultural landscape, that the indiscriminate violence, moral decay, and social fragmentation that fester behind the seamless official narrative of the war have become principal features of life in the United States as well. Vietnam not only has informed American sensibility of the blacker aspects within the national soul, but also has enhanced and legitimized them.

What Stone's veterans discover is that the new survival skills forged within the history lesson of Vietnam are mandatory in an America where greed and violence are omnipresent. Illusions of national virtue and good will have been scoured away by the concentrated mixture of American will and idea in Vietnam; new attitudes and practices are already set in place and operating without resistance. Converse summarizes the war not as moral crusade or geopolitical necessity but as pedagogic device and reality principle: "This is the place where everybody finds out who they are." Hicks responds to his associate's Americanization of Vietnam with the simple observation, "What a bummer for the gooks," but Converse extends his

thought with a statement that both speaks to the national loss of innocence and suggests why postwar America will be its own redefined
war zone: "You can't blame us too much. We didn't know who we
were till we got here. We thought we were something else" (57).

For Hicks and Converse, the educational quality of Vietnam and
the persistence of its lessons at home make the veteran's personal regeneration a nonissue. Life in Stone's postwar America is neither the
successful ordering of the past nor a coherent envisioning of the future, but the moment-to-moment practice of the art of self-defense.
Stone achieves his horrible vision of cultural shift by tracing how a
historical narrative such as the Vietnam War inflicts not only its substance but also its tone and style on its authors and readers. The return home of Converse and Hicks is not the beginning of recovery
from a terrible historical moment but a new encounter with its domestic variant, which is presented as a larger version of the affliction.

Stone's novel is horrific because his characters do not even hope
for personal regeneration after the war. Stephen Wright's *Meditations
in Green* achieves its chilling effects by assuming the same cultural
continuity between war and postwar sensibility that Stone does—the
proposition that the war is not a bracketed aberration of American
history but the new imprint of what the culture has become. Wright's
hero, returned veteran James Griffin, however, strives to reintegrate
body, mind, and spirit in an America that is no less a new wasteland
than the extended battlefield of *Dog Soldiers*. Stone's nightmare is an
America of only two classes: parasites and their victims. The darkness
in Wright's narrative resides in Griffin's failed attempt to become a
self-generating third proposition: a survivor who, surrounded by urban decay and trapped within disordered, ghastly memory, can claim
some variety of healthy organic life. The threats to his project are not
only the residue of what he became in Vietnam, a heroin-addicted,
fragmented sensibility, but also the present influences in his un-
named American city that encourage continued dissolution, paranoia,
and alienation. The war was the most jarring historical education, but
the contemporary urban existence that follows it is postgraduate
work in booby traps and defense perimeters. For Wright's veteran,
postwar America is not fertile ground for personal retrieval but the
likelihood that the cultural possibilities that the war illustrated and
energized will achieve increasingly virulent permutations.

Griffin's aides-de-camp in his attempted postwar recovery are Dr.
Arden, a therapist who is the author of a pastiche of botanical sci-

ence, pop psychology, and mystical musings called *The Psychology of the Plant*, and Huette "Huey" Mirandella, a young social worker who, as Griffin's confidante and part-time paramour, is a concentrated example of the surreal combinations and bizarre pathways of the contemporary American self-help project. Griffin's main conduit to the rootless survivalist sensibility already set in place in America, Huey— her name an ironic reference for Griffin to a helicopter, another instrument of American mobility—is both reflection of and encouragement for the hero's desperate improvisations:

> When I met her she was twenty-two years, she studied Chinese, played electric guitar, read a science fiction novel every two days, practiced a lethal form of martial arts once a week with a garageful of women, painted vast oil abstracts she called soulographs, and speculated that if there was another Renaissance lurking about the bloody horizon of our future then she was a candidate to be its Leonardo—"the smart clichés of a pop life." (5)

A personality already acclimated to a postwar cultural climate in which substance has given way to pure style, coherence to contradiction, depth to surface, Huey is the perfect critic and editor for Griffin's attempt to write a new personal history.

The chief architect of Griffin's desired reintegration, however, is Arden, "the messiah of the advent of vegetable consciousness" (88), who selects for each of his patients a personal flower, or "flow-image," on which the subject focuses his daily meditations. Hoping to find both release from the horrible iconography of Vietnam and a pathway to an acceptable future, Griffin listens to the therapist's exhortation to "Think green!" and strives to apply the guru's "organic calculus" as a corrective for personal dissolution and fragmentation. The mental discipline of visualizing the self as a healthy flower is a less powerful historical antidote, however, than Griffin's renewed acquaintance with the hallucinatory qualities of the real plant called the poppy. Huey's brother Rafer, an urban analogue to the jungle guerrilla, is the executive officer of a local street gang with whom Griffin has spent time "comparing scars, tattoos, chatting about the effects of various arms and pharmaceuticals" (6). Arden may encourage the broken hero to undertake an arduous mystical path to regeneration that even Griffin suspects to be a happy delusion, but Rafer, the "adolescent able to weld a connection into the high-voltage Oriental drug terminals" (7), provides Griffin with heroin, the true link between wartime and postwar states of mind. As Griffin breathes in again, in the novel's opening sequences, the substance that centered his personal history in Vietnam and that now is the most powerful mnemonic device, he offers himself to the reader as the most problematic historian, "your genial storyteller, wreathed in a beard of smoke" whose service it is to "look into the light and recite tales from the war back in the long time ago" (8).

Wright's creation of a narrator whose oral history is a series of horrific memories suspended in drug reverie—the essential interpenetration of a fragmented past and a disordered present—would seem to recommend *Meditations in Green* as the most recent candidate for James Wilson's "dope and dementia" bookshelf. Like Michael Herr, Wright argues that the essential history of this war cannot be communicated in detached reporting or revisionist glossing but through the necessary inventions by which consciousness traces the link between original experience and continuing influence on the deepest emotional and psychological levels. Wright reexamines through his botanical metaphors the challenge of building the necessary aesthetic equipment with which the unique cultural significance of Vietnam may be articulated, but, with Griffin's postwar project of personal regeneration, he also extends Herr's final assertion in *Dispatches* that the war continues to exert mythic pressure long after it has been tagged and filed away within official narrative.[2]

The returned veteran in Wright's America discovers that moving beyond the memory of the war experience is as unlikely as the successful ordering of it. As a continuing influence, Vietnam dictates the terms of the peace and creates real upheaval when its essential data are ignored or artificially reconciled. Griffin's reacquaintance with heroin may wrap memory in a hallucinatory haze, but it also heightens its colors and sharpens its contours. An apparent historical escape mechanism, a deflection of horror and guilt, Griffin's addiction, like the national amnesia that Caputo describes, is also a guarantee of deeper confrontations with the war, the exacting of unpaid debts. Walter Kendrick notes in his discussion of the novel that for Griffin and his peers, "the past will not fade; it masters them still" (24). But Wright applies the same proposition to the culture that receives the returned vet. Its failure to confront the history it has inscribed with bombs, chemical agents, and the blood of its warriors ensures its continued dissolution, its evolving psychosis.

As the "genial storyteller," Griffin transports the reader back to a

Vietnam War that is a gradual descent into historical madness, a deep encounter with American will exercising its darkest compulsions. He begins his tour of duty in a safe, sequestered position as an "image interpreter" for the 1069th Military Intelligence Group. It is his job to examine film negatives in order to locate the enemy and to assess the quality of the air strikes called in on them: "Wherever he put circles on the film there the air force would make holes in the ground" (43). He is later assigned to report the effects of the herbicide program. As one instrument of a new historical practice, he begins as an innocent among innocents: "The first time I heard of Agent Orange," Griffin tells the soldier educating him in the workings of chemical death, "I saw a piece of fruit wrapped in a trenchcoat" (131). But his is not the only ingenuous sensibility. He examines one of the defoliation aircraft and sees the inscription WE EAT FORESTS and rows of small trees drawn with red Xs through them. When he asks the pilot if the new chemicals are safe, the redefined combat ace charting his prowess in slain vegetation dips a finger into the flowing defoliant and sticks it into his mouth. Like Griffin, the other agents of American improvisation—the 4-H Club, as the crews call themselves—cannot begin to guess the full nature of the historical imprint they are carving in the green jungle.

Griffin's distance from the effects he charts and interprets begins to produce uneasiness, fragmentation, dark intuition. The images he studies square inch by square inch, he senses, are dead signifiers of the deeper history lessons dwelling behind them, a play of light and shadow that offers surface without depth. He fills his empty hours by educating himself in the effects of other chemical agents, and as he moves from dabbling in pot to daily sessions with heroin, he experiences a growing need to move from the periphery of his war to its beckoning center. When he goes aloft with one of the aerial photographers, he sees first hand the Ho Chi Minh Trail, whose images he has studied so often, and is "astonished at the difference between the insignificant tracings on a map and the broad avenue of actuality" (216). When his plane is hit by ground fire and nearly downed, he receives immediate evidence that the confidence he helps to foster in official history is unwarranted, that holes in the ground and chemically induced scorched earth do not signify an imminent or even distant victory.

At one juncture, Wright offers his storyteller's retrospective vision of what has become of the intelligence compound after the

American withdrawal from Vietnam—a projection in which the triumphant enemy is assisted by the regenerating vegetation that the herbicide dispensers had tried to expunge:

> No, I can see them still, those huddled ramshackle structures. They didn't even bother to dismantle them, torch the planks with souvenir Zippos. The ultimate insult: they ignored them, left all that Western redundance and engineered craziness to time and rain and wind. . . . Between the floorboards poke the tender tips of new life, shoots of marijuana, naturally. There is growth everywhere. Plants have taken the compound. Elephant grass in the motor pool. Plantain in the mess hall. Lotus in the latrine. Shapes are losing outline, character. Wooden frames turn spongy. The attrition of squares and rectangles. The loss of geometry. Form is emptiness, emptiness is form.
>
> Mind is a magpie. (145–46)

In his postwar urban landscape, Griffin cannot achieve the self-generating power he grants in reverie to his former adversaries. As he attempts to beat a hallucinatory retreat from the war, he finds only new evidence of its continuing hold on him. Memory, an incessantly chattering bird, allows the veteran no peaceful historical sleep.

Griffin's recording of the war as a terrible hallucination is but one intersection in the grouping of threatened sensibilities that Wright creates; his double movement deeper into his own disordered consciousness and into the horrific reality of Vietnam is reflected and complicated by other confrontations with the educational qualities of new American history. Claypool, "the single character lacking from their B-war . . . The Kid" (26), is an almost pure innocent who becomes a foot soldier despite promises of a desk job, witnesses the electrical torture of prisoners, and participates in an ill-fated patrol in which his peers are blasted to pieces before his eyes. Unknowingly administered mind-expanding drugs for several days, he retreats into a vegetable state and is evacuated finally to Okinawa, where "he could spend the remainder of the war, sitting in a closet and drooling in his shoe" (238). Like Griffin, Claypool undergoes through intimacy with violence and chemical agents a one-way passage to the most terminal form of historical consciousness. His reduction to the status of a living vegetable is Wright's most grotesque example of the organic power of Vietnam to reshape its participants. Claypool is the unseeking victim of what Griffin self-consciously explores, but the former's death-in-life is only a more heightened variation of the latter's doomed regeneration. As history lesson, Vietnam is the deepest cultural inscription whose capacity for surreal improvisation marks innocent and experienced alike.

Griffin and Claypool begin their tours in Vietnam seeking only to weather the historical nightmare that eventually absorbs, reshapes, and processes them in the most permanent way, but Wright presents characters whose faith in experience, order, and control proves their undoing. Major Holly joins the Military Intelligence Group after the previous commanding officer has been killed in a plane crash that seems more than an accident. Assessing war as "incredible boredom punctuated by exclamation marks of orgiastic horror" (96), he attempts to cultivate unit professionalism by having his men repaint buildings, plant flower gardens, and receive unwanted medals, but he discovers that this war will not conform to ideas of order, that its most persistent lessons sprout from beneath his cultivated surface like the ever-encroaching jungle girding the compound. Sensing finally that there are too many exclamation marks within the boredom, he is reduced to building tunnels to protect himself from his own men, his brightly painted, symmetrically perfect camp having become a shimmering but imprisoning delusion.

Kraft, a CIA operative who has been "spooking" since the early romantic days of the war, has seen the nasty growth of the American presence in Vietnam. A figure who has practiced and witnessed the ghastliest forms of covert activity, he is Claypool's historical antithesis, a symbol of recklessness, experience, and continuity who assumes that Vietnam holds no more surprises. Kraft achieves true communion with the war, however, when his helicopter goes down in the jungle and a rescue mission is organized to save the old warrior and his secrets from falling into enemy hands, an endeavor that becomes Griffin's essential education at the war's dark center as well.

The rescuers do not find Kraft, the "spook" who has disappeared into the jungle that their herbicides cannot expunge, but they are afforded the vision of the helicopter's crew and other passengers strung upside down from its rotors and horribly mutilated. The encounter in the jungle provides Griffin with the terrible subtext that has always resided beneath his high-altitude film negatives. The image interpreter has joined the search because "he wanted to experience some portion of the madness as his own" (275). Like the rest of Wright's immersed sensibilities, he discovers that the deadly organicism over which American overreach assumes control is capable of administering its own narrative control. Griffin is confronted in the jungle not by the neutrality of a celluloid image, but by "a Green Machine larger and more efficient than any human bureaucracy or mechanical invention," one that "would promptly initiate the indifferent processes of converting flesh and dreams into plant food" (277). The herbicide program that would deny such persistent truths is the final symbol of American obsession, Wright suggests. Griffin's response to the historical method of the jungle is an illustration of the collective refusal to identify limits:

> The whole stinking forest should have been sprayed long ago, hosed down, drenched in Orange, leaves blackened, branches denuded, undergrowth dried into brittle paper. The mountain was surely overrun with VC and their camouflaged crops, secret manioc fields, banana groves, rice paddies, water wells. Who permitted these outrages, where was the technology when you needed it? No wonder we were losing the damn war. In spite of the sweat in his eyes, the raw sore rubbing open on his left heel, he discovered he was smiling. Yes, you too, you fucking American. (278)

Griffin returns without Kraft but with dreams "of chemical showers, of winged nozzles sweeping the provinces from end to end, of 100 percent coverage" (294-95), but within his visions of absolute defoliation, he has moved irrevocably from observer to subject. He has become a component of the nightmare rather than its detached assessor. He feels in the jungle that "he had become a photograph, a new image to interpret" (279), but when he returns to his duties, he immerses himself completely in the new visions of heroin that soften the historical lessons but that also serve as memory's cocoon: "The war encapsuled him in peace. Events arranged themselves into machines of quiet harmony. Objects tended to rest in the serenity of an ancient comprehension. All things simply slowed slowly slowing except the days, of course, and the days, they went zip" (301).

Kraft eventually returns from his communion with the jungle alive, but a transformed sensibility. Refusing to move, even to come out of his room, he is no longer the outrider as "spook," the reconstituted Natty Bumppo in a remythologized American frontier. Returned from a dark wood that is filled with the most real and demanding historical shades, he is the most debilitated Goodman Brown, a figure who can only say softly to the few interested in his

report, "The plants . . . They're so . . . the trees . . . I . . . I
don't know" (321). Wright's Vietnam is a work of the American
imagination that doubles back to afflict and to haunt its creators. As
one of them, Griffin benumbs himself until the end of his tour, but
he fails to exorcise his new devils. Wreathed in a smoky haze and
imprinted with a shared nightmare, he returns to America as one
sensitive recording device among many, "a looped reel wound through
his head. A sequence of images projected onto a cold screen. The
computers awaiting final interpretation" (299).

How Wright manipulates his botanical metaphors to explore the
links between experience and memory is the special achievement of
Meditations in Green, its main claim to be read as a unique form of
interpretive history. Pamela Feinsilber noted in the *Saturday Review*
that Wright's treatment of Vietnam is "a hybrid hallucination of the
evening news and *Apocalypse Now*," an acceptable summary of how
Wright pressurizes poetically the confrontation of fact and imagination as historical document. But she also asserted that he "does not
express a point of view or insight into what occurred as much as he
conveys what the war felt like" (61). Her distinction between point
of view and the varieties of personal imprinting and retrospection that
Wright offers limits artificially the tools of the Vietnam War historian; it is the same distinction that the most rigorous and visionary
novelists and memorialists cast out in their prologues and prefaces.
Wright concentrates, heightens, and extends dramatically and metaphorically the experience of the war into a nightmarish realm no less
absolute in its evil than Kurtz's in *Heart of Darkness*. His method
neither falsifies his data nor results in merely another jarring sequence
of horrific images. The tone in which he offers the historical experience of his characters, what Peter S. Prescott calls "barely controlled
hysteria" (90), is an aesthetic strategy by which the discrepancy
between the power of the historical transmissions and the ability of
the individual to collect and to interpret them is most effectively inscribed. Griffin as a threatened, transformed sensibility is a familiar
figure in Vietnam writing, and Wright's evocation of him, inventive
and powerful as it is, is a variation on a theme. Griffin as a rare Vietnam War Proustian figure, the burrower within memory whose
historical narrative is an organic process of endless revisions, is the
historical link among the other modes of historical writing in Vietnam War novel and memoir.

Griffin's memory of the war is energized by more than his heroin addiction and his perception of his American urban landscape as a redefined war zone. Trips, another returned veteran of the intelligence unit, enters Griffin's postwar existence and attempts to recruit him for one final search-and-destroy mission, the extermination of a sergeant who killed his dog, Thai, in Vietnam. Trips finds his historical continuity not in heroin but through a revenge scenario that, like Griffin's recording device, is a volatile blend of memory and delusion. The figure who "couldn't warm his fuses except in relation to uniformed authority" (71), he is another illustration of the war as unfinished business and ongoing obsession, his all-consuming search for a dog killer the narrative line on which the larger nightmare is hung and explicated.

As he is drawn slowly into Trips's surreal vendetta, Griffin charts as well his own inability to extricate himself from the hold Vietnam maintains on him. The fifteen interchapters called "Meditations in Green" are a high-relief map of Griffin's internalized postwar battlefield. Like Griffin's lived experience in Vietnam, they trace with a plenitude of botanical correspondences his passage from initial hopefulness through guilt, vindictiveness, and alienation to the debilitating dreams of heroin addiction. Remarkable concentrations of poetic suggestiveness, they reveal the chambered structure of Griffin's memory and serve as objective correlatives for the buried emotional history of the war, the returned American veteran's true cultural boon to his nation. Having become his own image to interpret, Griffin reveals in his meditations that the veteran's struggle to order his history is much like Wallace Stevens's project of describing the blackbird. Discovering an abundance of sight lines, an overflowing of emotional response and constructive possibility, he logs within memory how any single perception is complicated by the intrusive, conflicting announcements of the remainder.

In "Meditation in Green: 1," Griffin as plant explores his "stunted growth" within his urban environment. Trapped within a concrete postwar hothouse, the veteran as regenerating organism admits, "I feel old. I take light through a glass, my rain from a pipe" (3). He dreams of the unattainable climatic factors that promote healthy growth, but he discovers only a cultural atmosphere of "cracked beds, stale air, enervations, apathy, loneliness" (3). The second meditation, an alphabetized list of enemies of botanical well-being, concludes with a statement on the veteran's special problems of readjustment: "And these are merely the threats to common house and garden plants. Consider the problems of backwoods survival" (16).

The meditations also allow Griffin to place himself on the receiving end of American engineering in Vietnam. As former agent, he becomes a victim like the Vietnamese plant life assaulted by bombing missions and defoliants, offering in "Meditation in Green: 4" a pointed chemical quatrain:

> 2,4-dichlorophenoxyacetic acid
> 2,4,5-trichlorophenoxyacetic acid
> 2,4,6-start the engines, pull the sticks
> 2,4,6,8-everyone evacuate (70)

In the fifth interchapter, he becomes "a fortress of botanical nastiness," a metaphorical correspondence that speaks to the new cultural status of the veteran. If contemporary American history is capable of producing a new strain, he is it, "a blot upon the landscape. A visual, tactile, olfactory blot. An indelible vulgarity" (85). In "Meditation in Green: 6," the veteran envisions himself retreating from his history into an embryonic state, "bounded by a nutshell then, secure in the vise of the earth, a unity whole, free, and organic, a voyager beyond time." The desire to bury memory, however, is only that. Griffin as plant asserts that "happiness is a pristine seed coat" (99). Even the power of metaphor is insufficient to liberate consciousness from historical control.

Other meditations explore additional aspects of victimization, isolation, and regeneration, but Arden's therapy fails to produce the desired effects: "My botanical life has become a shade unruly," Griffin tells fellow survivalist Huey. "Things grow whether I want them or not" (180). What sprouts freely within the hero's postwar life, his city as "terrarium," are two tangible renewals of the war. Griffin joins Trips in his final mission against the hated sergeant when the avenger mistakes a man on the street for the killer of his dog. Griffin receives an unexpected Purple Heart when he is stabbed while preventing Trips from murdering the wrong man. As he is rushed by ambulance to an emergency room, he receives a new lesson in how his nation perceives the Vietnam veteran:

> Someone offered me a whiff of oxygen. Someone took a history, nodding approvingly. Everyone got hurt these days, accident, dis-

ease, organs breaking down, and no one had proper coverage. Living was expensive enough but dying now was a luxury. A veteran, though, he's got his own hospitals, his staff, his lab tests, his food, his paid care, his security, yes a veteran, why he was home free. (319–20)

Griffin's other renewal of the war, one with greater duration and even more powerful effect, is his unique application of Arden's suggestion to add real flowers to his home. Covering the entire floor of his elevated urban cell with fresh humus, Griffin enfolds memory in a harvest of truly mind-expanding agents, a crop aided by his and Huey's fertility rites atop the seeded surface. "Meditation in Green: 15," a small instruction manual, is the final flow-image in Griffin's bout with history, the culminating application of metaphor to the postwar survivalist's true needs and desires:

1. Remove the latex from the capsules with a flat blunt metallic blade, taking care not to scrape the epicarp.
2. Place coagulated gum in bowl, cover with rice paper.
3. Set bowl in sun for period of two weeks.
4. Roll into balls.
5. Insert ball into pipe.
6. Ignite.
7. Who has a question for Mr. Memory? (340)

Wright concludes with an image of the veteran as the new character within American folklore, a reshaped Johnny Appleseed who volunteers to bring a new boon to his culture. Exploring the new visions that the harvest within his urban greenhouse provides, Griffin—former agent, victim, and scapegoat—suggests from his smoke-filled room his new historical function:

In the spring I'll wander national highways, leather breeches around my legs, pot on my head, sowing seeds from the burlap bag across my shoulder, resting in the afternoon shade of a laurel tree.

At night I carve peace pipes from old cypress branches.

Everywhere the green fuses are burning and look now, snipping rapidly ahead of your leaping eye, the forged blades cutting through the page, the transformation of this printed sheet twisted about a metal stem for your lapel your hat your antenna, a paper emblem of the widow's hope, the doctor's apothecary, the veteran's friend: a modest flower. (341–42)

Meditations in Green does more than renew national acquaintance
with the original planting of American will and idea in Vietnam.
The darkest remembrance of an ill-begotten cultural enterprise, the
novel suggests what the necessary link between the experience and
the final record must include. As the genial storyteller, Griffin argues
that, although retrospection is the most difficult organic process, the
Vietnam War is not a bad crop to be rooted out, boxed, and sent to
some distant marketplace. As Wright's veteran knows best, what
grows anew within native soil must be assessed finally as a permanent
feature of the national landscape.

When Saigon fell in April 1975, two years after American troops had
departed, the new Communist regime celebrated a victory that was
much more than the final routing of ARVN forces offering little
resistance or fleeing in panic before the advancing columns of NVA
and Vietcong forces. The taking of the southern capital was the
closure of a national narrative that had taken two millennia to write,
an epic of tenacity and sacrifice whose major characters included
Kublai Khan as well as William Westmoreland and whose cast of
extras were Chinese, Japanese, French, and, finally, American. Against
the final foreign power, the victors fell back on old historical lessons,
knowing well that patience, improvisation, and a willingness to endure horrible losses were the available weapons. American technological might was an unconquerable foe, but the commitment that
had placed the immense power in Vietnam could be loosened,
chipped at piecemeal, and, finally, removed from Vietnamese soil.
The victors played a waiting game against the United States, one
that produced uncountable casualties for NVA and Vietcong forces.
But for them, it was only a short chapter within a larger text, and
when Saigon received the new appellation of Ho Chi Minh City, the
great goal was realized. Vietnam was finally a unified, independent
state unshackled from outside interests and foreign control. Its future
history was, for once, its own.

Ready to contend with the Americans for decades, if need be, the
victors were less prepared, however, to live with the peace that followed. The regime that exulted in its triumph in 1975 suffers years
later from a variety of ills: insufficient agricultural production; con-

tinued hostility with China and the terrible legacy it has helped to write in Cambodia; a per capita income lower than that of India; persistent ideological and cultural divisions between North and South; an unwieldy military budget; and an ineffective Communist bureaucracy that rests atop the residue of the Confucian and French ones that preceded it. In *Vietnam: A History*, Stanley Karnow recounts a conversation with Prime Minister Pham Van Dong in which the official admitted, "Yes, we defeated the United States. But now we are plagued by problems. We do not have enough to eat. We are a poor underdeveloped nation. *Vous savez*, waging a war is simple, but running a country is very difficult" (127–28).

Vietnam has not yet written the bright future to which so much human life and sacrifice were dedicated. Instead, dark specters haunt its cities and rural areas, both in the North and in the South. An uneasy relationship with the Soviet Union, the blot on the land of the reeducation camps, the economic necessity of the black market, and applications by hundreds of thousands of citizens for exit visas are not the legacy of the war envisioned by the victors or their supporters. American myth had great difficulty validating its presence in Vietnam during the war, but postwar Vietnam is another study in the discrepancy between facts and fictions. If the losers must continue to explain to themselves a war that cost them $140 billion, 58,132 lives, and 303,000 wounded, the victors have a greater challenge. They must create an equitable, humane society with the same patience and dedication they used to build and to maintain the Ho Chi Minh Trail. If they do not, Karnow's assessment of the conflict will continue to be a postwar truth: "In human terms at least, the war in Vietnam was a war that nobody won—a struggle between victims" (11). Like the American veterans who returned to the United States to find renewed animosity or uneasy silence rather than mythic embrace, the leadership in Hanoi must build the necessary links among past, present, and future.

Amid their present economic, social, and ideological troubles, however, the victors are not plagued by the kind of debilitating retrospection characteristic of the American veteran. The singleness of purpose that allowed North Vietnamese and Vietcong soldiers and cadres to withstand American might remains a source of pride and even nostalgia, for the historical text they lived for so many years in the jungles and villages did not manifest the narrative inconsistencies and mythic slippage of the American one. If they are trapped by the past at all, their imprisonment resides in the postwar complexities that do not lend themselves so easily to pure visions.

In his article in the *Atlantic*, an account of his return to Vietnam fifteen years after he served there as a Marine officer, William Broyles, Jr., compares the substance and quality of retrospective visions:

> I talked to Viet Cong veterans several times about American veterans. I tried to explain post-traumatic stress syndrome—the flashbacks, the blackouts, the bitterness, the paralysis of will, that still seem to afflict many Americans. It was incomprehensible to them. "We had to rebuild our country. We had too much to do to think that adjusting to peace was a problem," Tran Hien, a former Viet Cong company commander, told me. "Life goes on." Simple ideas, believed without question, sustained men like Hien then, and sustain them now. Truly nothing, in their minds, is more important than independence and freedom. Their memories of war are remarkably unconfused. I had the sense of being with men and women who had done extreme and even terrible things but whose consciences and hearts are limpidly clear. They do not look into their selves and see angst or guilt or confusion, if they do look into their selves, in our Western, self-infatuated way, at all. They did their duty, like everybody else. For them the war is over. Life *does* go on. (114)

In the account of his journey into both past and present realities, Broyles charts the many troubling discrepancies between the victors' wartime vision and their postwar accomplishments, but as one of those in whom the unreconciled American narrative still dwells, he can deny neither the power of his former adversary's remembrances nor the disturbances that his own continue to create:

> As I listened to his memories, my own memories came back: of ambushes and booby traps and days and nights in the jungle looking for Hien, for an enemy we never seemed to find; of all those men, so young and brave, being wasted for nothing. All in all, I would rather have his war memories than mine.
>
> Hien asked me politely how the airport had changed since I was last here.
>
> "It's a lot quieter," I said. "And it's yours." (115)

When the narrator makes his return to Vietnam at the conclusion of Ward Just's *The American Blues*, he, too, considers the relation of Vietnamese memory to his own and concludes, "There was no connection between them. I began to think of the war as a parenthesis inside a far-going sentence, the parenthesis in English but the sentence itself in a language I did not know and could not decipher. I understood finally that I was on my own" (201). The speaker, a journalist who covered the war and now carries his intimate knowledge of it in the form of a narrative albatross, a 600-page history without a final chapter, is Just's postwar historian–quester, the sensibility whose self-imposed task is to discover a pathway out of an experience that will be neither ordered nor forgotten. Like Wright's Griffin, Just's nameless journalist hero lives a postwar existence marked by continual retrospective disturbances, but the narrator of *The American Blues*, rather than attempting to escape the war by natural or artificial means, is compelled to travel once again to its center to eradicate with pen and ink its infestation of memory.[3]

Revealing the nature of his obsession as he invites the reader to join his journey, he confesses on the first page,

> This is not a story of the war, except insofar as everything in my unsettled middle age seems to wind back to it. I know how much you dislike reading about it, all dissolution, failure, hackneyed ironies, and guilt, not to mention the facts themselves, regiments of them, *armies*. But I must risk being a bore at dinner for these few opening pages, for the life of the war is essential to the story I have to tell. And that is not about the war at all but about the peace that followed the war. (1)

Residing in a postwar America no less contaminated by unreconciled memory than Griffin's, the narrator describes how he and his family became voluntary exiles in a remote section of New England, the "frontier" that, with its "natural environment, clean air, safe schools, wood stoves, and a preindustrial economy," seemed the antithesis of their life in Washington, the chief nexus of new American history that has become "some monstrous contagion." His rejection of contemporary cultural imperatives, however, proves no escape from Vietnam. Watching the final days of the war via the single network he receives in the outlands, he discovers an intensification rather than a diminution of old bonds:

In 1975 it was my own memory on film, and this memory was crowded with fear and ardor, hot and bittersweet as an old blues,

> You told me that you loved me
> but you told me a lie.

They were diabolical memories, hard to communicate and ever harder to share. Yet my feet beat perfect time to the music, everyone said so. The war, the war, the war; for a while, we thought it would go on forever, a running story. And how fascinating that it was an American responsibility, supervised by our best minds. Surely somewhere there was consolation. (3)

The narrator experiences other invasions that correspond to the renewed assaults within memory: the pristine quality of his natural frontier is eroded by foreign investors, condominiums, and ski resorts. When a Huey helicopter occupied by real-estate developers scouting for new targets buzzes the previously sequestered valley, it forces an epiphany within the historian whose last chapter still will not come: "As the sound of the chopper faded and then ceased altogther, I understood that I had been living inside my history of the war, my feverish memory of it; this year was that year relived, but in a cold and lonely climate" (16). His mood darkening, his marriage deteriorating, he likens his obsession to a ship in a bottle and admits, "To release the ship I would have to break the bottle, and that I was unwilling to do—was afraid of doing—but until I did I would have no rest, nor would she" (18).

The narrator realizes that he must leave his family and the valley, which has become "a colony, like the Costa Brava or Nassau, its economy controlled by absentee landlords" (25), if he is to finish his history and to make a peace with memory. Gathering up the unwieldy manuscript and the Buddha's head that serves as a silent, taunting paperweight, he lights off for a new wilderness, the farthest northern reaches of Vermont near the Canadian border where his friend and fellow writer Quinn keeps his "American office," a snowbound retreat that Just fashions into a variety of historical battlefield. Quinn, the creator of the popular journalist hero Tom Plumb, is another creature of time. A hybrid British-American sensibility who pens a new novel each year, "always writing the final sentence the day after Christmas; he was as disciplined as Trollope" (29), he specializes in meeting deadlines as he appropriates, reshapes, and dispenses history in a romanticized form to a receptive audience:

Like Ian Fleming, who created James Bond at the precise moment when secret agents replaced army generals as heroes of the cold war, Quinn created Tom Plumb at the height of the Indochina war, when newspapermen replaced novelists as the most reliable interpreters of public reality and menace. With the advent of Watergate, the success of the series was assured. Tom Plumb became as well known as Nero Wolfe or George Smiley, and Quinn became a millionaire. (29)

Quinn's talents as a "connoisseur of parliamentary atmosphere, where casual conversation was as deadly as a knife fight" (29) are not relegated to his timely fictions, however. As someone who believes that real life should approximate the intriguing possibilities of art, he brings together the obsessed narrator and a young free spirit named Marty Neher, "a modern woman come of age in the peace that followed the war" (83), to help his friend break his historical logjam and also to see what a romantic generational confrontation might engender. The narrative structure that Quinn's improvised plot line begins to manifest, a pressurized interchange that is both personally draining and historically instructive for participants and observers alike, also serves for Just's narrator as a vital series of linked epiphanies, the catalyst for his return to Vietnam and his reimmersion in the pool of memory that may allow the final chapter to be written.

As the narrator and Marty, representatives of vastly different cultural perspectives, become entangled romantically, his obsession is highlighted for examination by her relation to recent American history. Too young to have been affected deeply by what Vietnam wrought within contemporary culture, she has been nurtured within a new sensibility with little knowledge of its difficult birth and its violent development. Her personal attitudes and practices—supreme independence; belief in simple, readable historical cause and effect; confidence that mobility and will power can keep the individual free from cultural inertia—are opposed to those of the narrator, the mired, suffering personality for whom Vietnam dictates both present and future possibilities. For the narrator, Marty is the paramour who "was not old enough to remember chapter and verse, thank God. Her memory would be a perfect small room in an unfinished mansion, the room filled with pretty, unbreakable objects" (63). Their immersion in each other does lead to the narrator's final chapter, but in a way that neither the blocked historian nor Quinn, the instigating adventure writer, anticipates, for Marty's theories of historiography and those of the narrator prove to be antipathetic. Like Sarkin and Berlin of *Going After Cacciato*, their interchange becomes more a statement of positions that a true dialectic.

Marty was a student of both physics and history in college but, as she admits freely, is suited to neither discipline. She retains, however, a firm conviction in the coming perfection of human knowledge: "I thought I had the temperament for it because history's *reliable*," she tells the narrator, "you can depend on it" (145). Probing but incapable of understanding his professional and personal infirmities, she offers a happy synthesis of her former disciplines that is both the principal summary of her general theories and a pointed, antagonistic diagnosis:

> "History's prophetic, you can use it to foretell the future. It's like watching a random quark, if you could watch quarks. A quark out of control, and if you plot it long enough you can predict its behavior—or that's the theory—no one's actually done it, though there's no good reason why it can't be done. You can plot history because you know where it's been. All that needs doing is to factor in the variables. Then you'll know where it's going. All you have to do is get the variables straight, which no one ever will, probably, in my lifetime. So for now it's not an exact science, that's the zippy thing about it. It's more like an art or a craft. I'm pretty satisfied with it, though America seems so exhausted to me now, all those old men. With their loopy memories." (145)

She displays her true historical movement, however, on the slopes near Quinn's as she flies down the mountain on skis, avoiding obstacles, achieving transitory perfection with agility and concentration, defying gravity and danger with her finely tuned ability to finish the run upright and unscathed. Her nostalgic visions linked to "Leave It to Beaver" rather than the Tet offensive or the invasion of Cambodia, she is afflicted by none of the narrator's dark memories, and, without the context necessary to understand his imprisonment, she negates the treacherous twists and turns of historical narrative as she would the hazards of the slope. Dispensing with ambiguity by staying a step ahead of it, she can assert finally, "You make it such a big deal. . . . And it isn't" (101).

In the face of such absolute confidence, the narrator's apprehensions of past complexities and ongoing disturbances become acute.

What Marty seals with categories of reconciled cause and effect, he perceives as tension-ridden narratives of real power and elusive connection. His imaginative sorties, both retrospective and prophetic, are suggestive of meaning but resistant to absolute linkage, to one-to-one correspondence. The principal characters who populate his personal archive are bit players in hers, and as he explores one vector into the past, he also discovers referents for their generational opposition:

> Nixon was no threat, he meant no more to her than Jim Morrison did to me. They were both messengers of cultural infantilism, the signal of collapse as surely as any disintegrating keystone or club-footed Mercury. Of course this was not to say they did not possess a certain aggressive, malignant genius. A certain comfortable purchase on our disordered national will. They went to the heart of things, give them that; their beat was strong, the little devils. (100)

What Marty perceives as finished business is the source of his own variety of prophetic visions. The free-flying historical positivist does not perceive the narrator's obsession as more than debilitating retrospection; nor does she assess the power of experience in terms of its likely future impact, its projected evolution. At one juncture in their tryst, the narrator thinks, "With her I was me without memory" (134), but her sense of an eternal, undefiled present, the quality that affords him temporary escape from his furies, is the one factor that contributes most both to the end of the affair and to the decision to return to Vietnam. He knows that the war is not only a present but also a future reality, and, contemplating the boat people, he isolates one small open text within the larger one, an additional example of how postwar America will continue to discover signs of its achievements:

> One more legacy from our brave little war, I thought; human beings scattered like driftwood throughout Asia, washing up now on this beach, now on that. I thought that for the rest of our lifetimes, wherever we go, we will find Vietnamese. No corner of the earth will be too remote. We will find them in Asia, in Europe, in Latin America, in Africa and Australia, and in towns along the Mississippi. Asian children will grow up learning to spell M-i-s-s-i-s-s-i-p-p-i. There will be a literature and in time a Vietnamese Mark Twain, a Twain to celebrate the necessity of lighting out for the territory. Ho Chi Minh as Aunt Sally, the United States as the

great river itself, vast and indifferent. Come back to the raft ag'n, Nguyen. (104)

Like Wright, Just illustrates that the veteran's task is to find acceptable closure for his personal narrative of the war in such a way that neither the integrity of the original experience nor the necessary personal explorations and improvisations within it are diminished. In *Meditations in Green*, Wright arranges his clusters of botanical metaphors to reflect in his narrative structure Griffin's synthetic operations within memory. Both imprisoned and free, his hero attempts to subject the persisting story—the set of images already imprinted within consciousness—to the power of individual creation, and, if not a seamless whole, *Meditations in Green* reveals a high degree of synchrony between form and idea. Just is no less successful in discovering appropriate figures for his mnemonic treatment of the war. During one interlude between Just's historical trysters, the narrator's attention becomes fixed on Quinn's piano playing, and he offers a small history lesson:

> I said, "Listen to Quinn." He was replicating Jimmy Yancey. I started to say something else, then didn't. . . . Instead, I began to describe the music, Chicago rent-party piano, and the men who played it. It was music drenched in sadness and fatalism, and the dignity that comes with the certain knowledge that the past is prologue. It was antique music, and the old black men who made it were dead before Marty Neher was born. I wondered if it was advantage, knowing nothing of it. (68)

The narrator's memory, itself an intricate mixture of structure and improvisation, sadness and fatalism, finds in the music not only a suggestive blend of fixed form and individual variation, but also the emotional tones that speak to his obsession. Michael Herr's probing of the original experience of Vietnam is cast in a supercharged rock-'n'-roll idiom, but Just's quieter retrospective narrative finds its form in the blue pigments of an even more deeply entrenched national song. Recalling Quinn's explanation of the music he plays so expertly, the narrator considers how one narrative pattern may suggest possibilities for others:

> "Those bars are made of iron, the American blues." He said, "The theme is announced in the first four bars. Then it's repeated, with

variations. First four bars are straight, second four aren't. The theme is answered in the final four, which are all blue. Those final four bars are instructive, like the couplet ending a sonnet. That's the consolation, when there is any." I thought of that now, as his fingers tapped the coffee table. Within the form everything was improvised, always pushing, always ambitious. There was freedom so long as you stayed inside the form, obeying its laws; it was remarkably spacious, though its limits were fixed. Revels in a penitentiary. (111–12)

Marty and the narrator end their liaison as respectful, ungiving historical adversaries, their statements of positions having produced both discernible wounds and vital knowledge. "Peace is at hand" (169), declares the narrator as the oppositions that have powered their exhaustive interchange dictate finally their departures toward independent futures, and, finding in the debris of the affair the stuff of emotional purgation, he senses as well a new resolve toward the unfinished manuscript:

> I knew then that I did not exist beyond the war. I was a creature of it. And I could not end it. I could not *conclude* it. I wondered if it had no conclusion; perhaps it would go on and on, living as long as I did. No: everything has an end. Loves does. Life does. War does. If there is a beginning, there has to be an end, though modern physics would contradict that theory. To hell with modern physics. (183)

Leaving Quinn's snowbound retreat, journeying home to his family, to New York, to the "monstrous contagion" of Washington but finding that things remain unresolved, he secures a visa to the one destination where he might hope to compose the final four bars of his personal blues, the missing chapter of his collective history. His return to Vietnam is less desire than need; he knows that "only there on the ground would I find the answer to the war's ultimate questions. How had the people fared, and what was the metamorphosis of their collective memory? Were they consoled? And what was the price? Really, it was all one question" (196).

What the narrator confronts in postwar Vietnam, however, is not historical clarification but new categories of mystery, additional signifiers of his aloneness.[4] "It seemed like a different state altogether and, without my countrymen, inscrutable. I realized then how much I had depended on the Americans for my news. Even the lies and misapprehensions were American, rising from the American character and obedient to it; the history was American" (200). Understanding that he is both individual agent and self-appointed representative for a sealed national narrative, his need to achieve a decent ending is intensified. Falling ill, then recuperating in Ho Chi Minh City, he explores newly translated documents, texts official and opaque, and sends personal dispatches to Marty, to Quinn, and to his son. Struggling with his manuscript, he writes a letter to an old friend, a diplomat who, like himself, must correlate the data of past actions with present concerns; one-half of his elusive closure, his dispatch is also a response to another writer from another war, for as the narrator takes issue with one American author's long-standing imperative, he states what the new one must be:

> For many years I had accepted the thesis, half a century old now, that the large abstract words such as glory, honor, courage, and cowardice, were obscene. That which was chaste was factual, in the instance of the war, the details of the weather, the geography, the weapons, the battle groups, and the statistical apparatus that supported it all. Now I knew I was mistaken and in this war all we had were the large abstract words. It was difficult to state them without mortification, but I had a skull filled to overflowing with facts—untainted, innocent—and none of them described the war, except who had won and who had lost and in this war that was only a detail. Only the large words were equal to experience, in which the sacrifice was so out of balance and the results so confounding. Glory or disgrace, sacred or profane; pick the words you want. Only in this way would the deepest secrets, those closest to the heart, be disclosed. They were the only secrets worth disclosing. (203–4)

The narrator's final gesture in *The American Blues* is an unwritten dispatch, for as he contends with the silhouette of Frederic Henry, he perceives as well a body of more contemporary voices: "I saw ghosts in the shadows; it seemed to me that multitudes were gathering beneath my window, waiting for a signal to mobilize. What a mighty army they would be, free at last" (204). Seeking the crucial link among past, present, and future, he stands at the balcony of his quarters late at night and envisions the vast army of imprisoned souls standing below on the surface of a new Vietnam. His final communication, one willed as much as discovered, suggests finally that experience and memory may be reconciled, that private and public records must cease to be bitter adversaries:

> Do you see it now? I was so tired, and in order to advance I would have to travel through the multitudes, from the present into the past, counting, weighing, measuring, listening. They had given so much and wanted so little in return; they only wanted an acknowledgment of the debt. They wanted a secure place in the public memory. None of us must be forgotten, and in that way the future is guaranteed and our sleep untroubled. So we must ask for mercy, and it was in the asking . . .
>
> Listen, I said. Everything's going to work out fine. (205)

Just's blue consolation and Wright's green metaphor meet at the same historical junction. Like Wallace Stevens's use of those same shades of color—one the realm of the imagination, the other the lived world with which it contends—their postwar remembrances speak anew of the cooperative process of experience and creation that lives at the core of any historical document, that enfolds all possibility of personal or collective peace. In their retrospective visions, Just and Wright address a tradition that began long before Alden Pyle's arrival in Vietnam. Ultimately, they cast their attention and impart their lessons to the archive of novel and memoir that extends to Khe Sanh but that threads backward to Inchon, Normandy, Belleau Wood, Gettysburg, and Lexington. Like Halberstam, O'Brien, Caputo, and the other practitioners of compensatory history, they inscribe aspects of necessary closure only to identify the powerful organicism of memory, the dim, receding outline of the missing chapter. Nothing will erase what happened to national innocence and virtue in Vietnam, they insist, but convenient revision or willed forgetfulness would be the most unacceptable legacy to future generations. As literary point men, they have walked a long distance with their necessary cultural news. Persistent nightmare, American dream, Vietnam has come home to stay.

Afterword

TOWARD AN AMERICAN PEACE

The return to Vietnam of Ward Just's narrator in *The American Blues* is only a prefatory gesture in a larger collective rite, one that begins with the recognition that the Vietnam War will remain a permanent feature within the American cultural landscape. There is much more than the black granite memorial in Washington to remind us of that presence; the thousands of boat people from Southeast Asia now living on native grounds—the new Americans from Vietnam, Laos, and Cambodia—demonstrate daily that the war remains a living seed within national consciousness, that true historical experience is never a static condition. Grafted together in the most tragic way, Vietnam and the United States are now like one of Stephen Wright's botanical metaphors, a hybrid cultural organism whose growth patterns cannot be prophesied.

Recent American fiction indicates how strong a presence the Vietnam War continues to be, how much aesthetic exploration and cultural explanation remain to be achieved. The novels of Robert Olen Butler feature American protagonists connected in a deeply personal way to Vietnam and its people. *The Alleys of Eden* is the narrative of a deserter who returns with his Vietnamese mistress to America, where both discover that they are spiritually and culturally displaced, strangers in a transformed historical landscape. Butler's most recent work, *On Distant Ground*, offers an American CIA officer who returns to Vietnam at the moment the South is falling to search for the son he has fathered during the war, a reflection of the new child he and his wife have just produced in America. Butler's hero, preparing to return home at novel's end with a new addition to his American family, is a symbolic reminder of how much care and nurturing healthy historical memory demands. Works such as Joan Didion's *Democracy* and Jayne Anne Phillips's *Machine Dreams* explore aesthetically how the Vietnam War infected national consciousness through time, affecting family relationships and generational continuity in the most telling ways. And Robert Stone's *A Flag for Sunrise* symbolically links America's past and present, the Vietnam War hovering constantly within Stone's mythical war-torn Latin American country, a powerful reminder in art of the persistence of old historical dreams to become new cultural nightmare.

The prime theme within the finest of the most recent fiction is how much native American grounds remain imaginative ghost country for the returned veteran, and three new novels are worthy of special note. Larry Heinemann, Bobbie Ann Mason, and Philip Caputo extend and deepen the aesthetic exploration of the war in novels that are true rites of healing, retrospective peace missions into the heart of America and into the tortured soul of unreconciled historical memory. Heinemann's *Paco's Story* was awarded the 1987 National Book Award for fiction, and the spare contemporary parable of one shattered veteran's attempt to correlate recent collective horror with present individual pain and alienation is the most problematic and disturbing of the new fictions. Heinemann's main character remains a half-realized shade throughout the novel, a postwar grunt Everyman who wanders his homeland with cane and thousand-yard stare. Heinemann's strategy is aesthetically risky, for the reader never learns Paco's personal history or even his last name; what is most striking in the novel is the narrative voice with which Heinemann describes Paco's death-in-life drifting from one small town to another, an aimless postwar trek that becomes a dark picaresque of visible and hidden wounds, a cycle of bus tickets, odd jobs, crumbling hotel rooms, and bad dreams.

A well-modulated instrument of quiet rage and tired regret tinged with persistent street-smart cynicism, Heinemann's narrative device is the collective voice of new American ghosts, for Paco is the only survivor of a hell hole called Fire Base Harriette where an entire company is wiped out in a single soul-destroying night. *Paco's Story* is a novel without real closure, however, for Heinemann's blistering, haunting diatribe against his country's inability or unwillingness to see its new invisible men is finally a demand rather than a plan for peace. Reaching the brink of despair, Heinemann's electric prose revitalizes the demand for more considerate visions. *Paco's Story* is charged eloquence waiting still for a clear historical reply.

Bobbie Ann Mason's *In Country* offers the most unusual new Vietnam veteran, seventeen-year-old Samantha "Sam" Hughes, who in 1984 undertakes two special operations: learning about her father, who was killed in the war, and resurrecting the spirit of her debilitated Uncle Emmett, who went to Vietnam to avenge her father's death. Spending his days playing video games, watching reruns of "M*A*S*H," and suffering from a skin condition possibly induced by Agent Orange, Emmett is a figure trapped within guilt and pain, a character whose past has voided his future. Told continually by the veterans of her Kentucky town that she will never understand the past, discovering within her father's diary that he had been transformed by the war from a good country boy into a callous killer, Sam attempts to discover the deadly secrets of Vietnam by spending a night "in country" within a swamp on the outskirts of town, an imaginative venture in which a cooler of soft drinks becomes her GI canteen, and canned pork and beans, her field rations.

Sam's mission does not replicate fully the lost war she seeks; like Paul Berlin, she discovers the limits of the imagination. Her night operation does produce an emotional catharsis for Emmett, who searches for her and finally reveals the details of the terrible fire fight in which he lay waiting for rescue among the bodies of his dead buddies. The night in country is only the first of two historical epiphanies, however, for Emmett, Sam, and her grandmother journey to the Vietnam Veterans Memorial in Washington, a necessary rite that links generations, engenders expiation and understanding, and begins to write a meaningful peace. In the final moving images of the novel, Sam's grandmother touches the name of her son on the black granite, Emmett restores the flow of time as he confronts his lost unit within new spiritual terrain, and Sam, the youngest veteran, finds another "Sam Hughes" listed among the dead, Mason's cluster of symbolic gestures revealing that the pain of historical knowledge is the necessary price for a credible American future.

In Country is a peace offering of the most significant kind, and its themes of confrontation and forgiveness are the core as well of

Philip Caputo's *Indian Country*, an aesthetic coming-to-terms with the issues of personal transgression and guilt, which permeated his personal memoir ten years earlier. A *Rumor of War* is classical auto-biography as painful confession; *Indian Country* is the novel as healing ritual, a work in which Caputo becomes shaman for personal and collective historical afflictions. Like Mason's young heroine, Caputo's Christian Starkmann is a seeker within 1980s postwar America. His need, however, is not to re-create a war imaginatively but to resist retrospectively the power of its most terrible revelations. Starkmann goes to Vietnam to defy his militant pacifist father and to repay a debt to Bonny George St. Germaine, an Ojibwa Indian who saved his life. He brings about his boyhood friend's death, how-ever, when he transmits the incorrect coordinates for an air strike, an act that festers within him years after the war as he attempts to begin his life anew in Michigan's Upper Peninsula, the scene of the fishing trips that afforded him his first contact with Indian culture.

The title of the novel is telling, for "Indian country" is both the grunt's designation for dangerous terrain in Vietnam and the geo-graphical matrix of fading Ojibwa belief and ritual in America. Wawiekumig, the grandfather of Bonny George, is the last caretaker of native mystical rites, connections between Nature and Spirit that are disappearing as quickly as the forests stripped from the land by the logging company that employs Starkmann. Two kinds of domestic defoliation—one physical, one spiritual—are the specters for Stark-mann's internal struggle, one that bears more than small resemblance to the postwar psychological plight of Hemingway's hero in "Big Two-Hearted River." Caputo's suffering vet, however, is incapable of writing his new historical report within the private camping and fishing rituals of Nick Adams. Besieged by guilt and paranoia, ex-changing Great War victimization for admissions of violent agency, Starkmann begins to imagine himself communicating with the spirits of dead comrades and slowly transforms his Michigan homestead, his Indian country, into a defense perimeter, one in which he plans to sacrifice himself and his painful memories to police in a cathartic confrontation.

Starkmann's estranged wife returns to avert the incipient fire fight in the Michigan pine forest, but his subsequent attempts at readjust-ment within a veterans' group do not hasten his recovery. Instead, he finds the beginning of true expiation only in a new American vision quest—the confession of his transgression to Wawiekumig deep within the Indian's ancestral lands and the cleansing of self within the cold, rapid waters from which he was saved by Bonny George. Caputo's aesthetic resolution not only completes a small, personal circle, but also links *Indian Country*—and all the works by the finest Vietnam point men—with a larger native tradition. Threading its way through the contemporary, ritualized forest of Christian Starkmann is a well-worn path passing through the spiritual terrain of Nick Adams and opening finally on the clearing where Natty Bumppo walked between virtue and violence, natural innocence and historical experience. Purifying himself within familiar American currents, Caputo's new veteran in fiction not only symbolizes where the quickly rushing river of collective memory must flow, but also points upstream to the headwaters of a long, twisting heritage.

As fine as they are as purgative social rituals, the new fictions of Heinemann, Mason, and Caputo are only invitations to future writers to explore a national archive, to renew the aesthetic exploration of a crucial American event. Visions and revisions of Vietnam will continue to appear within popular culture, within official quarters, within the general marketplace of national will and idea, but the finest American novels and memoirs of Vietnam stand as the true memorials for a concerned, caring readership. Charles Durden's hero in *No Bugles, No Drums* finds in his war one national evolutionary movement—"from Valley Forge to Vietnam, two hundred years of tradition to produce a madman" (276)—and, certainly, writing and reading novels may be no permanent cure for collective historical psychosis. No novel or memoir can illuminate fully a complex historical experience, nor can the work of art declare what appropriate collective resolve or opinion should be. Cooperation and imagination outside the text are needed for those operations.

The creation of the novelist, however, remains a most valuable guide. Finding at long last the power to forgive, Christian Starkmann in *Indian Country* concludes a personal rite that is both a reply to Durden's Jamie Hawkins and a symbolic action for a much larger American unit: "When the echoes died away, he dressed, hoisted his pack, and started walking, though not toward home; he was already there, returned to himself. Home, the place he had not seen or been these many years. *Home*" (419). Within the tall pines of his endangered wilderness, the new veteran testifies that memory may be neither eradicated nor outrun; rather, it must be endured, listened to, and, finally, acted on.

There remain within consciousness the fading sounds of rotor blades, the eerie, residual illumination of a night flare—the dark American wood burgeons with the persistent devils and consoling spirits of historical experience. Cutting trails toward the peace table with the creative imagination, walking point, Caputo and the rest have placed the most important national report, the missing personal testimony, into their living pages. The remainder of secret history, they know, is graven in stone.

NOTES

INTRODUCTION

1. Ross's central term in "The Assailant–Victim in Three War Protest Novels" is especially useful for appraising the shift in perspective toward the American soldier in many Vietnam works. As the twin roles of the initiate as agent and victim often reach grotesque proportions, a new emphasis on and exploration of the soldier as dispenser of tragedy as well as imprisoned innocent is a major shift in the collective apprehension of war and history in American letters, a development that at least partly explains why the war has been the object of willed collective forgetfulness and why the transmutation of the returned veteran into historical animus within national myth should come as little surprise.

THE CAMERA'S EYE

1. Students and critics attempting to assemble a book shelf of the essential fiction and memoir of the Vietnam War can take heart in the fact that the present renaissance of interest in the war has encouraged publishers to reissue a number of the lost works. David Halberstam's *One Very Hot Day* resurfaced through Warner Books in 1984, and Avon offered new editions of Charles Durden's *No Bugles, No Drums*, James Park Sloan's *War Games*, William Pelfrey's *The Big V*, and others in the same year. Of course, what qualifies as a Vietnam War novel is subject to in-

terpretation. In *Vietnam in Prose and Film*, James C. Wilson lists forty-five important Vietnam War novels written by Americans. John Newman, including both more peripheral works and a number written by non-Americans, offers 116 titles in *Vietnam War Literature*. The expanding nature of the corpus and the problem of definition make the problem of discovering a reliable, current bibliography a real one for scholars. The publishing history resembles the war itself in more than textual aspects.

2. Beidler discusses American Vietnam War poetry, drama, and oral history as well as the novels and memoirs in *American Literature and the Experience of Vietnam*. His and James C. Wilson's works are the fullest treatments of Vietnam War writing currently available. John Newman's *Vietnam War Literature*, although less valuable as criticism, offers an important annotated bibliography.

3. In 1974, Haldeman published *The Forever War*, a work that garnered both the Hugo and the Nebula awards for the best science-fiction novel of the year. The narrative deals with the ultimate war of attrition, a 1,200-year-long conflict between humans and an alien race called the Taurans. The novel's protagonist faces not only continual dangers in the battle zone, but also the problem of successive readjustments to an earthly culture barely recognizable or receptive after his long years in deep space. It might be argued that in terms of both iconography and interpretation, *The Forever War* rather than *War Year* is Haldeman's self-conscious historical novel about Vietnam. The former work, less concerned with verisimilar effects than with associative extrapolation and interpretation, is another example, like Twain's *Connecticut Yankee*, of how a work of the fantastic may speak to history.

4. My analysis of Del Vecchio's work was published originally as "Diving into the Wreck: Sense Making in *The 13th Valley*," *Modern Fiction Studies* 30 (1984): 119–34.

5. Foucault's examination, in *The Archaeology of Knowledge and the Discourse on Language*, of the connections among knowledge, language, and action is a valuable critical tool for the opening up of layered texts such as *Moby-Dick* and *The 13th Valley*, nineteenth- and twentieth-century "digs" into the archaeological formations of "the unities of discourse."

THE MEMOIR AS "WISE ENDURANCE"

1. The exploration of the warrior cult is the core of a number of novels as well. Norman Mailer's D. J. is a Texas adolescent who finds a grotesque American manhood on a surreal, high-tech bear hunt in the Alaska Brooks Range in *Why Are We in Vietnam?*, a work that offers violence as generational rite and cultural inevitability. The character of

Hicks in Robert Stone's *Dog Soldiers* is a natural gladiator fighting an existential battle in an American cultural landscape grown dark with corruption, drugs, and historical entropy; through him, Stone suggests both the historical necessity and the natural defeat of the warrior impulse. It rises, only to be expunged by the conditions that nurture it in a deadly cycle of cultural imperatives. Both James Crumley's *One to Count Cadence* and William Eastlake's *The Bamboo Bed* offer their respective protagonists as blunted mythic heroes; Crumley's Slag Krummel, a descendant of a long line of warriors, seeks combat from the weight of tradition and natural inclination, but he discovers moral and spiritual roadblocks in the murkiness of the latest American overreaching. Eastlake's Captain Clancy, the most fantastic historical projection in many of the works, parachutes from the sky wearing a helmet with a Roman crest and wielding a sword and shield. Consumed by the dark historical repetitions of which Vietnam is the most recent, Clancy is the cyclical warrior impulse confronting historical circumstances that absorb its very energy and confidence. Eastlake's warrior is more universal than Mailer's culturally nurtured one, but none of the four novelists suggests that historical exposure and deflation of the warrior strain by the American experience in Vietnam indicates its permanent demise.

2. The discrepancy between histories of the war from the perspective of high-ranking officers and from that of soldiers in the field is a major theme in many works. Josiah Bunting's *The Lionheads*, however, is one of the few works to offer an upper-level commanding officer as a major character; Bunting creates in General Lemming an opportunistic professional soldier with little concern about the men who live and die within his grand tactical schemes. Removed from the immediate facts of war, he can write and read a detached, euphemistic historical narrative, the very sort O'Brien and Caputo work vigorously against. Portraiture of the general staff as systems analysts and business managers in many Vietnam works emphasizes not only economic and political positions, but also a genuine class consciousness as a prime tool for reading. The subculture wrought by what Gloria Emerson calls the "caste system" is more than eager in many works to supply counterstatements to those who write the official versions of the war.

HEARTS OF DARKNESS

1. Although the inverted logic of *Catch-22* is cited by more than one Vietnam writer as art prophesying future history, Pynchon's dark historical wasteland blasted of human value to usher in the Age of Rocket seems closest in tone and message to the aesthetic visions of the most able Vietnam black humorists. For at least one of the new stylists, Heller falls short

of the necessary cultural fragmentation, surrealism, and entropy that Vietnam signified: says Charles Durden's Jamie Hawkins in No Bugles, No Drums, "I remember readin' a book called Catch-22 and I said this dude's gotta be crazy" (207). Pynchon's hero, pursued relentlessly across The Zone by nameless forces known only as "They," is the focal point of a struggle waged not for political or ideological reasons, but for economic and technological leverage. Avatar of a threatened class in an inescapable historical bargain, Slothrop is the embodiment of the postmodern argument that the possibility of paranoia is precluded by a growing list of real threats.

2. Peter Aichinger, assessing in The American Soldier in Fiction, 1880–1963 the aesthetic strategy of black humor, argues for a recognition of the limits of the negative energy that powers the mode: admitting that black humor "is a means of coping with the horror of war" that "momentarily relieves the trauma" of violent history, he warns also that it "does not offer a consistent alternative to the social creed that requires the individual to participate in the slaughter" (46–47). The black humorist, however, is a spokesman for those historical victims who with good reason have come to distrust the confident assertion of codes, creeds, and lists of required sacrifices. The aesthetic enhancement of the absurd may appear from one critical perspective to be revolution without a program, but it also bears implicitly a standard of humanism struggling to free itself from unreflective, enervating cultural configurations.

3. It is not surprising that Stanley Kubrick—director of Dr. Strangelove: Or, How I Learned to Stop Worrying and Love the Bomb—chose Hasford's work as the aesthetic source for his cinematic version of the Vietnam War, Full Metal Jacket. Kubrick's 1964 black-humor masterpiece—a deck of surreal images, including Sterling Hayden protecting America's "precious bodily fluids" and Slim Pickens, a nuclear buckaroo, riding a hydrogen bomb down on a Soviet missile complex—made a stronger ideological statement in art than did either On the Beach or Fail Safe, more conventional film treatments of nuclear issues.

THE WRITER AS ALCHEMIST

1. In Why We Were in Vietnam, Norman Podhoretz argues for the unusual nature of Safer's report at the time it was broadcast:

So much attention has been paid to Morley Safer's film of August 1965 on CBS showing marines using their cigarette lighters to set fire to the Vietnamese village of Cam Ne . . . that almost everyone thinks the networks were as skeptical about the war in the early years as some of the major newspapers, and as hostile to it as they themselves indubitably were in the

later years. But careful studies have shown that the Cam Ne program was
a rare exception. (125)

Safer's report, however, was a portent of what was to become the extensive antagonism between official and media versions of historical truth in
Vietnam. Murray Fromson notes that even in 1965, when television coverage was generally supportive of the master narrative, "the government's
reaction to the broadcast was excessive. After viewing it, Arthur Sylvester,
then the deputy secretary of defense for public affairs, called Fred Friendly,
the president of CBS News, and asked, 'Now that you have spit on the
American flag, how do you feel?' " (87).

    2. George Reedy has suggested why the established tools of the media
often proved inadequate for the historical configuration that evolved in
Vietnam:

> The daily press—print or electronic—is inherently event-oriented, and it
> may be impossible to recast it into another form. This means that journal-
> ists cover wars in terms of what is regarded as a *significant pattern* of events
> such as troop movements, battles, major destruction of property and lives,
> occupation of key territories, and surrender of armies. For World War I,
> World War II, and even Korea (where there were front lines) this pattern
> held, and journalistic performance could be judged by its success or failure
> in supplying answers to the questions implicit in the formula. . . . In
> Vietnam, the so-called significant pattern had very little significance. . . .
> Fundamentally, the war was a struggle for allegiance rather than strategic
> position—and this is not readily portrayed in the traditional block para-
> graphs of journalism or in the kind of film that electronics reporters can
> gather by accompanying a convoy. (120–21)

    3. The American anticipation of Khe Sanh as a decisive engagement
that, one way or the other, would repeat historically the French-Vietminh
drama at Dien Bien Phu was probably not a notion shared by the enemy.
In *Vietnam: A History*, Stanley Karnow describes how, during the siege,

> Pentagon specialists had constructed a sand-table model of the Khesanh
> plateau in the basement situation room of the White House and Johnson,
> dressed in a bathrobe, would prowl around the chamber during the night—
> reading the latest teletype messages from the field, peering at aerial photos,
> requesting casualty figures. In one of the oddest demands ever imposed by
> a president on his top officers, he insisted that the joint chiefs of staff sign
> a formal declaration of faith in Westmoreland's ability to hold Khesanh.
> (541)

But Karnow notes that General Vo Nguyen Giap, the chief designer of
the Tet campaign, argued later that Khe Sanh achieved such prominence
in the American mind only because it was perceived as a test of prestige.
In the same passage, Karnow tells that

a lower-ranking Communist officer, who had fought at Dienbienphu and Khesanh, underlined a point that seemed to me to be credible: "At Dienbienphu, the French and ourselves massed for what we both expected to be a final battle. The Americans, however, were strong everywhere in the south. Thus we realized from the beginning that we could not beat them decisively in a single encounter at Khesanh." (542)

4. A viewer need only compare the serious probing of moral and historical ambiguities in films such as *Coming Home* (1978), *The Deer Hunter* (1979), and *Apocalypse Now* (1979) with the simplistic remythologizing of American virtue through the single focus of the MIA issue in recent offerings such as *Uncommon Valor* (1983), *Missing in Action* (1984), and *Rambo: First Blood Part II* (1985) to determine how deep seems to be the collective desire to inscribe the war in comforting aesthetic and historical terms. Although all the films in the earlier grouping can be faulted for particular distortions or omissions, the directors— Hal Ashby, Michael Cimino, and Francis Ford Coppola—make attempts to confront the unpleasant reverberations of new American history. The new MIA films reduce the war to a revisionist dream of America as the victimized historical subject, a species of Vietnam War interpretation that had been absent from the screen since the cultural wish fulfillment of John Wayne's *The Green Berets* (1968).

SHADES OF RETRIEVAL

1. The Vietnam veteran in novel and memoir is more likely to address specific postwar problems and oversights than he is to draw larger blueprints for how the economic, political, and social institutions contributing to his war might be restructured, but the American tendency to illustrate specific abuses while failing to enunciate coherent collective responses is a long-standing pattern.

In *Exile's Return: A Literary Odyssey of the 1920s*, Malcolm Cowley assesses the slow return to America and to degrees of normalcy of the literary expatriates. Identifying the crucial split between their personal aesthetic and collective social visions, Cowley describes the American protest sensibility after World War I as one that was essentially retrospective rather than visionary:

> They formed a persistent opposition, a minority never in power and never even united in its opinions, except for a short period during the Spanish civil war; that was the one issue on which they agreed. On other fronts their rebellion was not only individual and unpolitical, in the narrow sense of the word, but also essentially conservative. They didn't look forward, really, to a new collective society based on economic planning and the in-

telligent use of machines; they were skeptical and afraid of bigness; in their hearts they looked toward the past. Their social ideal, as opposed to their literary ideal, was the more self-dependent, less organized America they had known in their boyhoods. Dos Passos was speaking for almost all of them when, in the last days of his uneasy alliance with the Communists, he described himself as "just an old-fashioned believer in liberty, equality, and fraternity." (295–96)

2. A reader might surmise that Wright's portrayal of the veteran as drug addict is fortification of rather than corrective for the two-dimensional figures populating postwar American popular mythology, but Griffin's struggle for personal regeneration is connected directly to aspects of national virtue and innocence that shape his past, control his present, and prophesy his future. One effective way to expunge a stereotype, insights Wright, is to place it into a context of significant depth and complexity so that its insufficiency may be clearly and permanently fixed.

In *Backfire: A History of How American Culture Led Us into Vietnam and Made Us Fight the Way We Did*, Loren Baritz demonstrates the split vision many historians use in assessing the unique cultural developments of Vietnam. Baritz contends, "Most of the veterans returned home reasonably whole, as whole as returning veterans from earlier wars. The majority were not dopers, did not beat their wives or children, did not commit suicide, did not haunt the unemployment offices, and did not boozily sink into despair and futility" (319).

Baritz takes care, however, to note the specific differences between Vietnam and previous American wars; on the issue of hard drugs, he argues,

> Nothing in all of military history even nearly resembled this plague. About 28 percent of the troops used hard drugs, with more than half a million becoming addicted. This was approximately the same percentage of high school students in the States who were using drugs, but they were using softer stuff. In Vietnam, grass was smoked so much it is a wonder that a southerly wind did not levitate Hanoi's politburo. (315)

His observations, seemingly contradictory but essentially accurate, illustrate the necessity of historical reports such as Wright's, documents that attempt to mediate between statistical reports and complex sensibility.

3. Just is one of the very few writers on the war who offers a canon of Vietnam works in which the author's vision of historical continuity and change may be examined through time. *To What End: Report from Vietnam*, Just's "description of the atmosphere and some of the events I saw in South Vietnam from December, 1965 to May, 1967," is a memoir that charts the American doom in Vietnam at the time of its unfolding. Published in 1968, the work begins with a telling epigraph from playwright Harold Pinter, a portion of which reads,

A character on the stage who can present no convincing argument or information as to his past experiences, his present behavior, or his aspirations, nor give a comprehensive analysis of his motives, is as legitimate and worthy of attention as one who, alarmingly, can do all these things. The more acute the experience the less articulate the expression.

The thematic cores of *To What End*, a memoir of first-person immediacy, and *The American Blues*, a retrospective novel, are notably similar. Each offers a speaking voice seeking order and understanding as it itemizes the cultural obstacles to those very commodities. When Just's narrator returns to Vietnam in the latter work, he repeats word for word the last sentence of Pinter's contention, indicating that as an ongoing concern, Vietnam's power to affect and to resist historical narrative remains undiminished.

4. The narrator's postwar recognition of his continued entrapment within American visions is Just's most recent restatement of what he contends in all his works is a principal cause for the American disaster at the time it occurred. Natural misunderstandings originating in American-Vietnamese cultural opposition, Just argues, are most readily observable in the violent lexicons from which larger cultural propositions are built. In *To What End*, Just recounts meeting an old French-speaking Vietnamese official in the Delta who offers him a short course in communications theory:

He said that language was the *sine qua non* of cooperation, and until the American learned that lesson there would be two separate lives, American and Vietnamese, and the war would never be won, or ended, and progress never made. I said we would probably not know the importance of language until the war was over and all the memoirs written. The old man smiled at that. (105–06)

In *Stringer*, Just's 1974 Vietnam novel concerning an intelligence agent's mission to destroy an enemy supply convoy, the hero listens to a conversation between two old Vietnamese that illustrates the distance between American and Vietnamese cultural practices and the problem of reading in a war in which friend and foe cannot be easily distinguished:

The two of them were otherwordly comical, squatting in the middle of the road, gesturing and sliding off each other with words. The language was so difficult and imprecise, it was a language of hints and rumors of hints, heavenly in metaphor and soft in line. Stringer listened with effort, he thought he was getting about every third word. Then he gave up, he had to concentrate on other things. (47)

In Just's analysis, the factors that ensured an American tragedy in Vietnam are the same ones that make the writing of its final act so problematic.

WORKS CITED

Aichinger, Peter. *The American Soldier in Fiction, 1880–1963: A History of Attitudes Toward Warfare and the Military Establishment.* Ames: Iowa State University Press, 1975.

Arlen, Michael. "The Effect of the Vietnam War on Broadcast Journalism: A Critic's Perspective." In *Vietnam Reconsidered: Lessons from a War.* Ed. Harrison E. Salisbury. New York: Harper & Row, 1984. 101–05.

Arnett, Peter. "The Last Years and the Aftermath." In *Vietnam Reconsidered: Lessons from a War.* Ed. Harrison E. Salisbury. New York: Harper & Row, 1984. 132–35.

Baber, Asa. *The Land of a Million Elephants.* New York: Morrow, 1970.

Baker, Mark. *Nam: The Vietnam War in the Words of the Soldiers Who Fought There.* New York: Morrow, 1981.

Baldwin, Neil. "Going After the War." *Publishers Weekly* 11 February 1983: 36.

Baritz, Loren. *Backfire: A History of How American Culture Led Us into Vietnam and Made Us Fight the Way We Did.* New York: Morrow, 1985.

Beidler, Philip D. *American Literature and the Experience of Vietnam.* Athens: University of Georgia Press, 1982.

———. "Truth-Telling and Literary Values in the Vietnam Novel." *South Atlantic Quarterly* 78 (1979): 141–56.

Bell, Pearl K. "Writing About Vietnam." *Commentary* October 1978: 74–77.

Bergonzi, Bernard. "Vietnam Novels: First Draft." *Commonweal* 27 October 1972: 84–88.

Bierce, Ambrose. *In the Midst of Life: Tales of Soldiers and Civilians.* Secaucus, N.J.: Citadel, 1946.

Boorstin, Daniel. *The Americans: The Colonial Experience.* New York: Random House, 1965.

Brown, Harry. *A Walk in the Sun.* New York: Knopf, 1944.

Broyles, William, Jr. "The Road to Hill 10." *Atlantic* April 1985: 90–118.

Bunting, Josiah. *The Lionheads.* New York: Braziller, 1972.

Burns, John Horne. *The Gallery.* New York: Harper & Row, 1947.

Butler, Robert Olen. *The Alleys of Eden.* New York: Horizon, 1981.

———. *On Distant Ground.* New York: Knopf, 1985.

Campbell, Joseph. *The Hero with a Thousand Faces.* Bollingen Series. Princeton, N.J.: Princeton University Press, 1972.

Caputo, Philip. *Indian Country.* New York: Bantam, 1987.

———. *A Rumor of War.* New York: Holt, Rinehart and Winston, 1977. Parenthetical references are to the Ballantine (1978) edition.

Clemons, Walter. "Killing Ground." *Newsweek* 1 January 1979: 60.

Coleman, Charles. *Sergeant Back Again.* New York: Harper & Row, 1980.

Cowley, Malcolm. *Exile's Return: A Literary Odyssey of the 1920s.* New York: Viking, 1951.

———. "War Novels: After Two Wars." In *Modern American Fiction: Essays in Criticism.* Ed. A. Walton Litz. New York: Oxford University Press, 1963. 296–314.

Crumley, James. *One to Count Cadence.* New York: Random House, 1969.

Cummings, E. E. *The Enormous Room.* New York: Liveright, 1922.

Davis, Peter. "The Effect of the Vietnam War on Broadcast Journalism: A Documentary Filmmaker's Perspective." In *Vietnam Reconsidered: Lessons from a War.* Ed. Harrison E. Salisbury. New York: Harper & Row, 1984. 98–100.

Del Vecchio, John M. *The 13th Valley.* New York: Bantam, 1982.

Didion, Joan. *Democracy.* New York: Simon and Schuster, 1984.

Downs, Frederick. *The Killing Zone.* New York: Norton, 1978.

Durden, Charles. *No Bugles, No Drums.* New York: Viking, 1976. Parenthetical references are to the Avon (1984) edition.

Eastlake, William. *The Bamboo Bed.* New York: Simon and Schuster, 1969.

Eisinger, Chester E. *Fiction of the Forties.* Chicago: University of Chicago Press, 1963.

Emerson, Gloria. "Our Man in Antibes: Graham Greene." *Rolling Stone* 9 March 1978: 45–49.

———. "Vietnam Veterans Speak—An Introduction." In *Vietnam Re-*

considered: Lessons from a War. Ed. Harrison E. Salisbury. New York: Harper & Row, 1984. 182–83.

———. *Winners and Losers.* New York: Harcourt Brace Jovanovich, 1972.

Epstein, Seymour. "Every Man Fights a Different War." *Saturday Review* 13 January 1968: 82, 87.

Ewalt, George, Jr. "Agent Orange and the Effects of the Herbicide Program." In *Vietnam Reconsidered: Lessons from a War.* Ed. Harrison E. Salisbury. New York: Harper & Row, 1984. 192–95.

Feinsilber, Pamela. Review of *Meditations in Green. Saturday Review* 9 December 1983: 61.

Fieldler, Leslie. *Love and Death in the American Novel.* New York: Stein and Day, 1960.

———. *Waiting for the End.* New York: Stein and Day, 1964.

Firestone, Bruce M. Review of *Going After Cacciato. Library Journal* 15 December 1977: 2513.

FitzGerald, Frances. *Fire in the Lake: The Vietnamese and the Americans in Vietnam.* New York: Random House, 1972.

———. "How Does America Avoid Future Vietnams?" In *Vietnam Reconsidered: Lessons from a War.* Ed. Harrison E. Salisbury. New York: Harper & Row, 1984. 301–05.

Foucault, Michel. *The Archaeology of Knowledge and the Discourse on Language.* Trans. A. M. Sheridan Smith. New York: Pantheon, 1972.

Freedman, Richard. "A Separate Peace." *New York Times Book Review* 12 February 1978: 1, 21.

Fromson, Murray, Lawrence Lichty, and John Mueller. "A Television War?" In *Vietnam Reconsidered: Lessons from a War.* Ed. Harrison E. Salisbury. New York: Harper & Row, 1984. 86–88.

Fuller, Jack. *Fragments.* New York: Morrow, 1984.

Giovannitti, Len. *The Man Who Won the Medal of Honor.* New York: Random House, 1973.

Grant, Zalin. "Vietnam as Fable." *New Republic* 25 March 1978: 21–24.

Greene, Graham. *The Quiet American.* New York: Viking, 1956.

Groom, Winston. *Better Times Than These.* New York: Summit, 1978.

Halberstam, David. *One Very Hot Day.* Boston: Houghton Mifflin, 1967. Parenthetical references are to the Warner (1984) edition, which includes a new Afterword.

Haldeman, Joe W. *The Forever War.* New York: Ballantine, 1976.

———. *War Year.* New York: Holt, Rinehart and Winston, 1972.

Hasford, Gustav. *The Short-Timers.* New York: Harper & Row, 1979. Parenthetical references are to the Bantam (1980) edition.

Heinemann, Larry. *Close Quarters*. New York: Farrar, Straus and Giroux, 1974.

———. *Paco's Story*. New York: Farrar, Straus and Giroux, 1986.

Heller, Joseph. *Catch-22*. New York: Simon and Schuster, 1961.

Hellman, John. "The New Journalism and Vietnam: Memory as Structure in Michael Herr's *Dispatches*." *South Atlantic Quarterly* 79 (1980): 141–51.

Hemingway, Ernest. *The Short Stories of Ernest Hemingway*. New York: Scribner's, 1953.

Herr, Michael. *Dispatches*. New York: Knopf, 1977. Parenthetical references are to the Avon (1978) edition.

If I Die in a Combat Zone. Review. *New Republic* 12 May 1973: 30.

Jameson, Fredric. *The Political Unconscious: Narrative as a Socially Symbolic Act*. Ithaca, N.Y.: Cornell University Press, 1981.

———. "Postmodernism, or The Cultural Logic of Late Capitalism." *New Left Review* 146 (1984): 53–92.

Janowitz, Morris. *The Professional Soldier: A Social and Political Portrait*. Glencoe, Ill.: Free Press, 1960.

Just, Ward. *The American Blues*. New York: Viking, 1984.

———. *Stringer*. Port Townsend, Wash.: Graywolf, 1974.

———. *To What End: Report from Vietnam*. Boston: Houghton Mifflin, 1968.

Karnow, Stanley. *Vietnam: A History*. New York: Viking, 1983.

Kazin, Alfred. "It was Us vs. Us." *Esquire* March 1978: 120–23.

Kendrick, Walter. "Drugged in Vietnam." *New York Review of Books* 6 November 1983: 7, 24.

Klein, Joe. "A Novelist's Vietnam." *New York Times Book Review* 15 August 1982: 16.

Knightley, Phillip. "The Role of Journalists in Vietnam: A Feature Writer's Perspective." In *Vietnam Reconsidered: Lessons from a War*. Ed. Harrison E. Salisbury. New York: Harper & Row, 1984. 106–09.

Kovic, Ron. *Born on the Fourth of July*. New York: McGraw-Hill, 1976.

Littell, Robert. *Sweet Reason*. Boston: Houghton Mifflin, 1974.

McInerney, Peter. "Straight and Secret History in Vietnam War Literature." *Contemporary Literature* 22 (1981): 187–204.

Mailer, Norman. *The Armies of the Night*. New York: New American Library, 1968.

———. *Why Are We in Vietnam?* New York: Putnam's, 1967.

Marin, Peter, "Coming to Terms with Vietnam." *Harper's* December 1980: 41–56.

Mason, Bobbie Ann. *In Country*. New York: Harper & Row, 1985.

Mason, Robert. *Chickenhawk*. New York: Viking, 1983.

Mayer, Tom. *The Weary Falcon*. Boston: Houghton Mifflin, 1971.

Meshad, Shad. "The Treatment of Vietnam Veterans." In *Vietnam Reconsidered: Lessons from a War*. Ed. Harrison E. Salisbury. New York: Harper & Row, 1984. 202–05.

Miller, Wayne Charles. *An Armed America: Its Face in Fiction*. New York: New York University Press, 1970.

Naperschek, Martin. "Vietnam War Novel." *The Humanist* July–August 1979: 37–39.

Newman, John. *Vietnam War Literature*. Metuchen, N.J.: Scarecrow, 1982.

O'Brien, Tim. *Going After Cacciato*. New York: Delacorte, 1978. Parenthetical references are to the Dell (1979) edition.

———. *If I Die in a Combat Zone*. New York: Delacorte, 1973. Parenthetical references are to the Dell (1979) edition, which includes O'Brien's revisions.

Pelfrey, William. *The Big V*. New York: Liveright, 1972.

Phillips, Jayne Anne. *Machine Dreams*. New York: Dutton, 1984.

Plummer, William. "Moby Dick in Vietnam." *Newsweek* 26 July 1982: 71.

Podhoretz, Norman. *Why We Were in Vietnam*. New York: Simon and Schuster, 1983.

Prescott, Peter S. "War Without Winners." *Newsweek* 3 October 1983: 89–92.

Pynchon, Thomas. *Gravity's Rainbow*. New York: Viking, 1973.

Reedy, George. "Difficulties of Covering a War Like Vietnam: II." In *Vietnam Reconsidered: Lessons from a War*. Ed. Harrison E. Salisbury. New York: Harper & Row, 1984. 120–23.

Ross, Frank. "The Assailant–Victim in Three War Protest Novels." *Paunch* 32 (1968): 46–57.

Roth, Robert. *Sand in the Wind*. Boston: Little, Brown, 1973.

Safer, Morley. "How to Lose a War: A Response from a Broadcaster." In *Vietnam Reconsidered: Lessons from a War*. Ed. Harrison E. Salisbury. New York: Harper & Row, 1984. 158–63.

Sale, Roger. "Love and War." *New York Review of Books* 22 February 1979: 19.

Santoli, Al. *Everything We Had: An Oral History of the Vietnam War by Thirty-Three American Soldiers Who Fought It*. New York: Random House, 1981.

Schroeder, Eric James. "Two Interviews: Talks with Tim O'Brien and Robert Stone." *Modern Fiction Studies* 30 (1984): 135–64.

Sheed, Wilfred. "En Route to Nowhere." *New York Times Book Review* 7 January 1968: 1, 45.

Sloan, James Park. *War Games*. Boston: Houghton Mifflin, 1971.

Smith, Steven Phillip. *American Boys*. New York: Avon, 1975.

Solotaroff, Theodore. "Memoirs for Memorial Day." *New York Times Book Review* 29 May 1977: 9, 21.

Stone, Robert. *Dog Soldiers*. Boston: Houghton Mifflin, 1973.

———. *A Flag for Sunrise*. New York: Knopf, 1981.

Styron, William. "A Farewell to Arms." *New York Review of Books* 23 June 1977: 3–5.

Swiers, George, " 'Demented Vets' and Other Myths." In *Vietnam Reconsidered: Lessons from a War*. Ed. Harrison E. Salisbury. New York: Harper & Row, 1984. 196–201.

Taylor, Gordon O. "American Personal Narrative of the War in Vietnam." *American Literature* 52 (1980): 294–308.

Terry, Wallace. *Bloods: An Oral History of the Vietnam War by Black Veterans*. New York: Random House, 1984.

Tetlow, Joseph A. "The Vietnam War Novel." *America* July 1980: 32–36.

Thomson, James. "United States National Interest in Vietnam." In *Vietnam Reconsidered: Lessons from a War*. Ed. Harrison E. Salisbury. New York: Harper & Row, 1984. 15–18.

Trumbo, Dalton. *Johnny Got His Gun*. New York: Monogram, 1939.

Tuchman, Barbara. *The March of Folly: From Troy to Vietnam*. New York: Knopf, 1984.

Updike, John. "Layers of Ambiguity." *New Yorker* 27 March 1978: 127–33.

Vonnegut, Kurt. *Slaughterhouse-Five or The Children's Crusade*. New York: Dell, 1969.

Walsh, Jeffrey. *American War Literature: 1914 to Vietnam*. New York: St. Martin's Press, 1982.

Webb, James. *Fields of Fire*. New York: Prentice-Hall, 1978.

White, Hayden. *Metahistory: The Historical Imagination in Nineteenth-Century Europe*. Baltimore: Johns Hopkins University Press, 1973.

Wilson, Edmund. *Patriotic Gore: Studies in the Literature of the American Civil War*. New York: Oxford University Press, 1962.

Wilson, James C. *Vietnam in Prose and Film*. Jefferson, N.C.: McFarland, 1982.

Wright, Stephen. *Meditations in Green*. New York: Scribner's, 1983.

INDEX